The Birds
of Scotland

The Birds of Scotland

Emilio Dicerbo

LOCHAR PUBLISHING · MOFFAT · SCOTLAND

© Emilio Dicerbo. 1991

Published by Lochar Publishing Ltd, Moffat DG10 9ED

All rights reserved. No part of this book may be reproduced, stored in an information retrieval system now known or yet to be invented, or transmitted in any form or by any means, mechanical or electrical, photocopied or recorded without the express written permission of the publishers except by a reviewer wishing to quote brief passages in a review either written or broadcast.

British Library Cataloguing in Publication Data
Dicerbo, Emilio
The birds of Scotland.
I. Title
598.29411
ISBN 0-948403-74-8

Typeset in 10 on 11 Photina by Origination, Dunstable, Beds. and printed in Scotland by Eagle Colourbooks

Photographs by Emilio Dicerbo and Robert T. Smith
Design by Alan Hamp.

CONTENTS

INTRODUCTION

Scotland is a beautiful country. Relatively unspoilt by urban development, most of the landscape is composed of hill moors, Highlands and mountains, patterned with sparkling hill burns, clean rivers and jewel-like lochs. Together with the heather moors and ancient pine forests, these assets combine to make Scotland exceptionally attractive to both birds and birdwatchers.

Within the last quarter of a century we have seen the return to Scotland of some fine raptors: the Osprey to many Highland lochs, the Hen Harrier to young forestry plantations, the cat-like Snowy Owl to the Shetlands, the ferocious Goshawk to mature forests, and the magnificent White-tailed Eagle to the Western Highlands. The latter has been successfully reintroduced from Norway, and there are similar plans afoot for the Red Kite, so that, perhaps within the next decade, the first pairs for many years will once again breed in Scotland.

Although only a mere fraction of the old Caledonian pine forests remain, the combined area of Abernethy and Rothiemurchus (which in ancient Scots means 'Great Plain of the Pines') is large by today's standards guaranteeing a future for the Scottish Crossbill, Crested Tit, Siskin and Capercaillie. At the same time, forestry policy and changes in planting procedure in the southern parts of the country where the woodlands already contain stands of beech and old oaks, are ensuring that future generations of birds and people will benefit from the planting of long-term hardwoods.

The Flow Country in the north of Scotland is the only area of its kind left in Europe and is one of the world's outstanding eco-systems, with some of our rarer birds, such as the Divers and Greenshank, and less common wildflowers dependent upon it for their survival. Recent forestry encroachment has proved that in order to retain this unique habitat, the planting of conifers should be held in check.

Although the romance of the Edwardian era has long since faded into the Highland mists, the grouse moors still provide sport for those who are prepared to pay substantial fees for the privilege of bagging a brace or two of Scottish Red Grouse, and although on occasion the odd predator pays the price, the vastness of the grouse moors provides a habitat for a greater number and variety of species than would be supported in the same area if it were covered with mature conifers. Scotland today has woodland birds in plenty while moorland species are dwindling in numbers, and although afforestation increases the populations of some typical woodland birds, their good fortune is frequently at the expense of the less-numerous birds of the hill moors. Somewhere between 'to plant' or 'not to plant', there is hopefully, a compromise which suits everything as well as everyone concerned.

The Scottish mainland and islands have between them over 1,000 miles of coastline, from sandy beaches to sea cliffs over three hundred metres in height, where immense colonies of seabirds thrive. The remote island of St Kilda in the Atlantic houses the largest gannetry in the world, adding its numbers of over 40,000 pairs to other notable island gannetries around our coasts, and giving Scotland the largest number of Gannets worldwide.

The Northern Isles of Orkney and Shetland also have many attractions to offer the birdwatcher. In addition to the Snowy Owls, there are Great and Arctic Skuas, Storm Petrels, Whimbrel and Red-necked Phalaropes and there is hope that in the future sandeels will return in sufficient numbers to support the colonies of Arctic Terns, Puffins and Kittiwakes as they did in the years prior to their disappearance.

The Hebrides, for their part, are the last Scottish stronghold of the Corncrake and, though seldom seen – even by more dedicated ornithologists – the Leach's Petrel carries out its nocturnal nesting activities on these remote islands.

Many fine estuaries around our coast are excellent places for waders and wildfowl where winter birdwatching is most rewarding, and during the summer months sometimes up to a dozen Osprey can be seen in the air at the same time above the Moray Firth.

In the south-west corner of the country the Solway Firth is notable for its wintering wildfowl including over 10,000 Barnacle Geese – the entire Spitzbergen breeding population – together with Greylag, Pinkfeet, Pintail, Wigeon, Whooper Swans and others, as well as a multitude of waders wintering in and around the Wildfowl and Wetlands reserve at Caerlaverock.

There are many other splendid bird, and wildlife reserves throughout the length and breadth of the country. In and around, the snow-capped Cairngorms, for example, Golden Eagles, Dotterel, Ptarmigan and Snow Buntings find sanctuary on the high tops, while lower down the pine and juniper woods, moorlands and lochs support Crossbills, Crested Tit, Capercaillie, Greenshank, Osprey and Goldeneye, to name but a few of the interesting birds on the Scottish list.

Nowadays more people are concerned about the environment and the wildlife it supports than at any other time in the history of the world, and in the British Isles this concern is shown by the many thousands who support natural history societies, preservation societies, and many other organisations and clubs where the common aim is to preserve our national and natural heritage for future generations.

The membership of most societies and trusts consists mainly of people who simply love the scenic beauty of the countryside, its trees, flowers, animal and birdlife. Closer to home in gardens large and small, rural and urban, millions more help our birds survive the winter by providing them with food and water, in return for which we can enjoy the beautiful colours and entertaining antics of the many species which take advantage of a little human support.

With all these people, as well as more regular birdwatcher, in mind, I have endeavoured to illustrate in words and photographs some 200 birds found in every type of habitat throughout Scotland, most of which I have had the privilege of observing from the close proximity of a hide. One of the aspects of photographing from such a situation that I find most gratifying is not, as one might expect, the resulting good photograph – which is, of course, the whole point of the exercise – but simply the opportunity to sit and watch the subject arrive at the nest and carry on with its domestic duties as though I were not there at all.

Whether it be a Tree Creeper a metre-and-a-half distant, or a Buzzard only fifteen metres from my lens, great care must be taken at all times, for no two species react in the same way when confronted with a camera. In fact, no two individuals of the same species can be relied upon

to react in a similar fashion, and any nervousness displayed by the subject is a signal to abandon photography by removing the hide as soon as possible

This book contains over 100 colour plates, the quality of which is reflected in the fact that many have been shown in various Scottish Salons of Photography. As the majority of my own photographs were taken in the south of Scotland, my friend and colleague Mr Robert T. Smith, has kindly supplied the remainder, so that a good cross-section of Scottish birds is illustrated.

The birds are presented in the order in which they appear in the *Field List of British Birds*, produced by the British Trust for Ornithology, since this is the recognised order accepted by most of todays birdwatchers. The information charts, covering most of the included species, contain details of status, habitat, nest, eggs and food, and will also prove helpful in 'sizing' the bird, which in each case is compared to a familiar species.

CHAFFINCH
Comparative size Slightly larger than House Sparrow.
Status Resident.
Habitat Woodlands, Gardens, Parks.
Nest Cup-shaped. Moss, lichens, wool, hair, feathers.
Eggs Greyish-stone. Slightly spotted/streaked brownish. Clutch 4-5.
Food Insects, caterpillars, seeds.

'Status' refers to the bird's appearance in Scotland, and though many are listed as 'Resident' there can be a seasonal movement within the country, with large numbers arriving from northern countries. For the Chaffinch, for example, 'Resident' means that the bird can be seen in Scotland in every month of the year. For the swallow 'Summer Resident' indicates that it arrives in Scotland from Africa in the spring, breeds here and then returns to Africa in the autumn. For the Waxwing, 'Winter visitor' tells us that the bird arrives in Scotland in autumn, winters here, and leaves again for its northern breeding grounds in the spring.

By following this simple plan, you will soon establish that twice a year, in spring and autumn, there are huge northerly and southerly movements of birds up and down the country.

Spring migration brings our Scottish summer residents to where they will nest and rear families, while at the same time the birds that have wintered with us, will return to their northern breeding territories. During the autumn migrations the entire situation is reversed, with the birds, like grains of sand in two gigantic eggtimers, turned first one way, north to south, and then, approximately six months later, south to north.

During the migration periods, birds that breed beyond Scotland can at times be seen on our coasts, and the more regular of these are listed as 'Passage migrants'.

Habitat describes where we are most likely to find the bird, either breeding or feeding.

The information on **Nest** and **Eggs** is for average nest construction, clutch sizes and colouring of eggs, and should not be taken to be exact.

The Red-throated Diver incubates two eggs in her nest which is always situated near the waters' edge.

Red-Throated Diver
Gavia stellata

Black-Throated Diver
Gavia arctica

The Red-throated Diver is 60cm in length and perfectly designed for its aquatic lifestyle, as is its close and slightly larger relative the Black-throated Diver, at 65cm.

In autumn, following the breeding season both Red and Black-throated Divers head for the coastal waters, where they spend the winter. In this environment they are difficult to tell apart, as in their winter plumage both appear dull greyish-brown with a white throat and neck, and it is only at relatively close quarters that the slightly upturned bill of the Red-throated Diver can be distinguished.

In summer plumage the Red-throated Diver's throat is, as its name implies, a rich, dark red with its head and sides the of its neck a smokey grey. Contrasting uniform lines of grey and white run down the back of the neck merging into the upperparts which are brownish-grey and completely lacking in the conspicuous chequered pattern noticeable on the backs of the other Divers in summer. Both sexes are similar in colouring.

The **Red-throated Diver** is the most common and best known member of its family, in the breeding season frequenting small tarns and pools in the Scottish Highlands. Like the Black-throated Diver, it can also be found on the larger lochs, and at times the watcher may find it difficult to distinguish between the two species especially on a dull, grey day when the birds swim low on the rippling waters.

Since the pool in which they choose to rear their young is too small to provide enough fish for the family, the breeding habitat of the Red-throated Diver is within flying distance of the sea or larger lochs and in their breeding haunts in the far north the birds' peculiar call as they circle high above their territory is said to forecast rain – hence their local name of 'Rain Goose'.

The two rather elongated eggs are usually laid in June, and the nest, typical of the Divers, is merely a flattened depression on a hummock among the sedge or heather. It is usually situated on a small islet and always close to the water's edge, as the parent birds are extremely ungainly on land due to the position of the legs and webbed feet, which are set well back in the body – awkward on land, but perfectly positioned for swimming, both on and under the surface of the water. Submerged, while in the pursuit of fish or fleeing from some intruder. Divers swim much faster than they do on the surface, and although they may at times use their wings for extra speed, it is more usual for them to rely on their feet for propulsion.

In the air their flight silhouette is unmistakeable, as they fly with outstretched neck and head held lower than their hump-backed bodies, and – unlike the duck family, who drop their 'undercarriage' when alighting on the surface of the water – divers 'plane-in' on their breasts.

The **Black-throated Diver** in summer plumage is also an attractive bird with its head and the back of its neck slate grey. The throat is purplish-black and down the sides of the neck are even, contrasting, streaks of black and white. The upperparts of the body are blackish, streaked and spotted with white, and the underparts are pure white. The black bill is straight and pointed and the legs are black and grey.

The nesting habits of the Black-throated Diver are similar to those of the Red-throated Diver, except that the former breeds on larger lochs

---

RED-THROATED DIVER

Comparative size Similar size to Mallard.
Status Resident, winters in estuaries and coastal waters.
Habitat Lochans and tarns.
Nest Scant vegetation near water's edge.
Eggs Elongated; olive brown, dark spots; clutch 2.
Food Fish.

BLACK-THROATED DIVER

Comparative size Slightly larger than Mallard.
Status Resident, winters in estuaries and coastal waters.
Habitat Large lochs in northern Scotland.
Nest Scant scrape near water's edge.
Eggs Olive brown, dark spots; clutch 2.
Food Fish.

which are more capable of providing for the family's dietary needs, thereby lessening the need for the parents to leave the vicinityof the nest. Both Black-throated and Red-throated Divers are aggressive in defence of their breeding territories, driving off any other of their species that may appear.

The third member of the family occasionally seen around Scottish coasts in summer is the Great Northern Diver and, as its name suggests, it is noticeably larger than our two resident Divers (its two predecessors), being fully 80cm in length.

Great Crested Grebe

Podiceps cristatus

The Great Crested Grebe is indeed an attractive bird in summer plumage, when the dark, spiky crest and frilly, chestnut feathers with darker tips – called 'tippets' – which hang down each side of the face, are in full display. The longish, slender throat, breast and underparts are snowy-white, the upperparts greyish-brown and the wings slightly darker, with two conspicuous white patches. Although there is no noticeable tail. the birds are 48cm long, with the bill slender and dagger-like. The feet are 'lobed', that is, that each toe resembles a small paddle. The sexes are similar in colouring.

A further attraction of these birds is their fantastic mating display, called the 'weed dance' when the pair face each other on the water and perform exaggerated movements, accompanied by a great deal of head shaking. Then one or other of the pair crouches low on the surface with half-open wings, while fluffing its feathers and spreading its crest, as its mate stands upright with its beak pointing downwards. They then swim away from each other, dive and resurface with beakfuls of weed, then, coming together, they stand erect on the surface, their breasts touching, while paddling furiously to remain in this position for some seconds before one or other drops the weed and, following more headshaking, patters off across the water towards some reedy area where they probably intend building their floating nest.

The nest is a bulky affair which looks like a floating heap of water weeds, but it is cleverly constructed and is usually placed in such a position that it can rise and fall with the water level while remaining moored to some surface plant. If the sitting bird is disturbed while incubating, it will carefully cover the eggs with some nest material before slipping into the water, thus ensuring safety and that the humidity helps to keep the eggs from becoming chilled.

When hatched, the young take to the water within 36 hours; they, too, are very attractive in their black-and-white-striped, downy coats. To see two or three young Grebe carried 'cradle-wise' on one of their parents' backs, as is the habit of these birds, always holds a special appeal for the watcher.

While rearing their young, Great Crested Grebes indulge in a quaint habit called the 'feather game' while cruising on the surface of the water. One or other of the parents will pick a small, downy feather from its breast or from the surface of the water and present it to the chick which in turn allows it to float away again; the feather is then retrieved by the parent and again passed to the chick. This procedure is repeated about half a dozen times before the parent finally swallows the feather as an aid to digestion!

The recovery of the numbers of Great Crested Grebe from the late nineteenth century low is one of the success stories of the natural world, as they were almost shot to extinction for the sake of their plumes which were used to adorn ladies hats while the warm, downy breast feathers were employed as a cosy lining for muffs.

The Seabirds Protection Act of 1869 brought an end to the slaughter and from the 40 or so pairs that were left in the country at that time numbers have now risen to over 4,000 pairs, with a fair percentage residing in Scotland.

Great Crested Grebes are plentiful in the south of Scotland, but as one travels northwards they become more scarce, and they are totally absent from the north. Reservoirs, lochs and gravel pits are their haunts, and if the winter is not too severe many Grebes will remain where they have reared their families. Severe winters, however, force the birds to move to estuaries, where they

---

GREAT CRESTED GREBE

Comparative size smaller than Mallard.
Status resident, winters in estuaries.
Habitat Fresh water lochs, reservoirs, gravel pits.
Nest Floating heap of aquatic vegetation.
Eggs 3-6 white, soon becoming stained!
Food Fish, molluscs, crustancea.

The Great Crested Grebe incubates her eggs in a raft-like nest which rises and falls with the level of the water.

find their 'fishy' diet more readily. During the winter months both their 'tippets' and attractive colouration are discarded and on viewing the birds on the water they appear to be simply dark grey and white.

Little Grebe
Tachybaptus ruficollis
Slavonian Grebe
Podiceps auritus

The **Little Grebe** or 'Dabchick' is a round, dumpy little bird which is almost tailless, and at only 26cm in length it is about half the size of the Great Crested Grebe.

It is the smallest and most abundant of the Grebe family, frequenting ponds, lochs and reservoirs of all sizes, as long as there is plentiful reed or other vegetation, or aquatic plant cover

in which to build its nest. It also prefers relatively shallow water where it can dive for small fish, insects and other small aquatic creatures.

In summer plumage the upperparts are dark brown with the underparts a shade paler and the cheeks and throat chestnut. There is a conspicuous yellowish-green patch on the base of the black bill and the legs are greenish. In autumn the chestnut turns to pale brown – the general colouring of the Little Grebe's 'winter coat'.

'Tippets' (see Great Crested Grebe) and crests, which are a prominent feature in the courtship display of other Grebes are totally absent in the Little Grebe and consequently these birds are more vocal as they chase each other over the water, uttering their high-pitched trilling whistle which can be heard throughout the spring months.

The breeding habits resemble those of the Great Crested Grebe. A similar type of floating nest is built using aquatic vegetation which the Little Grebe dives under the surface to collect, very often mooring the nest to an overhanging willow frond. Little Grebe also cover their eggs when leaving the nest unattended for any length

The Little Grebe incubates her eggs in a floating nest which is usually moored by overhanging willow branches or reed stems.

of time, but as sometimes happens in nature, there is the odd exception to the rule and I was fortunate enough to witness one of these while undertaking some photography.

As I watched a female Little Grebe sitting on her eggs, she rose as if to turn them, but instead slipped into the water with barely a ripple and headed away from the nest leaving her eggs exposed. I watched curiously as she swam away, and it was then that I noticed that a Mute Swan had approached the island and was cruising about ten metres from the nest. The Little Grebe swam on the surface of the water until she was only five metres from the swan; she then submerged, and seconds later a very surprised swan rose almost clear of the water, simultaneously turned in a semi-circle and then hastily swam off in the other direction. The Little Grebe surfaced at the spot from which the Swan had made its hasty retreat, and I can only assume that 150gm of Litle Grebe had successfully torpedoed 12kg of Mute Swan – for she then returned to the nest, carefully straddled her eggs and continued incubation, droplets of water glistening on her back in the evening sunlight.

In winter Little Grebes frequent lochs, reservoirs and estuaries as well as quiet stretches of river, where they have the most annoying

---

LITTLE GREBE

Comparative size Smaller than Moorhen.
Status Resident.
Habitat Fresh water ponds, tarns.
Nest Heap of floating aquatic vegetation.
Eggs 4-6, creamy-white, becoming stained.
Food Aquatic insects, crustaceans, small fish.

SLAVONIAN GREBE

Comparative size Smaller than Mallard.
Status Resident, (scarce) winters on coast.
Habitat Fresh water ponds, tarns.
Nest Heap of floating aquatic vegetation.
Eggs White, becoming stained, clutch 3-5.
Food Fish, crustaceans.

---

habit of diving under the surface as one approaches. Waiting for the bird to reappear can be a fruitless task as they usually surface among vegetation or swim further away with only their heads showing above the water.

At 35cm in length, the Slavonian Grebe is somewhat larger than the Little Grebe. In summer it is a beautifully coloured bird with rich chestnut flanks and neck, a black head and decorative yellow ear tufts, projecting horn-like from behind the eye out past the back of its head.

The upperparts are blackish with a white wingbar, and the underparts are white; the bill and legs are bluish-grey. The sexes are similar in colouring.

The Slavonian has a similar courtship display to the Great Crested Grebe, including the mad, dashing 'weed dance' and it is also quite vocal, with a low trill being the main breeding call. Nesting habits are also similar. Outside the breeding season Slavonian Grebes are marine in their habits favouring sheltered estuaries and bays as well as inland lochs.

Swimming high in the water they resemble the Great Crested Grebe in many ways and following a rather awkward, pattering take-off once airborne the flight is strong with rapid wingbeats.

In winter their colouring is greyish-black and white, and some confusion can arise as they closely resemble the Black-necked Grebe, which can at times be found wintering in the same habitat, diving for fish, crustaceans, molluscs and other marine life.

Only a few remote and secluded lochans in the north of Scotland are the breeding haunts of this beautiful bird, which is rare in the British Isles.

Fulmar
Fulmarus glacialis

Manx Shearwater
Puffinus puffinus

The **Fulmar** is somewhat gull-like in appearance and may be mistaken for one at a distance. The mantle is grey, shading to darker on the long, narrow wings but there are no black wing-tips. The head, neck and underparts are snowy-white with a small dark patch in front of the eye. The sexes are similar in colouring and are both about 47cm in length.

The yellowish-green bill has tubular nostrils, or rather a horny tube, attached to the top of the somewhat complex beak from which the Fulmar can emit a noxious substance – its old northern name 'Tube Nose' obviously relates to this feature as does the ancient Norwegian of Fulmar, which roughly translated means 'foul gull'.

Watch a Fulmar in flight as it makes use of the up-draught of air currents in a bay among the sea cliffs, and as it twists and glides you will soon learn to distinguish it from the Herring Gull and other species that usually inhabit the same cliffs, for the Fulmar is among the most graceful and spectacular of fliers, never ceasing to please the watcher. That is, until you inadvertently get too close to a sitting bird, because if alarmed the 'Tube Nose' turns nasty and you will discover all too quickly the purpose of the curious beak.

Fulmars feed almost entirely on floating refuse from the sea. In days gone by, whalers always had their share of attendant Fulmars and today fishing boats are followed in much the same way, when fish alive or dead are eagerly taken. In the course of digesting this fish and offal with plankton the Fulmar produces a penetrating, foul-smelling, sticky, oily substance which it is capable of spitting, or rather shooting for a distance of up to about three metres – and if you are unfortunate enough to be 'shot' your garments may well have to be discarded, especially if they made of a woollen or tweed material. Even young birds a few weeks old are capable of defending themselves in this manner.

Fulmars spend most of their lives on the open seas, only coming ashore to breed, usually from May to August. There is little or no effort to build a nest, and the single white egg is laid on a bare ledge or in a crevice, generally being secured by a few strategically placed pebbles. When the chick hatches it is tended by both parents for about four weeks, and when it finally leaves for its oceanic life it will probably be three or four years before it returns to land, with a further two years passing before it is mature enough to mate.

FULMAR
Comparative size Smaller then Herring Gull.
Status Resident, winters on open sea.
Habitat Sea cliffs, oceans.
Nest Bare ledge.
Eggs White; clutch 1.
Food Fish, fish offal.

The Fulmar's single egg is laid on a bare, rocky ledge or steep grassy slope high above the crashing waves.

Prior to the evacuation of the St Kildans in the 1930s, Fulmars played a large part in the island's economy. As well as the eggs being harvested, full-grown young and adults were taken for food, oil and bedding.

During the late nineteenth century St Kilda was home to the only significant Fulmar colony around Scotland, but by the early 1960s not only had the St Kilda population reached about 40,000 pairs but the Fulmar had extended its range to all round the coast of Britain, where they can now be found breeding in colonies ranging from a few pairs to many thousands.

The **Manx Shearwater** is much smaller than its close cousin the Fulmar, being only 34cm in length. The upperparts are black while the underparts are white, merging into greyish-brown on the head and neck. The slightly hooked bill is black with similar curious, tubular nostrils. The webbed feet are pinkish and the wings are long, narrow and pointed.

A truly oceanic species, the Manx Shearwater comes ashore only to breed and this they do mainly in colonies.

They gather just offshore in large numbers, sometimes as early as February, and, following a period of reluctance to leave their watery sanctuary, they land, somewhat awkwardly, and commence excavating a nesting burrow in soft earth, about a metre long with a nest chamber at the end. Rabbit burrows are also used.

A single white egg is laid in May and following an incubation period of some seven weeks, the downy chick is reared by both parents for another eight weeks before it is finally abandoned. After this it lives on its fat for about ten days until hunger finally drives the youngster seawards – very awkwardly, and in total darkness.

While the young are in their burrows, the parents also rely on the cover of darkness to allow them to approach the colony without fear of being predated by Great Black Backed Gull or Great Skua. Large numbers will gather just

offshore in the failing light as they return from their fishing trips; then, as darkness falls, they land and scramble to the safety of their burrows, from which all comings and goings are strictly nocturnal. As one would expect, the Manx Shearwater is an expert swimmer, using its wings for propulsion in the water, but it is in flight that these Shearwaters really excel, sweeping low over the waves, twisting and gliding as they 'shear the water'. The Western Isles and the west coast are favoured breeding haunts, although occasionally they are carried far inland by severe westerly gales, when odd birds are found exhausted.

Manx Shearwaters are expert navigators and they also possess an unimaginable homing sense as one individual female proved when she was removed from her burrow on Skokholm, Pembrokeshire and flown (by plane) to Boston USA where she was released – and found back in her burrow 13 days later, a distance of over 2,500 miles.

Storm Petrel
Hydrobates pelagicus

Leach's Petrel
Oceandoroma leucorhoa

The **Storm Petrel**, and **Leach's Petrel** are small oceanic birds, so small in fact that the Storm Petrel, at 16cm, is only Sparrow-sized, while the Leach's Petrel is slightly larger. Both birds are similar in colouring, having dark brown plumage with white rumps, and both have the typical slightly hooked bills and tubular nostrils of the Petrels, though the larger Leach's has longer wings and a distinctly forked tail.

Leach's arrive just offshore at their breeding haunts in the Outer Hebrides in April, about two weeks before the Storm Petrels make their appearance in waters around their territories in

MANX SHEARWATER

Comparative size smaller than Herring Gull.
Status Resident, winters on open sea.
Habitat Islands and oceans.
Nest Burrow in soft earth.
Eggs White; clutch I.
Food Fish.

STORM PETREL

Comparative size Size of house sparrow.
Status Resident, oceanic.
Habitat Islands and oceans.
Nest Burrow or rock crevice.
Eggs White, Clutch 1.
Food Plankton, small fish.

the Northern Isles. Their nesting habits are similar, both species only venturing ashore after dark to select a nesting hole in a wall or among rocks or to excavate their own burrow in peaty soil, a task undertaken by the male, at the end of which process a solitary chick is reared.

During incubation the male and female share the hatching of the egg for about five or six weeks, each bird sitting for periods of three or four days at a time, neither leaving the nest or taking food, while the mate remains at sea feeding on plankton, small fish and crustaceans. After about 60 days and many nocturnal visits to the nest by the parents, the young of both species are abandoned to the elements and the entire colony becomes oceanic once again.

The dainty Storm Petrel has earned the name of 'Little Peter' as it follow in the wake of ships, skimming and turning in erratic, bat-like flight and appearing to 'walk on the water' as it flutters its wings only centimetres above the surface, feet touching the crests of the waves as it pick tiny morsels brought to the surface by ships' propellors.

Leach's Petrel, on the other hand, avoid the ships, preferring the open sea where it spend many months feeding from and resting on the rolling waves of the South Atlantic.

Gannet

Sula bassana

The **Gannet** is a magnificent seabird, one of the largest in the British Isles, and is unique both in appearance and performance.

The Gannet's plumage is predominantly brilliant white, with yellowish-buff colouration on its head and neck. The long, narrow wings are tipped with black and the white tail is pointed. The sexes are similar in colouring. The bill is formidable – long, straight, dagger-like and extremely efficient – and the dark legs and webbed feet, of which all four toes are included in the web, remind us that the Gannet is related to the Pelican. The length of these birds is an impressive 95cm, making them larger than any of our Gulls, and their wingspan is almost 2m.

Although the Gannet is essentially an oceanic species, it does not venture as far from land as most of our other oceanic birds and can be seen round our coasts throughout the year. March or even February finds the Gannets returning to the

The Gannet never ceases to impress the watcher as it dives headlong into the sea or as it soars and glides on wings spanning almost two metres.

gannetries, most of which are extremely well known both for the massive numbers of birds and for the inaccessibility of the colony, which is usually situated on an isolated offshore rock stack.

Most Gannet colonies consist of thousands of birds, with the nests being built just out of pecking distance of their neighbours and, as one would expect in such a situation much squabbling and thieving of nest material takes place even though one or other of the pair usually stands guard.

However nests are eventually completed, being constructed from seaweed, grasses and anything else that may be of use, and the solitary egg is laid around the middle of May. The egg is pure white, soon becoming stained, and as it is incubated for about 45 days it is extremely dirty before it hatches. The young are naked and ugly at first but are soon dressed in an attractive white, downy coat, and they develop fast on the fish brought and fed to them by regurgitation from both parents.

On land the Gannet is an awkward bird as it shuffles about, but once airborne it is a true master and its performance almost unrivalled as it turns and twists, hovering in the wind, gliding and soaring. It is while feeding, however, that Gannets present their most exciting spectacle and the watcher is held in fascination as these magnificent divers plunge into the sea to catch their prey. If the shoal of fish is relatively near the surface the dives are made at an angle and from only a few metres, but if the shoal is at a greater depth the Gannet will drop from a height of about thirty metres, only folding their wings, arrow-like, at the very moment that they pierce the surface, giving them a deeper and more efficient dive. Once submerged, their binocular vision comes into play and they are able to pursue and secure the fish, which is swallowed as soon as it is caught unless it is too large, when it is brought to the surface and eventually swallowed.

```
GANNET

Comparative size Larger than Herring Gull.
Status Resident, winters on open sea.
Habitat Seas and cliffs.
Nest Bulky, seaweed, grasses.
Eggs White, later stained, Clutch
1-2 (normally 1).
Food Fish.
```

Nestling Gannets, fed continuously, eventually outweigh their parents and it is at this time that they are left to their own devices. At first they stay where they are, but as the days pass they lose weight while at the same time developing their wings and plumage. Finally, an ungainly – and apparently suicidal – step finds the young Gannet bobbing about on the surface of the sea, where it is usually another day or two before it can catch fish for itself.

Young Gannets take about four years to mature. At first they have an all-dark plumage, but each year they develop the typical white plumage of their kind to a greater degree. This leads to numbers of immature birds at various stages of development being present in, or rather around active gannetries where they watch and learn in preparation for the time when they will inhabit the gannetry themselves.

Not so long ago Gannets provided food for the inhabitants of some of the Scottish islands, who risked their lives attempting to reach the birds' breeding haunts. This practice has now ceased and the Gannet is a plentiful bird, with notable colonies located on the Bass Rock in the Firth of Forth and on Ailsa Craig off the Ayrshire coast, to name but two from a list of at least a dozen spectacular Scottish gannetries.

Cormorant
Phalacrocorax carbo

Shag
Phalacrocorax aristotelis

Although mostly a marine bird, the **Cormorant** is equally at home in fresh inland waters.

The plumage is glossy black except for the distinctly white throat and cheeks, and in the breeding season white patches on the thighs are conspicuous, especially when the birds are in flight. It has a slightly downcurved beak covered with yellowish skin at the base and the four toes are all joined by the same web, forming an extremely effective paddle. The sexes are similar in colouring and about 90cm in length.

The Cormorant moves awkwardly on the ground and when rising from the water take-off appears difficult, but once airborne it is a powerful flier as it crosses over the water with outstretched neck.

The Shag, or 'Green Cormorant', builds a bulky nest with flotsam and sea weed in which the eggs soon become stained and chalky.

On the coast nests are usually built among rocks or on rocky ledges on cliffs, but inland Cormorants can be found nesting in trees which at times become skeletal – withered prematurely by the birds' droppings. Cormorants seen perching on such trees convey to the watcher an almost prehistoric vision.

The nest is very bulky, covering a fair area and built of sticks, seaweed and any other convenient pieces of vegetation, thus resembling a small compost heap and smelling even worse as incubation progresses. Incubated in such a bed for a period of 28 days, the clutch of white eggs soon becomes stained. The stench in the Commorant colony increases as morsels of half-digested fish inevitably get scattered around the edge of the nest as the chicks, fed by regurgitation, force their entire heads down their parents' throats to reach their meal.

Cormorants really excel at diving and fishing, being able to stay submerged for over 60 seconds as they propel themselves through the water to secure their prey. On returning to the surface the fish is swallowed whole – sometimes following a severe battering!

It is this method of fishing that is exploited by the Japanese. Nowadays, they use the catching of fish by Cormorants only as a tourist attraction, but in earlier times when fish were more plentiful it provided them with a lucrative business. The fishermen would row out onto the river as darkness fell with a few Cormorants in a cage. A torch would be lit and hung from a pole in the stern of the boat, and the Cormorants would then be placed on the water, attached to the side of the boat by a thong about four metres long. This thong was attached to the base of the birds' neck by a neck-ring or collar, preventing the Cormorant from swallowing the fish which it dived for and caught, attracted to the glow from the torch. After a night's fishing the collars were removed and the birds were fed with some of the smaller fish.

The Cormorant adopts a characteristic stance following a bout of feeding. Standing on a rock or pole by the water's edge it holds its wings semi-spread in the sunlight or sea-breeze. More recently, Cormorants can be seen adopting this stance on top of high pylons, especially in the vicinity of fish farms which can be well inland from the coast.

The **Shag** or 'Green Cormorant' is, as its name suggests, closely related to the Cormorant, though at 75cm in length it is somewhat smaller with a thinner neck and more slender bill. Breeding all round the Scottish coast, it is truly a marine species seldom seen inland.

Although at a distance Shags may be confused with Cormorants, close up the Shag is a dark, glossy green, and lacks the white cheeks of the Cormorant. In the breeding season Shags have a tufty crest of spiky feathers at the front of the head and again the sexes are alike. Rocky outcrops on the shore provide nest sites for Shags, where they can be found in colonies of varying size. The nests are usually built in April by both parents using seaweed and any other suitable material, and the chicks are hatched in as smelly an environment as their cousins the young Cormorants.

If the watcher can find an elevated spot and is fortunate enough to have the sun in the right place, the sight of Shags in the sea pursuing their prey underwater presents an extremely exciting spectacle as they twist and turn at great speed, first in one direction and then another.

Shags feed mainly on small round fish and sandeels in mid-water, whereas Cormorants prefer to search for flatfish on the sea bed. In this way the two species do not compete for the same food source, even though they may nest close together.

CORMORANT

Comparative size Heron size, upright stance.
Status Resident.
Habitat Seas, lochs.
Nest Sticks, seaweed, on rocks or in trees.
Eggs Whitish, Clutch 3-4.
Food Mainly flat fish, rainbow trout (inland).

SHAG

Comparative size Smaller than Cormorant.
Status Resident.
Habitat Seas, rocky shores.
Nest Sticks, seaweed, on rocks.
Eggs Whitish, clutch 3-4.
Food Round fish, sandeels.

Grey Heron

Ardea cinerea

The **Heron** is one of our largest resident birds, being fully 94cm in length. The plumage is predominantly grey, shading to darker, almost black, on the rounded wings. Its white head is adorned with a black crest running down the back and the white breast and long neck have bluish-black markings. It has long legs and the yellow dagger-like bill is about 13cm in length. The wingspan is approximately 1.8m.

The Heron is best seen in its characteristic stance when it appears to be at rest, standing motionless by the water's edge or in shallow water. Then a sudden forward dart of the head, and a jab of the dagger-like bill seals the fate of some unsuspecting water creature, thus revealing the true character of this deceiver.

The prey could have been fish, frog or eel, or even a small mammal such as a water vole. Insects, worms and, on occasion, small birds also supplement the Heron's diet.

Heronries in Scotland are usually situated high in trees – fir, pine and beech being favoured – and although they can be occupied as early as February, it is usually into March before they are in full swing. Nests that survive from the previous season have extra material added, making them really substantial structures, while new nests are considerably smaller in size.

Although the eggs are laid in a deep cup they occasionally end up smashed on the ground when the tall, whippy trees are battered by spring storms, but thankfully if incubation is not too far advanced the hen will lay again.

In recent years a further and even deadlier menace has evolved to threaten the eggs or tiny chicks. Sadly, the diminishing role of the gamekeeper has meant an increase in Carrion Crow numbers with every heronry sharing nest sites with these opportunists, who rob the Herons' nests if they are left unattended for any length of time.

Herons nest in high trees early in the spring which can result in the contents of some of the nests coming to grief during severe storms.

Leaving heronries undisturbed until the young are well grown is the best advice for the enthusiastic watcher. Then it is a fascinating place for a visit – noisy and messy, with the nests containing almost full-grown young well marked with droppings, and downy, powdery feathers caught in the topmost branches as the young birds preen themselves continuously.

Observing a Heron approach the heronry you will notice that in flight the neck is well drawn in and the legs stretched straight out behind. The flight is slow and deliberate, but a considerable distance can be covered with surprising speed. The young birds greet their parents noisily, calling and clicking their beaks. The parents reply with a variety of sounds and, if alarmed, will utter a loud guttural 'fra-ank' – the sound which is responsible for the Heron's local name of 'Old Franky'.

The young are fed on regurgitated food taken from their parents' bills. Then, as the parents' visits to the nest gradually decrease, at about seven weeks old the young Heron will walk out along the spindly branches on equally spindly legs, spread their wings, and allow the breeze to lift them gently into the air.

Herons do not fare well in severe winters when their feeding grounds are frozen, and at such times some individuals can be approached to within a few metres before they reluctantly and laboriously take flight. Others, not quite so robust, will perish.

Herons are widespread throughout Scotland with a breeding population of over 1,000 pairs, and although most heronries are located in pine woods or other tall trees, about 10 per cent of Scottish Heron nest on cliffs.

In recent years, due to the advent of fish farms, Heron populations have decreased in some areas. Now fortunately, there are a variety of measures that can be taken to prevent Herons from raiding fish stocks.

GREY HERON

Comparative size Large, Stork-like.
Status Resident.
Habitat Open meadows with drains.
Nest Bulky, sticks and twigs in trees.
Eggs Greenish-blue, clutch 3-5.
Food Fish, frogs, small birds, small mammals, worms.

Mallard
Anas plantyrhynchos

Teal
Anas crecca

The **Mallard** is our best known wild duck, with practically every pond, loch, reservoir and river supporting resident populations. The 'Wild Duck', as it is also known, is the ancestor of most of our varieties of domestic duck, with many hybrids occurring on ponds in city and town parks.

The drake is an attractive bird, a trait that is found throughout the duck family. The dark green head and neck have a purplish sheen as has the browny coloured breast, the two separated by a thin white collar. The back and flanks are grey, and the upper – and under-tail coverts are black, with the tail pure white.

Both drakes and ducks have a black-edged purple 'speculum' which is bordered on both sides with white, forming a double wing bar in flight. The 'speculum' is a bar of bright colour, usually casting a metallic sheen, which is noticeable on the wings of surface-feeding duck and, to a lesser degree, on diving duck. The duck is mottled in browns and buffs, and as she incubates the eggs herself in her well-concealed nest among brambles, reeds, or other vegetation, occasionally in a large hole in a tree, she blends perfectly with her surroundings.

Mallards pair early in the year, possessing a well incubated clutch of about a dozen eggs by early March – soon to delight many thousands of children throughout the country as they appear on ponds with their tiny, floating brown-and-yellow ducklings scurrying around the mother while sifting the surface water for morsels of food.

In more out-of-the-way places duck Mallards, not quite so familiar with humans, tend to conceal their families from intruders by guiding them into cover as you approach the river or burnside and, if necessary, performing her 'broken wing' act to lead you away from her brood as they crouch together among the vegetation.

Mallards are widespread throughout Scotland with thousands more arriving from northern parts during autumn to spend the winter. It is mainly these arrivals that are sought after by wildfowlers, who lie in wait in 'butts' – concealed

The Mallard is the most familiar wild duck found on ponds, reservoirs, waterways and lochs.

places for shooters – listening for the whistling sound of their wings as they plane-in to land.

At 65cm the Mallard is one of the largest duck to frequent ponds, where they can become extremely tame, unlike our smallest member of the duck family, often found in the company of Mallards but by no means as trusting, the tiny Teal.

The **Teal** is widespread throughout Scotland and is our smallest duck, being only 36cm in length. Like the Mallard, whose company it apparently enjoys, it is a surface feeder or dabbling duck.

The drake Teal is as attractive as he is small. His rusty-brown head and neck have a broad

MALLARD
Comparative size Similar size to Herring Gull.
Status Resident, numbers increasing in winter.
Habitat Parks, ponds, most expanses of water.
Nest Twigs, grasses, feathers, down.
Eggs Clutch 9-12 (usually).
Food Water plants, aquatic creatures (wild); grain, bread, etc. (on town ponds).

TEAL
Comparative size Smaller than Mallard.
Status Resident, numbers increased in winter.
Habitat Lochs, ponds, marshes, moors.
Nest Grasses, bracken, down.
Eggs Pale buff, clutch 8-12.
Food Mainly seeds, insects.

fluorescent-green band from the eye down the sides of the head, with a white eyestripe which leads from the bottom of the eye forming the hint of a border. The back and flanks are finely decorated in contrasting thin, wavy lines of black and grey, and the speculum is black and green, above which is a conspicuous white bar. The breast is mottled with dark spots and there is a light patch under the buff-and-black-barred tail.

The duck is dressed in shades of light and dark brown, as she is the one who will incubate the eight to ten eggs in her nest concealed among the heather or moorland grasses in some well-hidden hollow, not too far from a source of water, to which she will eventually lead her ducklings.

The eggs are laid in April or May in the bracken-lined nest, and as incubation progresses the duck plucks downy feathers from her own breast to form an additional lining so that when the ducklings eventually hatch their first experience of life is to awaken in a cosy feather bed. All ducks line their nests in this manner as incubation progresses.

When disturbed, teal ducklings will more readily dive under the surface than young Mallards, and when crouching among vegetation on the open moor they are almost impossible to find. Teal are gregarious in autumn and winter, when they like to spend the day resting in some concealed place. Then, as evening falls they fly to their feeding grounds in a swift, direct flight.

Although all surface-feeding ducks spring clean from the surface of the water when disturbed, the Teal appears most agile and a spring of a dozen or so will rise almost vertically, as one bird, when alarmed.

Wigeon
Anas penelope
Gadwall
Anas strepera

Although the **Wigeon** is best known throughout the country as a wintering species, it now breeds in small numbers in practically every county in Scotland, mainly in the north.

The drake is a handsome bird, with a prominent yellowish-gold forehead and crown adorning the chestnut head. The mantle and flanks are grey, finely marked with slightly darker, fine wavy lines, and the pinkish-brown breast feathers merge into white underparts, which end abruptly at the base of the black tail. There is a white patch on the drake's forewing which is extremely conspicuous in flight, especially when a flock indulge in 'whiffling' – twisting, side-slipping, dropping a few metres and then levelling out before lowering the undercarriage and skiing to a halt before allowing themselves to settle – and though the duck is less conspicuous in her mottling of chestnut and brown, both birds sport a black, green and white speculum.

Wigeon are mainly grazing ducks, but they will dabble on ponds or other expanses of water where, when seen in the company of other surface feeders, the roundish head and shorter neck are noticeable.

Wigeon are quick to exploit the situation where a Mute Swan, while up-ending, provides them with morsels of water plants which float to the surface. This is known as 'commensal feeding': one species benefitting another.

On one such occasion while I was photographing a small party of Wigeon by the side of a pond, a Mute Swan sailed past and started up-ending to reach the bottom. Within moments the Wigeon approached and surrounded it, directly benefitting from the swan's efforts.

In Scotland Wigeon are late breeders, preferring heather moorlands or islands on lochs on which to nest, usually in May, and while the duck incubates the drake is always close by. Once hatched, the half dozen or so ducklings are tended by both parents for about six weeks.

Approaching a flock of Wigeon busily grazing in a field or coastal marsh, you can often hear the peculiarly attractive whistling notes before catching sight of the ducks themselves. They are extremely gregarious, and in winter large numbers can be seen resting together on any big expanse of water, either on the sea or inland.

WIGEON	
Comparative size	Smaller than Mallard.
Status	Mainly winter visitor.
Habitat	Lochs, ponds, rivers, fields.
Nest	Grasses, down.
Eggs	White, clutch 6-8.
Food	Grass, aquatic plants.

A lone drake Gadwall mingles with a group of Wigeon on the icy surface of a pond.

Almost 150 years ago the Gadwall was added to the list of British breeding birds, and from its place of introduction in East Anglia it spread slowly northwards, so that today it can be found breeding in Scotland from the south to the central regions on the eastern side of the country.

At 50cm in length Gadwall are slightly smaller than Mallard, and if a small number appear among other ducks on a pond one soon realises that here is the most inconspicuous drake among the entire duck family. But take a closer look, for he is every bit as handsome in his own way. Although his plumage is predominantly mottled greyish-brown, with the upper- and undertail coverts slightly darker, he sports a noticeable black-and-white speculum, as does his even more sombre coloured mate.

Both birds have contrasting white underparts, and when seen close up the drake's most attractive feature is the pattern on his breast: thousands of tiny crescents of greys, browns and black, seen to advantage when he treads the surface to exercise his wings.

Gadwalls swim high on the water and in the air the flight is direct, like that of the Mallard,

with a similar whistling sound as they pass overhead. Shyer than most ducks, Gadwall frequent quiet ponds, marshy pools, reservoirs and the like. Being dabbling duck, water plants picked from, or just under the surface form the bulk of their diet.

Certain of their display gestures are akin to those of the Wigeon, suggesting that the two are closely related, and in fact they can at times be seen together in suitable situations – the observation pond at the Wildfowl Trust Refuge at Eastpark in Dumfriesshire is one such place where I photographed the two species together. This type of habitat and amenity richly deserves further mention.

GADWALL

Comparative size Slightly smaller than Mallard.
Status Resident, numbers increase in winter.
Habitat Fresh water lochs, ponds, moorland.
Nest Sedges, grasses, down.
Eggs White, clutch 8-11.
Food Water plants.

Eastpark, Caerlaverock, Dumfriesshire

The refuge at Eastpark is inhabited entirely by truly wild species throughout the winter months. In fact, the reserve is open from mid-September until the end of April.

The main attraction is the population of Barnacle Geese numbering over 10,000 individuals, which arrive from their breeding grounds in Spitzbergen.

Large numbers of Pinkfooted Geese and to a lesser degree, Whooper and Bewick Swan, many species of duck and thousands of waders are all to be found and seen to advantage from one or other of the many well-concealed hides, or from the perfectly situated and comfortable observation towers.

To watch and observe the many species of duck, geese and swan from the observatory is a privilege and an opportunity no 'birdie person' should miss when in the county, whether novice or 'old timer'.

Other notable wildfowl wintering areas on the Scottish mainland

Location-Region	Species	Map Reference
Barons Haugh	Whoopers, Widgeon, Teal, Pochard, Tufted etc.	NS755552
Beauly Firth, Highland	Greylag, Pinkfeet, Snow Goose, Sawbills	NH600480
Cameron Reservoir, Fife	Pinkfeet, Greylags, Whoopers, Gadwall etc.	NO479123
Carron Valley Reservoir Central	Bean Geese	NS722838
Ken-Dee Marshes Dumfries & Galloway	Greenland Whitefronts, Greylag, Shoveler, Wigeon, Pintail, Goosander	NX648704
Loch Fleet Highland	Common and Velvet Scoters, Long-tailed Ducks, Red-Breasted Merganser	NH780970
Loch Leven – Vane Farm Tayside	Pinkfeet, Greylags (Mainly in autumn)	NT160991
Lochwinnoch, Strathclyde	Whoopers, Greylag, Goldeneye etc.	NS359581
Montrose Basin Grampian	Whooper & Mute Swans, Widgeon, Greylag, Pinkfeet, Shelduck, Pintail etc.	NO700580

Pintail
Anas acuta
Shoveller
Anas clypeata

The long 'pintail' of the **Pintail** makes it one of the more readily identifiable ducks, both on water and in flight. It has a long neck for a dabbling duck, with the back of the drake's being chocolate-brown, the same colour as the head and throat.

The upperparts are striped grey and black, the flanks are grey, and the breast and underparts are white. There is a continuation of the white breast feathers in the shape of a finger-wide stripe running up the sides of the neck and ending at the nape, and the speculum is bronze-green with a brown bar in front and a whitish one behind it. The undertail coverts are black, contrasting with

The Pintail's longish neck allows it to feed at a slightly greater depth than that reached by other dabbling ducks.

a creamy patch below. The duck strongly resembles a duck Mallard but her 'pintail' helps with identification.

Pintails enjoy the company of other surface-feeders and though their diet is similar, in the shape of water plants and other vegetation, they do not compete directly for food due to the length of their necks which makes it possible for them to reach the bottom at a slightly greater depth as they up-end.

Resident somewhat locally in Scotland, mainly on the eastern side of the country, their numbers are greatly swelled by visitors from north-eastern Europe during the winter months, when they can be found in large numbers both inland and on estuaries. Here their feeding is mainly nocturnal, though they also feed by day.

Pintail are quite tolerant towards others of their kind when breeding, and a few pairs could nest together in a small colony on an island in a loch. The nest is scant, a mere hollow among the vegetation lined with down, and the eggs are laid in May. The duck incubates alone for about 22 days with the drake never far away, and when the ducklings hatch they are tended by both parents for about six weeks.

One of the most impressive sights presented by wildfowl is to watch an evening flight of a thousand or so Pintail, having departed their roosting area, pass overhead towards their feeding haunts, usually on estuarial flats.

The remarkable spoon-shaped bill of the **Shoveler** gives rise to its name. The drake is a truly handsome bird, with his dark-green head and neck contrasting with a white breast and a further patch of white in front of the undertail coverts. The upperparts are dark, brown with a whitish line separating them from the chestnut-

PINTAIL
Comparative size Mallard size.
Status Resident, numbers increased in winter.
Habitat Lochs, estuaries.
Nest Slight hollow, lined down.
Eggs Cream, clutch 7-9.
Food Water plants, molluscs, crustaceans.

SHOVELER
Comparative size Smaller than Mallard.
Status Resident.
Habitat Shallow edges of ponds, lochs.
Nest Hollow lined grass, down.
Eggs Buffish, clutch 8-12.
Food Small aquatic life, water plants/seeds.

coloured flanks, and the wing has a front edging of pale green with the speculum green and white.

The duck, as is usual in the dabbling ducks, is mottled and streaked in shades of brown but at least she sports a little colour in the pale green forewing and green-and-white speculum.

The Shoveler looks unbalanced in the air, with his huge bill pointing downwards. He is extremely ungainly on land, but once in his natural element he is an excellent and lively swimmer.

The curiously shaped bill of the Shoveler is indeed a specialised aid as it contains rows of tiny tooth-like serrations called lamellae, which are extremely effective as a filter when feeding on minute aquatic life and fragments of water plants. The method of feeding also differs from the usual surface-feeding habit, in as much as the Shoveler does not favour up-ending but is content to scurry over the pond surface, moving his bill from side to side in the shallow, muddy water which passes through the bill and is filtered continuously.

If the area the Shoveler is working is not too productive, he will resort to a clever manoeuvre to obtain his meal. He picks a spot a few metres from the bank, not too deep, and swims around in a small circle, somehow producing the effect of a small whirlpool in reverse – the tiny insects and plant matter can then be collected from the surface. I was extremely fortunate on one occasion to photograph this entire sequence of events.

The nest is well concealed among reeds or other vegetation, usually near water. It is a slight hollow, lined with down and, when hatched, the ducklings are tended by their parents for about six weeks.

Shovelers are present throughout the lower half of Scotland, but they are absent from the north west.

Pochard
Aythya ferina
Tufted Duck
Aythya fuligula

Watch a party of **Pochard** on a pond as they doze and bob on the surface of the water and you will see a picture of serenity but, if alarmed the scene changes dramatically as these diving duck labour to become airborne.

Unlike surface feeders that spring clean from the water, diving duck patter across the surface, flapping their wings furiously to get into the air – a good pointer in identification:

Surface feeders = spring clean.

Diving ducks = require running take-off

The drake Pochard is quite colourful in his chestnut head and neck, grey vermiculated back and flanks, and black breast. Black is also the colour of his upper- and undertail coverts, contrasting with white underparts, and the grey speculum is barely distinguishable against the grey wings. The duck is less colourful, being dressed in shades of brown and grey with pale markings on her cheeks and throat.

When airborne, the flight is straight and rapid and there are no prominent wing bars or markings to be seen. In the water Pochard are excellent swimmers and divers remaining submerged for about 20 seconds as they scour the bottom at a depth of about two to three metres for the aquatic plants and water insects on which they feed.

Pochard prefer to nest near water and the nest which can be a bulky affair, is hidden among the dense cover of reeds or rushes at the pond edge. The six to ten greenish eggs are laid in April or May and incubated by the duck alone for about

POCHARD
Comparative size Smaller than Mallard.
Status Resident, numbers increase in winter.
Habitat Shallow lochs, reservoirs, rivers.
Nest Down-lined depression in vegetation.
Eggs Greenish grey, clutch 6-12.
Food Seeds of water plants, insect larvae, shellfish.

The Pochard is one of the more familiar diving ducks and is usually seen in the company of Tufteds.

24 days and, when hatched, she alone tends the ducklings for about seven weeks.

Pochard are not plentiful in Scotland, or even throughout the whole of the UK as a breeding species, but in autumn large numbers arrive from central Europe.

Pochard prefer to feed in shallower fresh water, but favour the safety of deeper lochs and reservoirs for roosting, often in the company of Tufted Duck.

The **Tufted Duck** is second to the Mallard for popularity on our lochs, reservoirs and ponds in town and city parks. Because they are able to exploit the many expanses of water created by man there has been a dramatic rise in their numbers over the past thirty years, but unlike the Mallard they have less tendency to hybridise, remaining true to their species to a higher degree.

The drake is unmistakable in his pied colouring. With a black head, back, breast and tail with contrasting pure white underparts, he also has a white wing-bar which is conspicuous in flight. He also has a crest of trailing black feathers and is the only duck to be adorned in such a way. The duck is dressed in dark browns, with paler flanks, but she also sports white wing-bars.

Tufted Ducks conform in many ways to the general pattern of behaviour of other diving ducks, and in the air, on the ground and afloat they are especially akin to the Pochard. On diving below the surface, Tufteds can slip underwater almost without a ripple, while at other times they submerge in an explosion of spray similar to the dive of the Pochard. When under the surface, at a depth of some three metres, Tufteds feed on a variable diet of vegetable and animal matter such as small fish, aquatic insects, worms and even frogs, so they do not compete directly with the Pochard.

In the breeding season a number of pairs can be found nesting together among the vegetation on an island in a loch, usually not too far from the water's edge. The nest is a mere hollow, lined with grass and rushes, and when the clutch of up to a dozen eggs are laid their greenish colouring contrasts strongly with the lining of dark down in the nest. Following an incubation period of about 24 days, the hatched ducklings are tended solely by the duck, and are independent at the age of seven weeks.

Tufted Ducks are resident throughout Scotland, with large numbers migrating here in the autumn from Iceland, Scandinavia and north-east Europe, when our native population is increased by many thousands.

Scaup
Aythya marilla

Long Tailed Duck
Clangula hyemalis

Smew
Mergus albellus

Although there are about a dozen authentic records for **Scaup** breeding in the north of Scotland at the turn of the century, ever since then it has been absent as a breeding species. However, it more than makes up for this summer absence through the large numbers that spend the winter around our shores, arriving mainly from Iceland and northern Europe.

A compactly designed diving-duck accustomed to battling the maritime elements, the Scaup is at once seen by the watcher to resemble the Tufted Duck, but the light grey (not black) back soon rectifies any mistaken identity. As well as having a grey back, the drake's head, neck, tail and tail coverts are black, contrasting with white flanks and underparts. The duck is much browner in appearance, with a conspicuous white patch at the base of her bill, giving her a pale-faced look.

Essentially a sea duck, Scaup are seldom seen inland. The shallow coastal waters of the Forth and Solway are two favoured wintering areas, though numbers in the Forth around Leith have decreased dramatically since the disappearance of enormous quantities of waste grain from local breweries. Islay, however, offers somewhat

---

TUFTED DUCK

Comparative size Smaller than Mallard.
Status Resident, increased in numbers in winter.
Habitat Fresh water lochs, ponds.
Nest Depression lined with grass, down.
Eggs Greenish-grey, clutch 7-12.
Food Molluscs, crustaceans, small fish.

The Smew, a scarce winter visitor from the USSR, is the smallest member of the three sawbills which occur in Scotland.

similar fare, with barley waste from distilleries being sought after by many hundreds of wintering Scaup. Some observers have remarked on the tameness of this species and how they could be approached to within a few metres – perhaps the ducks were slightly tipsy?

Scaup are a very sociable species, and as well as feeding together, large numbers will roost together in shallow estuaries and bays. The take-off from the water, especially in a slightly choppy sea, is extremely laboured, the birds pattering over the surface with great effort to become airborne.

In their breeding haunts Scaup remain sociable, nesting in colonies usually situated on an island in a lake, and the nest, a mere hollow on the ground lined with feathers and dow,n is never far from water. The six to ten greenish-grey eggs are laid in May or June and when the ducklings appear they are led to water as soon as they are dry, and are then tended by both parents for some six weeks, after which time they become independent.

Principally a wintering species found around the Northern Isles, the **Long-tailed Duck** is also found down the east coast in varying numbers, and it was not until recently, due to their habit of favouring the open sea, that the existence of greater numbers than previously believed came to light: a study of sea-going duck in the Moray Firth area showed that approximately 12,000 Long-tailed Ducks wintered there annually.

SCAUP

Comparative size Smaller than Mallard.
Status Winter visitor.
Habitat Coasts, estuaries.
Nest Down-lined crevice in rock.
Eggs Olive grey, clutch 8-12.
Food Molluscs.

In winter, when we are most likely to see the Longtail, the drake is brown and white. His head, neck, underparts and flanks are white, with the remainder of his plumage dark brown, and he also sports a long, pointed, brown tail. In summer plumage he is a different duck entirely, dressed in rich shades of chestnut and brown but retaining white underparts, undertail coverts and cheeks. The duck's tail is much shorter and she is much browner at all seasons.

As one would expect from such a marine species, the Long-tail is perfectly suited for the open sea, being a buoyant swimmer and an expert diver. Something of an exception to the rule for diving duck, the Long-tail does not patter over the surface before taking off but springs clear of the water, in a style similar to that of the surface feeders. While they are gregarious, Long-tailed Duck prefer the company of their own kind.

In the air the bird has a characteristic rolling flight as it sways from side to side, alternately showing a brown back and then white underparts, while at the same time the wings on the up-stroke are held on a horizontal plane in line with the body.

Occasionally, on some inland loch, reservoir or smaller expanse of water a small, predominantly white diving-duck splashes down during the autumn or winter months, to add a real 'blue riband' tick to the watcher's list. The tiny **Smew** is only 26cm in length, extremely active, wary and difficult to observe, but do persevere – for this native of Russia has, for some reason or other, overshot his Dutch wintering grounds to delight those of us fortunate enough to be within viewing distance with every sighting in Scotland worth a mention in birdwatching journals. They are, in fact, somewhat more plentiful in south-east England where approximately 100 sightings are reported annually.

The drake's white plumage is broken by black lines on his back, breast and flanks, and a black patch below his eye. There is also a black centre to his wispy crest, and his tail and tail coverts are grey. The duck has a chestnut head and nape, grey upperparts, greyish underparts and white cheeks, so that she too is an attractive and distinctive bird, at times being dubbed a 'Redhead'.

The Smew is related to the Goosander and Red-breasted Merganser, with all three being classed as Sawbills, as the edges of their bills are serrated with tiny tooth-like spines. The 'teeth' point slightly backwards, making it almost impossible for any fish prey to escape: then they are brought to the surface and devoured.

LONG TAILED DUCK
Comparative size Smaller than Mallard. **Status** Winter visitor. **Habitat** Maritime lochs. **Nest** Grass, down lined. **Eggs** Olive buff, clutch 5-11. **Food** Crustaceans, molluscs.

SMEW
Comparative size Much smaller than Mallard. **Status** Winter visitor. **Habitat** Lochs, reservoirs, waterways. **Nests** Hole in tree, woodchips, down. **Eggs** White, clutch 7-10. **Food** Fish, aquatic insects.

Goosander
Mergus merganser

Red-breasted Merganser
Mergus serrator

The **Goosander,** the larger of our two breeding Sawbills, is a long, slender bird some 62cm in length. Sawbills are so called because their long, narrow bills with downcurved tips are edged with tiny, spiny, pin-sharp serrations which point slightly backwards making them extremely effective for catching and holding slippery fish, the Sawbills' only form of food.

The Goosander drake is indeed a handsome bird with his shiny, bottle-green head and neck, black mantle and wings, grey rump and tail, and white sides and underparts tinged with delicate salmon pink. The bill and webbed feet are deep red. The duck is predominantly grey, with a rich brown head adorned with a singular crest of spiky feathers.

Goosander are now common throughout most of Scotland, even though the first breeding was

The abundance of down in the Goosander's nest denotes that the eggs are well incubated and that hatching could take place within a few days.

recorded just over a century ago. For many years they did not enjoy the protection of the law, as they are detrimental to fish stocks on salmon and trout rivers, but thankfully now they are protected. Nevertheless, on some rivers in the south of Scotland with which I am well acquainted, Goosander numbers are exceptionally high, so perhaps some form of control will have to be implemented – hopefully not the method used in an attempt to curb their numbers in the past by one or two inadequate anglers, who blamed their poor baskets on every creature that ever caught and ate a fish. This was based on the fact that goosander ducks, when their eggs are well incubated, line the nest with a cosy lining of down plucked from their own breasts. The nest, when situated in a hole in a tree, is usually, but not always, near water and the duck sits very tight, hissing snake-like at any intruder. It is this reluctance to leave her eggs that had led to her demise on the odd occasion that I came across a nest where a few large stones covered both duck and nest contents.

On a happier note, many's the angler at the riverside who, out of the corner of his or her eye, would catch sight of a movement as a duck Goosander drifted downstream, hugging the far bank as close as possible as she led her brood of ten or so ducklings to safety. As soon as she was a few metres downstream from the standing figure she would erupt into action, flapping and scurrying further downstream with her family in close pursuit. Fifty metres or so further on she would pause, turn, collect her brood and, with a final glance as if to say 'Ha! Fooled you', continue on her way.

As with other duck, the drake Goosander goes through an eclipse period of moult when he strongly resembles the female. This eclipse can take about eight weeks from July to September, but once through the moult drakes of all species are truly resplendent.

In winter Goosanders are gregarious, with good numbers being seen on lochs, reservoirs and estuaries and there is always a resident population on our rivers unless the winter becomes too severe, when they move to larger expanses of water.

The **Red-breasted Merganser,** being 55cm in length is slightly smaller than the Goosander, and the drake is a much more colourful bird. His dark green head is decorated with a double crest of spiky feathers and he has a white collar with a white line running down his nape, which merges with his dark mantle. The lower back and flanks are streaked with grey and the wings are black and white. His breast is bright chestnut and the underparts, rump and tail are white. The duck has a brown head and neck with a smaller crest, greyish-brown back and white underparts, with the white markings on the wings being less prominent.

Mergansers are more inclined than Goosanders to frequent salt water where they fish at greater depths, but on rising from the surface both birds have similar difficulty in becoming airborne, having to patter furiously across the surface.

The nest of the Red-breasted Merganser is located on the ground, sheltered by rocks or an overhanging bank, and the eggs are laid in a mere hollow lined extensively with the duck's grey down. The eggs are laid at least four weeks later than those of the Goosander, hatching similarly, so although they are both fed on similar tiny aquatic life, the broods of youngsters do not compete with each other in the early days when they are most vulnerable.

On the river the Merganser has a characteristic method of fishing, usually allowing himself to be carried downstream by the current while periodically poking his head under the surface to sight his prey. Family parties can also be seen feeding in this manner, and Goosander will also fish in packs, driving a shoal of fish towards a certain point and then diving together to catch their meal.

GOOSANDER
Comparative size Larger than Mallard.
Status Resident.
Habitat Rivers, lochs, reservoirs.
Nest Hole in a tree.
Eggs Creamy white, clutch 6-12.
Food Mainly fish

RED-BREASTED MERGANSER
Comparative size Mallard size.
Status Resident.
Habitat Rivers, estuaries.
Nest Hollow under overhang, lined down.
Eggs Greenish buff, clutch 6-10.
Food Fish.

Scoters

Bucephala clangula

Goldeneye

The **Goldeneye** gets its name from its beautiful golden-coloured eyes, which are even more pronounced as they are set amid the glossy greenish-black feathers of the 'buffel' (bushy) head.

The drake is a study in black and white, with a noticeable white patch between the eye and base of the bill. The back and tail are black with pure white sides and underparts, and there are white striped patches on the black wings. The duck is somewhat smaller being greyish-brown above, and though she displays white patches on her wings, she completely lacks the white face patch of her mate.

The Goldeneye is a robust little duck completely at home on loch or pond in all weathers, an excellent swimmer and diver, diving

The pied plumage, curious shaped head and golden eyes are striking characteristics of the drake Goldeneye.

at times to a depth of six metres, and when necessary they can leave the water with little difficulty to take flight. The flight itself is characteristic, strong and swift with a peculiar whistling of the wings, with which, when you are familiar, an overhead party can be identified by sound alone.

Goldeneye are a more solitary species than most ducks, preferring their own company or, at most, small parties. For the last 20 years Goldeneye have bred in central Scotland, encouraged by the proficient use of nest boxes on some Scottish lochs, and as their numbers increase hopefully they will spread further south,

---

GOLDENEYE

Comparative size Smaller than Mallard.
Status Scarce breeding resident, many arrive in winter.
Habitat Woodland lochs.
Nest Tree hollow/nest box, feather-down lining.
Eggs Bluish-green, clutch 7-12.
Food Crustaceans, molluscs, aquatic insects.

as occasionally Goldeneye pairs can be seen in courtship display on our southern lochs in late spring.

When feeding Goldeneye dive to a fair depth and while on the bottom the short, stubby bill is brought into use, turning over small stones and pebbles in search of the aquatic animal life on which they feed.

Once established as a breeding species, the same site can be used in successive years with only a sparse lining being required, as the nest soon becomes a mass of feathers and down. When the ducklings hatch they generally stay within the safety of the nest for about a day or so, then they tumble out of the hole and head towards the water where they are tended by the mother for about seven to eight weeks.

Common Scoter

Melanitta nigra

Velvet Scoter

Melanitta fusca

Surf Scoter

Melanitta perspicillata

All Scoters are predominantly black and by far the best way to study them is from a boat, but they can be seen from the mainland when large 'rafts' of birds appear off our shores in winter.

The **Common Scoter** is the most numerous and the drake's black plumage is striking, for here is the only all-black duck to appear on our waters, with the only other colour on the drake being a reddish patch on the upper mandible of the black bill. The duck, as with all ducks of the Scoter family, is much browner.

Typical duck of the open sea, the Common Scoter is sturdy, buoyant, an expert diver and a powerful swimmer and flier. When a large raft of several hundreds is located there is always continuous activity, some diving, some on the surface and some in low flight, leap-frogging from the rear to the front of the raft and then diving into fresh fishing grounds to scour the bottom for molluscs of all kinds, mussels being strongly favoured, though fish and marine plants will also be taken.

When watching a raft of Scoters, always be on the lookout for a flash of white amid the bobbing black mass. Look carefully for a prominent white wing-bar which identifies a close relative, the **Velvet Scoter,** who at 55cm is slightly larger than the Common Scoter, at 48cm.

The Common is the only Scoter to breed in Scotland, in a few of the northern regions, with the majority coming from Scandinavia and Russia to spend the winter off our coasts. The Velvet Scoter is entirely a winter visitor arriving from similar breeding haunts but in far lesser numbers. Wintering Scoters appear to favour the eastern sea coast, with huge numbers being recorded in the Moray Firth region.

The Solway is also a favourite wintering area for Scoters, with sea cliffs offering good vantage points, and when the onshore winds drive the birds closer to land this is the time to scrutinise the rafts with care, in order to see if you can spot the third and rarest of our Scoters – the **Surf Scoter,** which appears from time to time either singly or in small parties. This bird is easy to identify if you can hold him in focal distance for any length of time, the white forehead and nape confirming identification – on one occasion while I was observing four drakes on the Solway, an individual raised himself on the crest of a wave while facing seawards, showing that the white nape patch was conspicuous even at a fair distance.

Eider

Somateria mollissima

Shelduck

Tadorna tadorna

The shape, size and colour of the drake **Eider** in his summer plumage makes him unmistakable. He has a pure white mantle and breast, the latter tinged with pink, while his crown, flanks,

---

COMMON SCOTER

Comparative size Smaller than Mallard.
Status Resident, large numbers wintering.
Habitat Maritime and lochs.
Nest On ground, grasses, down.
Eggs Pale brown.
Food Molluscs.

The drake Eider is a striking bird and though the duck is drab by comparison the down plucked form her breast to line the nest during incubation is much in demand for Eiderdowns.

underparts and tail are black. There are pale greenish patches on the sides of the head and nape, and the wedge-shaped bill is also greenish. The duck also has a large wedge-shaped bill, but her colouring is a pattern of brown and black bars and markings.

Eiders are among the seabirds which can suffer extensively in the aftermath of that modern day curse, the oilspill, but thankfully these birds are on the increase, with practically the whole of the Scottish coastline and islands being frequented by potential breeders.

Visit a colony of Eiders in early May when they are indulging in their courtship displays, and you will witness some weird and wonderful sights and sounds as the drakes perform in front of the ducks. It seems that there are drakes everywhere, but a month or so later the picture is quite different – the drakes have disappeared, and you have to look closely to find the sitting ducks.

Nests can be made in a variety of places, but the most common site is in a grassy tussock or a cleft in the rocks. In both cases, when incubation is well under way with the ducklings due to hatch within a few days, the eggs are bedded in a mass of eiderdown, plucked from the duck's own breast a little at a time as she sat patiently over the previous three weeks. This is the origin of our cosy eiderdown quilts, and even today in Iceland colonies of many thousands of Eider are encouraged to nest by all manner of means, so that the down may be collected and marketed.

When the ducklings hatch they are taken to the water where they behave very independently, seeking protection only when alarmed. When a threat appears the ducklings will scurry to the

---

EIDER

Comparative size Size of Mallard.
Status Resident.
Habitat Rocky shores.
Nest Hollow on ground, lined feathers-down.
Eggs Creamy, clutch 4-6.
Food Mussels, crustaceans (marine).

nearest parent – not necessarily their own – so that sometimes a duck can be seen with a large brood of various sized youngsters, or alternatively a few mothers will group together and form a larger family party.

Outside the breeding season Eiders spend much of their time on the open sea, but they do come inshore to rest on rocky islets or ledges at the base of cliffs, and when a number appear close by a harbour wall or suchlike they present the watcher with a fine and entertaining specatacle as they dive under the surface up to a depth of about six metres to secure the mussels and crustaceans on which they feed.

The **Shelduck** is the largest member of the duck family but would fit more comfortably somewhere between the ducks and geese, as some of their characteristics and habits are quite goose-like. On land they walk easily and can become airborne with very little effort, and when in flight they present an unmistakably colourful study in black, white, chestnut and green.

The first noticeable feature the birdwatcher records that is more characteristic of geese than of ducks is the fact that both drakes and ducks are similarly coloured, having dark, bottle-green heads with white breasts and underparts. The white tails are tipped with black and the wings are black and white with a green speculum. From the lower breast a broad chestnut band encircles the body and the bills are deep red, that of the drake adorned with a curious knob at the base. Another noticeable goose-like feature when a flock of Shelduck is in flight is the fact that they fly in 'V' formation.

Shelduck are birds of the shoreline, seldom going far from land, and as such they choose to nest in a appropriate habitat. The nest is built in a rabbit hole among the sand dunes, being a mere scrape at the end of the burrow liberally lined with down, in which a dozen or so eggs are laid. The duck incubates alone for four weeks, but the drake is always close by. When breeding further inland, Shelduck can be found nesting in tree-holes, haystacks and holes in walls.

When hatched, the ducklings leave the nest almost at once, in single file, the procession heading seawards, with mother in the lead, then the ducklings and finally dad bringing up the rear. They are tended for about eight weeks by adult birds – not necessarily their own parents, for the Shelduck take their brood to a recognised 'nursery' on the shore, usually in a sheltered estuary, where there are always a few 'aunties' in attendance. These 'aunties' could be ducks with failed nests or non-breeders, but they do get left virtually 'holding the baby' or, more precisely, the broods. The crèche can contain half a dozen or so families of ducklings from a few days old to the free-flying stage, and the minders will tend them for as long as necessary. Meanwhile, their true parents have probably departed for their moulting grounds in the region of the German Bight, where for about six weeks – the time it takes to re-grow their main flight feathers – the birds populate the mudflats with rafts in excess of 25,000 individuals.

Following the moult, most of the British Shelduck return to spend the winter in their native waters, with the Scottish coastal mudflats providing the marine molluscs, crustaceans and insects necessary for their survival.

Grey Geese
Greylag
Anser anser

White-fronted Goose
Anser albifrons

Pinkfoot
Anser brachyrhynchus

Bean
Anser fabalis

Four species of grey geese winter in Scotland but only one is a regular breeder mainly in the north-western part of the country.

SHELDUCK
Comparative size Larger than Mallard.   **Status** Resident.   **Habitat** Coastal mud flats.   **Nest** In burrow, grasses-down.   **Eggs** Creamy white, clutch 8-14.   **Food** Molluscs, crustaceans (marine).

The **Greylag** is the largest of the group and from a distance appears as a typical grey goose, greyish-brown being the predominant colouring, with a conspicuous white rump and undertail coverts (small, broad feathers on wings and tail).

Greylags are the nearest relatives to farmyard geese and their calls are said to be somewhat similar. As there aren't too many farmyard geese with which to familiarise oneself these days, a couple of simple pointers to identification may help.

When observing a flock of grey geese in a field, firstly note the colour of the bill, then concentrate on the legs and feet, if the flock consists of hundreds of individuals with noticeably orange bills, pink legs and feet, then Greylag are your subject.

Wintering Greylag arrive in October, flying in in skeins (flights) of varying numbers in typical V formation until there are many thousands throughout Scotland.

Even in good light the pale grey forewing of the Greylag may be difficult to distinguish, but while planing-in to land, especially on water, the aerial evolutions of these large geese as they come 'whiffling' in is a good identification feature. The birds twist, side-slip, drop a few metres and then level out, before lowering their undercarriage and ski-ing to a halt on the surface, then allowing themselves to settle.

Greylags frequent salt and freshwater marshes, lochs, ponds and fields where they find the grazing to their liking. Breeding pairs build large nests among heather or rushes using sticks, heather and grasses with moss and down for the lining. The female incubates the eggs on her own but her mate is in attendance when the goslings appear, and then the family move off together to the nearest water course.

The **Whitefront** is noticeably smaller than the Greylag, and in general appearance is the darkest member of the greygoose clan.

A visit to an area such as the Ken-Dee marshes south of New Galloway in winter could well provide the birdwatcher with generous views of these birds, and as there are also flocks of Greylag in the area comparisons can be made.

Firstly, the white patch at the base of the bill will be noticeable, with the breasts of the Whitefronts having varying degrees of black markings in the shape of broken horizontal bands. The legs and feet are orange and the bill, on closer inspection, will also appear yellowish-orange, identifying the flock as **Greenland Whitefront,** birds which breed in Greenland and choose to winter with us in **south-west** Scotland. Migrating skeins fly in typical 'V' formation and in smaller, looser flocks, with their voice being the most musical (in a 'yodelling fashion'), of all the geese. **European Whitefront** from the USSR have pinkish coloured bills, and these birds winter further south, mainly in the Severn estuary.

Thousands of the smallest members of the 'greygoose' clan arrive in Scotland in late September and October to spend the winter here. The **Pinkfoot** has, as its name suggests, pink feet and legs. The bill is also pinkish coloured, but as it has a black base and tip it looks completely dark even from relatively short distances, especially in poor light. This is one of its identification features. The bill is also noticeably shorter and stubbier than the bills of other grey geese, making it more efficient for feeding on potatoes and other root crops, while stubble and arable land are also favoured.

In the evening, when large flocks fly from their roosting grounds on the sandbanks in the estuaries to feed in the fields, they present an awe-inspiring spectacle for the birdwatcher. On migration or flying from one feeding ground to another, Pinkfoot fly in usual chevron fashion or long angular lines, and as their 'honking' calls carry for great distances, the watcher looks skywards, firstly trying to assess their numbers,

GREYLAG
Comparative size Smaller than Canada Goose. **Status** Resident, large numbers arrive in winter. **Habitat** Fields, meadows, lochs, ponds. **Nest** Built on ground, sticks, grasses, down. **Eggs** Creamy white, clutch 4-6. **Food** Grasses, various vegetation.

PINKFOOT
Comparative size Smaller than Greylag. **Status** Winter visitor. **Habitat** Summer, Tundra and marsh: Winter, fields, including root crops **Nest** Shallow cup of vegetation and down. **Eggs** White, clutch 4-6. **Food** Grasses, cereals, root crops.

The Greylag is scarce as a breeding bird in Scotland but thousands spend the winter here, mainly arriving from Iceland.

then mentally forecasting the weather by noting the direction in which they are flying. This piece of old country lore has always left me somewhat quizzical, as skeins of Pinkfoot may be seen one day flying from the Solway area northwards, then a few days later the (same?) birds return!

The **Bean Goose** is one of the larger of the greygoose clan, being almost as large as the Greylag, with which it is often confused. However, although the colouring of the bill is orange, similar to that of the Greylag, it has a black tip and base, so much less of the orange is actually visible. The legs and feet are also orange, and in general appearance the goose is brownish-grey.

Bean are the scarcest of our grey geese, withjust a few appearing annually in south-west Scotland, but there is a flock of about fifty which winters on the Carron Valley Reservoir in Central Region about twelve miles west of Falkirk.

Canada Goose

Branta canadensis

The **Canada** is one of the members of the black goose clan, and at 95cm in length it is the largest of all our geese.

Introduced into England in the seventeenth century as an adornment to lakes and ponds in country estates and parks, it soon became established as a successful breeding species and spread accordingly. Although the overall British population is well into thousands, the Scottish contingent is merely a few hundreds, mainly in Dumfries and Galloway Region and Central Region, with a few being found further north.

The Canada is a very large grey and brown goose. The upperparts and wings are greyish-brown with paler edges to the feathers, with a paler shade of barred-brown on the breast and

---

CANADA GOOSE

Comparative size Largest of our geese.
Status Resident.
Habitat Reservoirs, ponds, marshes.
Nest Depression on ground, grass, leaves, down.
Eggs Creamy white, clutch 5-10.
Food Grasses, water plants.

underparts. The tail is dark brown, contrasting with the white hindquarters, and the head and neck are black with a white mark extending from the chin almost to the crown, then down to the base of the grey bill.

Canada Geese are gregarious, but in the breeding season they can become territorial and this controls the number of nests on any one expanse of water. In Scotland the Canada Goose appears slightly less tolerant towards humans and prefers to nest in out-of-the-way moorland or marshy ponds, preferably with a small islet where they feel relatively safe from predators.

The nest is usually built among dense reeds or other vegetation and is a depression lined with grass, leaves, feathers and down. The eggs are hatched by the goose alone, but the gander is always close by and together they tend the goslings for about seven weeks until they are ready to fend for themselves. Grasses of various kinds plus water plants and weeds form most of the Canada's diet, but they also have a liking for grain.

Like all geese, the Canada has a flightless period, when the major flight feathers are cast in unison. Over the years some Canadas have reverted almost to their original wild state, and as such they seek a haven where they can rest and feed until their flight feathers have re-grown. The Beauly Firth, north-west of Inverness, provides such sanctuary and numbers of up to 1,000 leave the West Riding of Yorkshire and the Midlands to spend high summer on Scottish waters.

Barnacle Goose

Branta leucopsis

The **Barnacle Goose** is the other member of the blackgoose clan to be found in Scotland, but only as a wintering species. 'Only' is perhaps the wrong word to use in any descriptive form regarding the Barnacle Goose, for every winter many thousands of people marvel at the beauty of the individual, and the majesty of the huge flocks as they flight back and forth between merse (the marshy area bordering the sea) and field to feed and roost.

The Barnacle Goose is perfection in black, white and grey. The crown, neck and breast are glossy black, with the underparts silver-grey barred slightly darker. The forehead and face are white as are the hindquarters, and the bill and legs are black.

Over 40 years ago Caerlaverock, on the Solway (later to become a National Nature Reserve), provided early sanctuary for the Barnacle Geese when their numbers totalled a mere few hundreds. Many successful years later, with the development at Eastpark Farm and competent management by the Wildfowl Trust, the numbers now wintering in the Solway are in excess of 10,000.

The Caerlaverock Barnacles are the breeding population from Spitzbergen in the Arctic Circle and they usually start to arrive in late September, delighting us with their presence for about six months. In their breeding grounds, Barnacle Geese provide us with a rather surprising revelation, as normally one thinks of geese incubating their eggs in nests on the ground. The Barnacles, however, nest on ledges on high cliffs, a precaution against predators such as the arctic fox.

Back in their wintering grounds there is always something of interest taking place. It may be a skein of some thousands flying low over the reserve, or hedge-hopping from one field to another, or simply grazing, with perhaps the odd albino adding further interest.

The breeding population of Barnacle Geese from Greenland winter on the RSPB reserve at Loch Gruinart, on the island of Islay, with a population almost double that of the Solway. There are also large numbers of Whitefronts that find the grazing much to their liking on the island and a visit to Loch Indaal will produce good sightings of many of our sea ducks and waders.

Over ten thousand Barnacle Geese, the entire breeding population from Spitzbergen, winter in and around the Wildfowl and Wetlands Reserve at East Park on the Solway Firth.

BARNACLE GOOSE

Comparative size Smaller than Canada Goose.
Status Winter visitor.
Habitat Fields, merses, estuaries.
Nest On rocky ledge, depression, lined grass, down.
Eggs White, clutch 3-5.
Food Mainly grasses.

Mute Swan
Cygnus olor

For sheer grace, elegance and power, the swan has no equal, with practically every pond and loch supporting varying numbers. In town and city ponds, **Mute Swans** become very tame, accepting titbits from anyone. A stroll in the park with the children prior to Sunday lunch generally includes the ritual of feeding the ducks and swans, especially in winter.

Everyone is familiar with this large white bird with the long neck and pinkish-orange bill, the male or 'cob' having a noticeable large black knob at the base, while the female or 'pen' possesses a similar bill but with the knob not so pronounced.

Mooching among the smaller residents of the pond, snatching and swallowing pieces of soggy bread crusts, the swan loses some of its dignity, but in a semi-wild state grace and elegance are restored.

In March, if there is no suitable nest site where they are they will leave, flapping furiously while paddling along the surface of the water to become airborne. Once in flight their flying power is demonstrated as, with head and neck stretched straight out in front and wings producing a musical humming sound, the pair head towards a more suitable breeding habitat. On arrival at their destination they soon commence building their huge nest close by the water, the cob bringing the nest material in the shape of sticks, rushes, roots and reeds and the pen arranging it to suit herself.

As a rule, five to seven large greenish-grey eggs are laid but larger clutches are not unusual. As soon as the clutch is complete both parents share the incubation period of about 35 days, and during this time the cob is extremely aggressive in defence of the nest and eggs. If you approach the nest he adopts a formidable appearance, hissing in defiance as he challenges the intruder with outspread wings arched over his back, ready for the attack. Usually the sight of the swan in this posture is enough to persuade the intruder to back off, but there are occasions when the cob has left the water's edge to strike a severe blow with his wing.

When the cygnets appear they are clad in silver-grey down and can often be seen riding on the pen's back, warm and safe. Later the down becomes darker, with cygnets being fully fledged in about five months. However, they must wait two years before attaining the pure white plumage of their parents.

Mute Swans will at times up-end while feeding, being able to reach the bottom, and the water plants and weeds on which they feed, at depths of up to one metre.

Found as residents throughout Scotland, swan numbers are greatly increased during the winter when they are joined by their arctic cousins, the Whooper from Iceland and USSR.

MUTE SWAN	
Comparative size Very large, 150cm.	
Status Resident.	
Habitat Ponds, lochs, rivers, reservoirs.	
Nest Bulky, sticks, roots, rushes, reeds.	
Eggs Large, greenish-grey, clutch 6-10.	
Food Water plants, weeds, some amphibia.	

Whooper Swan
Cygnus cygnus
Bewick's Swan
Cygnus columbianus

In late autumn, **Whooper Swans** arrive in Scotland from Iceland and practically every county has a regular flock, with the largest numbers wintering in the Outer Hebrides. Probably the world's heaviest flying birds, weighing up to 20kg, it is little wonder that they never cease to thrill the watcher as they bugle-call overhead, answering similar calls from their kin on the waters below, then veering and landing to swell their numbers.

The Whooper is similar in size to the Mute Swan, with the yellow base of the black bill being the best feature for comparison. At a distance, the upright head and neck stance of the Whooper also differs from the gentle curve of the Mute.

Although it is late autumn when Whoopers arrive in Scotland, they are reluctant to leave in spring; indeed, the odd pair linger, finding conditions to their liking, and stay to breed in the far north, their nest and habits being similar to those of the Mute Swan.

Bewick's Swans arrive from Russia and Siberia slightly later than the Whooper, and by

no means in the same numbers. They are noticeably smaller than the Whooper, with the yellow colour at the base of the bill covering a smaller area and having a rounded edging rather than the pointed one of the Whoopers.

The best method of identification is to see both species together on the same pond, which doesn't often occur. However, some winters find both species on the ponds at East Park, Caerlaverock and on one occasion at a local fish farm two Whoopers and one Bewick's spent about a month together on the stock pond, allowing me to photograph a Whooper and a Bewick's side by side with no other subject in the frame to cause distraction.

A few pairs of Whooper Swans occasionally breed in the far north of Scotland but hundreds more spend the winter here.

Golden Eagle
Aquila chyrsaetos

The majestic **Golden Eagle,** a resident of the Scottish Highlands and Western Isles, is truly a king among birds and unless one is privileged enough to watch a family at their eyrie, the most one can hope for when in eagle territory is to see one circling high above, riding the thermals.

With the increase in the Buzzard population over recent years sightings of 'eagles' have increased proportionately, and it takes an experienced eye to differentiate between the two high in the air, the better distinguishing features being, firstly, that the beak of the Eagle is much more pronounced than that of the Buzzard and, secondly, that the wings are longer, over two metres in length, with more of a spread to the flight feathers.

In general appearance the Golden Eagle is a huge bird, dressed in various shades of brown.

WHOOPER SWAN

Comparative size Similar to Mute Swan.
Status Mainly winter visitor: A few pairs breed in North of Scotland.
Habitat Lochs and sea inlets.
Nest Bulky, built with grasses and waterweeds.
Eggs Creamy-white, clutch, 3-5.
Food Mainly grass and waterweed.

The head and neck are disproportionately small for the size of the body, coloured in a lighter shade which reflects a golden hue in sunlight, hence its name. The powerful beak has a yellow cere (the bare, waxlike patch at the base of the upper-part of a bird's beak) and the legs are feathered their whole length to the yellow feet.

Golden Eagle nest sites are traditional, and some have been in existence for so many years that they have become truly massive structures of sticks, heather, roots and bracken. Like many other birds of prey, Golden Eagles use more than one nest site over the years, probably keeping up two or three but at times showing a continued preference for one more than another, and if this eyrie is in a pine tree rather than on a rocky

ledge it becomes extremely bulky, reaching approximately three metres in height and one-and-a-half metres in width.

Mating takes place early in the year, the two eggs being laid at an interval of two to four days. They are incubated immediately on the laying of the first egg, and this produces two noticeably different-sized young. In such situations only 20 per cent of eyries successfully produce two eagles, for in the other 80 per cent the first-born repeatedly attacks and pecks the younger eaglet with such savagery that it eventually dies. The remaining eaglet receives all further attention and food, which is brought by the male alone in the early days and left for the female, who tears off tiny strips of meat and fur and feeds it to her offspring. About seven weeks later both male and female bring prey to the eyrie, leaving the eaglet to deal withit itself. During the entire time the young eagle is in the eyrie, fresh green fronds and branches are brought in periodically by the male and laid round the perimeter, perhaps as some form of sanitation.

Young eaglets reach the free-flying stage at the age of about ten weeks but they stay in the vicinity for some time, learning from their parents the art of survival, and departing to make their own way the following spring.

Golden Eagles are catholic in their choice of food, from tiny weasles to partly grown fox cubs, from Dipper to Greylag Geese. Inevitably, Grouse are also favoured, but then so is carrion in the shape of dead ewes and lambs. It is pure speculation when observing a Golden Eagle carrying a lamb to the eyrie as to whether it was alive or dead when the Eagle picked it up.

Birdwatching can be a most disappointing pastime or extremely rewarding, as the following two examples will show. Firstly, 'don't count your chickens' certainly applied to a trip I took up north to 'see' Eagles, returning home two days and 400 miles with one 'could it have been?' entry in my diary. On the other hand, who would have thought that following such an experience I should be able to watch a pair of Golden Eagles only six miles from my front door on a March morning some years ago? Excerpts from my records are as follows:

At times the magnificent Golden Eagle can be seen among the hills of Southern Scotland only a few miles from the Scottish/English border.

17 March. While checking Raven nest sites in the Moffat Water Hills, I saw a large bird soaring above a linn. It flew, or rather glided towards the small group of rocks where I was crouching and I watched it as it flew overhead. After studying the bird in flight for a few minutes, I was convinced that the size, shape and colouring was that of an immature Golden Eagle.

Sunday, 21st March. While returning from the 'Grey Mare's Tail' (a waterfall in the hills of Moffatdale), Moffat Water, a large bird flew across the valley, and I soon established that it was the young Golden Eagle I had observed a few days earlier as the wing pattern was similar. After watching it for a few minutes another Eagle appeared from the other side of the valley and, after soaring for a while, it flew into a linn reappearing soon after carrying a rabbit.

This Eagle was in more adult plumage than the first and it flew across the valley, landed in a field on the hillside and commenced eating its kill. While it was feeding about a dozen crows gathered round as if awaiting their share, but every now and then the Eagle would dash at them, driving them off until there were only two left. Even standing together, the combined size of the two crows was dwarfed by the immense size of the Eagle. All the time that this Eagle was feeding the other was circling and soaring above, and I spent a further fifteen minutes watching the two birds.

During the following weeks the Eagles frequented the valley, favouring one or two linns and building my hopes that they might eventually settle. However, this was not to be. Was it due to too much disturbance, or were there not enough open hill moors left to support a breeding pair? Perhaps a bit of both, and I am left with a memory, ever-hopeful they will return – but a verse from one of my later poems reveals my inner thoughts.

I've watched the mighty eagle soar,
On out-stretched wings so still.
Then fold, and drop just like a stone,
Unseen beyond the hill.
To reappear with furry prey,
Then glide across the glen.
But Sitka Spruce and Larch ensure,
He'll ne-er come back again...

I sincerely hope to be proved wrong.

GOLDEN EAGLE

Comparative size Huge bird of prey, 80cm.
Status Resident.
Habitat Mountains, moorlands.
Nest In tree, rocky ledge, huge – sticks, roots, bracken, grass.
Eggs White, sparsely spotted, clutch 2, spotted, blotched with brownish-grey.
Food Mammals, birds, carrion

White-tailed Eagle

Haliaeetus albicilla

After an absence of over eighty years as a breeding species, the huge vulture-like **White-tailed Eagle** is once again established in the Western Highlands of Scotland.

Following an ambitious reintroduction programme in 1968, in which three young Eagles were brought to Fair Isle for acclimatisation there has been a steady reintroduction of the species from Norway bringing the total up to over eighty individuals.

The White-tailed Eagle has a wingspan over 0.5m longer than that of the Golden Eagle, giving the female a wingspan of almost 3m, and mature birds can readily be distinguished from the latter by their white tails, paler heads and massive beaks.

Recently, at least ten pairs have been showing signs of nesting, but as it takes at least four years for the birds to reach maturity only a few pairs have been successful to date in producing young. With more birds reaching maturity annually, however, the future looks promising.

Although fish is the favoured food of the White-tailed Eagle, seabirds and rabbits form most of its diet in this country, with the fishy supplement being supplied by obliging otters.

Buzzard

Buteo buteo

There is no doubt that changes in attitudes towards birds of prey are partly responsible for the current increase in **Buzzard** numbers, for as little as 20 years ago they were scarce in many areas.

One such area where there is a noticeable increase in the population is within the valley of Upper Annandale, Dumfriesshire with sightings of four or five soaring and wheeling together not uncommon. Habitat, nest sites and a good rabbit population are also in their favour.

The Buzzard is a large bird of prey, so large in fact that when seen soaring high in the air it can be, and often is, mistaken for an Eagle, but the much smaller beak and shorter, slightly more rounded wings help to distinguish between the two.

The plumage can vary considerably, ranging from a pale buff to dark brown, the more usual colouring being streaked, dark brown mantle and upper parts, with the lighter underparts boldly marked. The legs, feet and cere are yellow.

Although similar in colouring, the sexes differ in size, the female being larger than the male by approximately 5cm, making her about 58cm in length with a wingspan of 1.5m.

Buzzards are in their territories early in the year, but nest building does not take place until April, when it is not unusual to find nests containing eggs and by mid-May incubation will be underway in those which already contain full clutches.

Disturbance at this time should be avoided, as Buzzards do not take lightly to interference and early nests can be abandoned. The nest itself is well constructed of branches and sticks and lined with bracken, grasses and sheep's wool. Although three eggs is an average clutch, sometimes as many as four or even five will be laid at two- or three-day intervals, with incubation commencing with the first egg. This results in different-sized chicks being found in the same nest, a trait common throughout the birds of prey. The hatching of each egg takes about 30 days, with the young remaining in the nest for six weeks before they start 'branching' (leaving the nest and perching among the branches near the nest-site). At first the male brings the prey to the nest, but after a few days he is joined by his mate on hunting expeditions, with both birds bringing prey to the nest.

During the nestling period fresh greenery is constantly being added to the interior of the nest, and explanations for this include camouflage, sanitation (to help keep flies off any surplus food), or simply decoration – I feel inclined to go for sanitation.

Although Buzzards will perch on a vantage point for long periods of time, it is in the air that they are most often seen as their characteristic

---

BUZZARD

Comparative size Large bird of prey.
Status Resident.
Habitat Rolling hills, woodlands, farmland.
Nest In tree, rocky ledge, sticks, branches, grasses, wool.
Eggs Off-white, variably marked, reddish-brown, clutch 2-5.
Food Rabbits, rodents, birds, insects, carrion.

A Buzzard soaring high in the air is often mistaken for an eagle but the buzzard's beak is noticeably much smaller than that of an eagle.

shapes circle and soar overhead often accompanied by their plaintive 'mewing' calls, especially when you are in their breeding territory.

Given the right conditions the Buzzard can hover, but unlike the Kestrel – which vibrates its wings to maintain its position – this larger bird of prey literally hangs in the air, taking advantage of the updraught on a hillside with barely a movement of its outspread wings, which are held slightly upwards as keen eyes scour the ground below. At other times a soaring bird will half close its wings, falcon fashion, drop a considerable distance, level out when near the ground, and then start soaring and climbing all over again.

In different areas Buzzards adapt well to the situation, some birdwatchers finding their subject on sea or inland cliffs, where the nest is usually a bulky affair built on a rocky ledge. Throughout most of the country, however, they are more of a woodland species, nesting in trees and preferring low, rolling hill country with patches of mixed woodland and farms.

Rabbits, when available, undoubtedly form the major part of the diet, with other rodents also being taken. Carrion is also eaten and, to a lesser degree young birds, especially when the Buzzard are feeding their own young, and at one nest which I was photographing the main prey brought to the two well grown youngsters were young Rooks and Carrion Crows – if only more Buzzard would behave in this way.

Buzzards are widespread throughout Scotland with the Rough-legged variety occurring as a scarce passage migrant.

Sparrowhawk

Accipiter nisus

Prior to the Second World War **Sparrowhawk** were persecuted by gamekeepers but during, and especially after, the War numbers built up again due to the increase in afforestation and changes in the attitudes of many landowners.

The male has dark grey upperparts and a whitish breast and flanks, which are barred with pale brown tinged with orange. His tail is grey with broad dark brown bars and his tarsus (the part of the foot to which the leg is articulated) and toes are yellow. The female is slightly browner than her mate with the hint of a white eyestripe, but she lacks the orange tinge except for small patches on her flanks. As with other birds of prey, she is noticeably larger than her mate – at 38cm she is approximately 6cm longer with a wingspan of 66cm.

The Sparrowhawk population steadily increased until the late 1950s and then crashed, becoming almost non-existent in many south-eastern counties of England due to the extensive use of highly toxic chemicals to protect seeds against insect pests. In the south of Scotland the Sparrowhawk fared slightly better due to less intensive farming methods but even so there was cause for alarm. While photographing Lapwings in a recently sown local field in May 1962, I noticed a number of small buntings and finches participating in what appeared to be dust-bathing, but on closer inspection it became obvious that the birds were in their final death throes. I immediately sent two carcasses to the RSPB for analysis, and the results were as follows:

Mercury – 19 parts per million.

Dieldren – 4.40 parts per million

As these chemicals are persistent, they were also taken in by the Sparrowhawk and other predators in small doses with each bird they ate until they, too, finally died.

In 1961 a voluntary ban had been imposed on the spring use of organochlorine insecticides, and in 1962 a Special Protection Order was implemented, making it an offence to interfere with Sparrowhawks in any way, so by the mid 1960s the Sparrowhawk was once again on the increase and today they are plentiful throughout Scotland.

Sparrowhawks find the vast afforested areas of the south of Scotland much to their liking with many pairs in residence as they show a strong preference for conifers as nest sites. The nest itself is built by both birds, usually close to the trunk and about ten to twelve metres above the ground. It is a bulky affair, built with sticks and larch twigs, and then lined with dead leaves.

Four to six eggs are laid in May and incubated by the female alone, while the male brings her food; hatching takes about 35 days. As the eggs are laid at two-day intervals and incubation begins with the first egg, it is possible to find the oldest chick about eight days older than the youngest. This is not noticeable when the youngsters are 'branching', as the older chicks perch among the branches while the younger ones remain in the nest, in a manner similar to the Buzzard family.

When the chicks are very young the female broods them while the male catches food, such as a small finch or songbird, which he then carries to a plucking place near the nest and he removes the beak, feet and some of the plumage. He then calls quietly and the female glides down from the nest, returning with the prey and then tenderly tearing off small morsels to feed the family, each chick in turn receiving its share.

After about four weeks of tending her brood the female begins to accompany her mate while hunting, and the prey is brought to the family almost complete, perhaps minus the head, and left for the youngsters to dismember for themselves.

The Sparrowhawk is rather a crafty hunter, watching from the branches of a tree or perched on a stone wall, waiting for a small flock of finches or the like to appear. Then the chase is on: a few rapid wingbeats and a short glide brings Hawk and flock together, immediately scattering them in all directions. It is at this time that the Hawk's tenacity can lead to its downfall, as occasionally the small birds are near a window where the fluttering reflections cause the Hawk to

---

SPARROW HAWK

Comparative size Smaller than Pigeon.
Status Resident.
Habitat Open woodland, forests.
Nest In tree, large platform, sticks, larch twigs, dead leaves.
Eggs Bluish-white, blotched reddish-brown.
Food Birds from Wren to Wood Pigeon, small mammals.

smash into the glass, with a broken neck as the most usual outcome. I have received a number of carcasses for taxidermy from these mishaps and on one occasion a female Sparrowhawk shattered a metre square windowpane in the house of a forester friend, scattering pieces of broken glass five metres into the room. The Hawk was retrieved unconscious from under the TV set and the following day I liberated her, none the worse for her 'shattering' experience.

An intensive ringing programme is undertaken throughout Annandale with the result that most of the dead Hawks that are brought in bear BTO (British Trust for Ornithology) rings, and age,

The female Sparrow Hawk being larger than her mate is capable of taking prey as large as a Wood Pigeon.

movement, and so on can be learned from the numbers contained on them by contacting the BTO. The most interesting case I have known was a female found dead in our local park. On furnishing the BTO with the number on the ring, I received the history of the bird:

Ringed as a nestling near Beattock 26 June 1971.
Bred in Greskine Forest – 1975, 1980, 1981.
Found dead, Station Park, Moffat, 16 January 1982.

This made the bird 10.6 years old and the longest lived Sparrow Hawk on record in the British Isles to date, the previous record being 9.3 years. The mounted specimen, ring and Record of Ringed Bird are now in my possession.

Goshawk

Accipiter gentilis

Throughout the forests of southern Scotland a large raptor has appeared in certain areas where it has been absent as a breeding species for over 150 years. The bird is the **Goshawk,** favoured by falconers, loathed by gamekeepers, with those of us inbetween left to form our own opinions – for this is indeed a formidable killing machine, with the tenacity of the Sparrow Hawk and the size of the Buzzard.

Male and female are similar in colouring, being greyish-brown above with whitish underparts, boldly barred in brown. They have a white eyestripe and the long, white-tipped tail is grey, with darker bands, and when seen in a standing position the legs are noticeably shorter than those of the Sparrowhawk .

Averaging 60cm, females are 12cm larger than males and are capable of killing birds the size of Capercaillies and full-grown hares, though I have known falconers whose Goshawks avoided hares because during a previous encounter the hare gave the Hawk a rough time, in the shape of a severe kicking.

While hunting in the wild the Goshawk has much the same agility as the Sparrowhawk, flying and gliding through woodlands in search of prey and manoeuvring through the trees in total silence. Once prey is sighted a short burst of speed usually seals the victim's fate, and if some small bird is the unfortunate recipient of the grip from the powerful talons, life is crushed out instantaneously.

It is the prey of the Goshawk that gives rise to the controversy between gamekeepers and conservationists. Ask a gamekeeper what the Goshawk eats and pheasants will be top of his list; ask the same question of a conservationist and pigeons and crows will be his reply. For the sake of the Goshawk, I hope he keeps his 'feet clean', taking mainly pest species and mammals, for no living person can tell us what effect his presence once had on the birdlife of the countryside so many years ago.

Returning to the present we find that Goshawks are essentially birds of the forest, choosing to nest at various heights from ten to twenty metres. The nest is usually built under

Following a brief, swift chase a Goshawk feeds voraciously on a rabbit.

the canopy of a tree, close to the trunk and supported by a branch. It is a bulky affair built by the female, occasionally using a previous nest for the base and completing the structure with a lining of fine twigs and dead leaves.

When the eggs and young are in the nest, fresh greenery is added periodically as it is with other broad-winged raptors and, similarly, the female broods the young in the early days while the male undertakes the hunting, calling the female from the nest to collect the prey to take back to the chicks.

At the age of about five weeks, the young Goshawks are in the branches near the nest and even at this age young females are noticeably larger than their brothers. The youngsters stay in the vicinity of the nest for a few more weeks before finally dispersing.

Goshawk are now also established in some of our more northern forests.

GOSHAWK

Comparative size Buzzard size.
Status Resident.
Habitat Conifer forests, woodlands.
Nest In tree, bulky, sticks, branches, grass, dead leaves.
Eggs Bluish-white, clutch 2-5.
Food Birds, small mammals.

Hen Harrier

Circus cyaneus

The early stages of afforestation undoubtedly suit the **Hen Harrier** as they do so many other moorland species, but unfortunately once the young conifers reach one metre high the typical moorland species move out, leaving finches and thrushes occupying territory that previously supported an impressive list of birds.

Originally a bird of the rough heather moors, the Hen Harrier has fared well in some parts where forestry policy is to protect rather than persecute these attractive, exciting raptors, for – as we are informed by the media from time to time – there is no doubt that the Hen Harrier is not in favour with everyone, especially on grouse moors.

The male Hen Harrier is entirely different from his mate in his predominantly blue-grey plumage

with black wing tips and conspicuous white rump. His underparts are lighter, merging to white, and altogether the effect is a handsome bird indeed. The female is so different in appearance that one could not be blamed for assuming that they are two different species. She is mainly dark brown with paler streaks on the head, and has an almost white-rimmed spectacle effect round her eyes. Her underparts are streaked in dark and pale brown and, like her mate, she sports a white patch at the base of her long brown-barred tail. At 52cm in length, she is about 10cm larger.

Looking at the Hen Harrier eye-to-eye, so to speak, one can see a facial resemblance to the owls and, as Hen Harriers are reluctant to fly in wet weather, this characteristic also unifies the two families.

In their breeding territories the male performs quite spectacular aerial evolutions, including somersaulting and persistent diving during his mating display, but while hunting for prey the flight is leisurely and buoyant as he quarters the moorlands at low level. Hen Harriers are also expert at hovering, and when they decide to move to another location in search of further prey they glide with wings held in a shallow 'V', which is a good Harrier identification feature.

The nest is a slight hollow on the ground among the heather or young conifers, copiously lined with heather and grasses. The eggs are laid in April or May, and are incubated by the hen for about four weeks.

When hatched, the young are brooded until they are about two weeks old, when they leave the nest and wander off to hide among the vegetation. This is a safeguard against predators such as the fox, which is attracted to the nest site by the strong scent of waste food and droppings.

It is during this period that another aerial spectacular can be witnessed, when the male brings food for the young. He calls his mate to him and, as she approaches, he drops the prey in

---

HEN HARRIER

Comparative size Smaller than Buzzard.
Status Resident.
Habitat Heather moorland, young plantations.
Nest On ground, depression among vegetation, lined, heather, grasses.
Eggs Bluish-white, clutch 3-8.
Food Small mammals, birds.

---

mid-air for her to retrieve. She then grasps the prey in her talons and glides back down to where her youngsters are concealed.

Although Hen Harriers are widespread throughout Scotland, they are somewhat local in their distribution.

Hen Harriers find temporary sanctuary in young conifer plantations and heather moorland is also a favoured habitat.

Osprey
Pandion haliaetus

Robbed of their eggs by collectors and shot by hunters for mounting in glass cases, the **Osprey** ceased to be a British breeding bird around the end of the nineteenth century. During the 1950s the birds made a few attempts to re-establish themselves, but persistent robbing of their eggs halted any success, until the well-known RSPB reserve at Loch Garten, Speyside produced young in 1959.

The success story since then has become known worldwide, and besides being a boon for birdwatchers, the Scottish Tourist Industry has also benefited from thousands of tourists as well as birdwatchers visiting the Loch Garten site annually, where views of these magnificent fish-eating hawks are readily obtained.

As a predator, the Osprey is in a class of its own. It resembles a small eagle with a wingspan of 1.5m; when in flight the wings are seen to be somewhat narrow and distinctly angled, bearing prominent black patches on the whitish underside. Seen from above the Osprey is dressed in dark brown tinged in places with white, the same colours as the slight crest, and there is a dark line which runs from the eye to the back of the neck, joining the dark upperparts. The underparts are white with a brownish band round the breast, and the hooked beak is black, with the specialised fish-catching feet being greenish.

All four toes of the Osprey are equal in length, with the outer one capable of being reversed rather like those of the owls. Covered with spiny scales on the underside, the Osprey's feet are the ultimate for catching and carrying fish prey. At 56cm in length, the female is slightly larger than her mate, but both birds are similar in colouring.

Osprey nests are large affairs, even when first built, but as the same nests can be used year after year, with additional material added, some of them become quite massive. Thick canopied pines appear to be favoured in Scotland, a more suitable base than one finds in parts of America where any elevated situation or construction is accepted, such as a shed roof or a lamp standard, somewhat demeaning these majestic birds.

With obvious reason, the nests are sited near lochs or reservoirs with a clear view over fishing territories, and they are built mainly of sticks and branches lined with grasses and moss. The eggs

The characteristic shape of an Osprey in flight is becoming a more common sight throughout Scotland as numbers steadily increase.

are laid in late April or May, taking about five weeks to hatch, and for the following six weeks the chicks are fed by the female who tears off pieces of fish, brought in by the male, to feed to the young. When the young are old enough and capable of dealing with the fish themselves, both parents leave the nest to 'go fishing' together.

Watching Osprey fish is an unforgettable experience, especially at a fish farm where one of the stock ponds is allowed to be plundered for the sake of ensuring future visits from this summer resident who, when our salmon run upstream to their spawning grounds, will slowly but surely head south to spend the winter in West Africa. Although a few reports of migrating Osprey are recorded in the south of Scotland annually at the back end, the spring migration is by far the most productive, with birds turning up with some regularity at ponds and reservoirs. One or two are visited all through the breeding season, which makes me somewhat suspicious and – ever hopeful – that next season our pair of nesting Osprey will add to the Scottish breeding population of over fifty pairs.

Some years ago on a morning in early May I received a 'phone call regarding an Osprey which had apparently taken up residence in trees overlooking a well stocked pond on a country estate. I arrived about midday complete with camera and lenses, immediately taking up a position on a balcony only a few metres from the edge of the water. As I was about to attach the necessary lens, the Osprey left its vantage point, hovered momentarily approximately twelve metres above the surface of the pond and only fifty metres from where I was stationed, and then in a flash the wings were half-closed as the great bird plunged feet first, splashed and rose with a rainbow trout firmly grasped in its talons. A convulsive shake to rid itself of surplus water, and seconds later it was perched high in a tree on the far side of the pond, partly obscured by branches – and I hadn't fired a shot! Someone suggested that we take the Range Rover along the track to see if we could get an unrestricted view and perhaps a photograph, but the Osprey had lingered long enough. Possibly a female with a mate already in their breeding territory, the last I saw of her she was heading north with leisurely wingbeats, still clutching in her talons one of the Major's rainbow trout.

The RSPB reserve at Loch Garten, or the Scottish Wildlife Trust reserve at Loch of the Lowes on Tayside, are a must for anyone wishing to see these 'Eagles of the Lochs' throughout the summer months, for there they can be viewed to best advantage without any undue disturbance.

OSPREY

Comparative size Slightly larger than Buzzard.
Status Summer resident.
Habitat Lochs, estuaries.
Nest In trees or rocky islets, branches, sticks, grasses.
Eggs Creamy, blotched reddish-brown, clutch 2-4.
Food Fish.

Peregrine Falcon
Falco peregrinus

The mere mention of the name **Peregrine** throughout Britain today immediately induces the populace to think in terms of thousands of pounds, mainly because of coverage by the media whenever a nest is robbed of eggs or young.

Like the salmon, which in days gone was so plentiful that service staff on country estates refused to eat it more than three times a week during the season, the Peregrine was so plentiful that shooting by 'keepers and pillaging by egg collectors failed to inflict any real harm, and even during the war years, when they were destroyed by any possible means to protect message carrying pigeons, they still thrived. The slaughter ceased after the 1939-45 War and Peregrines could again be found in many of their previous strongholds, thriving and expanding their range.

Then came the organochlorine based insecticides of the mid-1950s and the Peregrine, like the Sparrow Hawk, was at the end of the food chain, receiving dose after dose contained in the bodies of their prey species, persistent and deadly. Mercury and Dieldrin was sprayed on seeds taken by finches and pigeons which in due course were taken by predators, causing death in some cases, and thin-shelled and infertile eggs in others. To add to the rate at which the Peregrine was giving cause for alarm, young were being taken illegally for falconry and numbers decreased still further.

Following the voluntary ban on such pesticides in 1961, and an extensive protection programme by the NCC and RSPB to the present day, Peregrine numbers are thankfully back to former levels, and on most days the birds can be seen in their rocky domains and along our shores.

The Peregrine is our largest falcon, magnificent in its mastery of the air and perfectly equipped for speed and accuracy of aim – thus it is the favourite of falconers throughout the world.

The male has slate grey upperparts with a dark crown, and the sides of the head are also blackish with a white patch. He has a distinct black moustachial stripe and his underparts are creamy, boldly barred in black. His wings are long and pointed and his cere and legs are yellow. The female is browner than her mate and as is usual among birds of prey, at 48cm, is larger with a wingspan of about 75cm.

Peregrines are early nesters and are usually on

eggs by mid-April and, unlike the broad-winged raptors that build substantial nests, falcons are content to lay their eggs in a slight hollow on a rocky ledge or, as is favoured in hill country, an old raven's nest. Both male and female take part in incubation, with the female taking the greater part, and the chicks hatch after a period of 28 days, being brooded by the female while the male catches the prey.

On one occasion I was sitting in a hide about twenty-five metres from a female and her solitary chick at her nest on a rocky ledge, when the male landed less than two metres from my right foot with the carcase of a pigeon. He commenced plucking the bird, allowing the feathers to be carried by the breeze past the peephole, and I hardly dared breathe lest I should startle him unduly, but all went well. A few minutes later he carried the plucked carcase to a point some 20m from the nest site, from where the female collected it and returned to feed the chick. Peregrines perched on rocky ledges can be spotted from a fair distance away as their light-coloured breasts reflect the sun – at times they

The 'stoop' of the Peregrine, as it drops from a considerable height towards its prey is one of the most thrilling sights in birdwatching.

are so still that one wonders if the lightish object is a bird at all.

At the other extreme is the 'stoop', the method by which the Peregrine catches its prey, and to be close enough to witness the sound and speed of this manoeuvre is one of the highlights of the birdwatcher's year. From some vantage point, or high in the air, the Peregrine fixes on its intended victim, almost closes its wings and drops with incredible speed, over 150 miles an hour, while at

---

PEREGRINE

Comparative size Smaller than Buzzard.
Status Resident.
Habitat Rocky and hilly country.
Nest Scrape on ledge, old Raven nest.
Eggs Whitish, blotched with deep red.
Food Birds, large and small, few mammals.

the same time producing a rocket-like sound, and the prey is struck in an explosion of feathers falling to the ground. From here it is retrieved, carried to a favourite plucking place and devoured.

Birdwatching on the Solway coast one Sunday morning in midwinter a large pack of Knot attracted my attention, and as I watched them twisting and turning in unison a Peregrine appeared high above. It folded and 'stooped', splitting the pack in two like someone cutting through an apple, but failed to make a strike, levelled out, and continued on its way, causing no end of panic among the shoreline waders. Meanwhile, the two halves of the Knot pack had joined together again, holding my attention for a few more minutes, and all was well.

Merlin
Falco columbarius

The **Merlin** is our smallest falcon, being barely larger than a Mistle Thrush.

It is a beautiful little falcon, having slate grey upperparts while the underparts are buff, tinged with orange and streaked with dark brown. The tail is shorter than those of our other falcons, blue-grey in colour with dark bands, with a broad black one immediately above the white tip. The female is slightly browner than her mate and her breast is much whiter. Like others of the falcon family, she is larger than the male by almost 5cm, making her approximately 30cm in length, with a wingspan of 45cm.

Merlins follow their prey species, and when the Meadow Pipits move from the hill moors to the coast they are followed by these dashing little raptors. In March and April when the pipits and larks return to their moorland habitat, the Merlins are close behind and, being one of our more agile raptors, their fantastic aerial displays are soon in full swing. Both birds fly and circle at over 150 metres above the ground, then stoop and dive at each other until they are almost at ground level, then off they go again, climbing and spiralling, to repeat the whole performance.

In most areas Merlins choose to nest on the ground among the heather, but in the south of Scotland the favourite site for many years has been in old Carrion Crow nests, where no material whatsoever is added. The eggs are laid in May, incubation taking about four weeks, and

for the first fortnight of their lives the female stays close by the nest, guarding and brooding the chicks. After that both parents pursue prey: when caught, it is taken to a favourite plucking place and prepared before being taken to the young by the female,. It will be about another two weeks before they leave the nest.

During the nesting season, Merlins are extremely defensive towards their eggs or chicks, and will mob and even strike much larger birds such as Ravens and Buzzards with such force that the odd feather has been seen to fly.

For hundreds of years the Merlin has been regarded as the ladies' falcon, being much in favour with Mary Queen of Scots, and in medieval times ladies would ride out side-saddle with their falcons on their fists, returning to their castles with a string of Skylarks possibly destined to end up in a pie.

In pursuit of Skylarks, Merlins use their speed and agility to the utmost, for the Skylark spirals ever upwards with its pursuer desperately trying to gain enough height to position itself above the Lark, which then plummets to earth, seeking cover, but more often than not the Merlin's stoop puts an end to the downward dash and freedom.

In their breeding territories it is almost impossible to maintain a focal distance using binoculars when the Merlins are in the air, as the speed at which they twist and turn, even in level flight, is almost unbelievable, indeed some say that the Merlin's level flight outstrips even that of the Peregrine.

One Merlin nest I located some years ago had a most interesting history, having been occupied by a series of tenants. A pair of Ravens built their bulky nest in a thick hawthorn tree on a steep hillside and, assuming that the Ravens would return the following spring, I was somewhat disappointed to find a pair of Carrion Crows in residence. Curiosity took me back to the site during the third spring, to find yet another species taking advantage of the security of the protective hawthorn, a pair of Buzzards, but their eggs proved to be infertile and in due course were abandoned being forsaken. Needless to say, the site was the focus of my attention the following spring, and it was then that I discovered that a Merlin had laid four eggs on the shallow platform. I decided there and then to attempt photography at a later date, as the nest could be seen quite openly.

In due course a hide was ready about 12 metres from the nest, and I was fortunate to be

Our smallest falcon, the Merlin is about the size of a Mistle Thrush. Larks and Pipits are the main prey species.

able to spend a pleasant June afternoon sitting behind the camera. The sun was shining, the chicks had hatched and all was quiet following the departure of my two assistants who, were under strict instructions to vacate the area, returning to relieve me in two hours' time.

Soon after their depature the female Merlin was back at the nest, shielding her brood from the sun. The first fifteen minutes were quite uneventful, with little action as the chicks had recently been fed, so I decided to rest my eyes for a moment, dropping my gaze to the grassy floor of the hide, and to my horror I discovered an extremely active ant hill. My assistants arrived to find me somewhat relieved at their appearance, having taken very few shots and spent most of the time with my legs held high my and behind rather painful – I can honestly say that I wasn't too disappointed at not being able to find time for a further photographic session.

The young flew successfully about three weeks later, and the following spring – wait for it – a pair of Kestrels occupied the site, rearing five young.

I look back with sadness when I review some of my old notes, recorded not too many years ago, for on a recent visit to this magic place, glen and hawthorns were lost among the conifers...

MERLIN

Comparative size Smaller than Kestrel.
Status Resident.
Habitat Open heather moors, coasts.
Nest Scrape on ground, old crow nest.
Eggs Whitish, blotched with reddish brown, clutch 3-6.
Food Small birds, small mammals, insects.

Kestrel

Falco tinnunculus)

The **Kestrel** is our best known and most plentiful falcon, being readily seen by millions of people daily as they journey up and down the country. No motorway drive is complete without viewing one or two Kestrel hovering above or close to the verges, as they provide a habitat for many small mammals and beetles, two of the Kestrel's favourite prey. Train journeys can be equally productive for the viewing of Kestrel, as they are extremely widespread and can be found in any type of habitat, rural or urban.

Kestrel are something of an exception to the rule among our raptors. In most cases the female is normally larger than her mate, but Kestrel sexes are quite similar in size being 38cm long with a wingspan of about 55cm.

The male is a handsome bird with a chestnut mantle and wings, spotted with black; his buffish underparts are also streaked with black. His head and rump are bluish-grey and his long pointed tail is also greyish with a broad dark band immediately above the white tip. The female is less colourful with head, mantle and upperparts reddish-brown barred in black; her long tail is also barred. Her underparts are paler with dark streaks, and in both sexes the legs, cere, and skin round the eyes are yellow.

The flight is leisurely and graceful, especially during the spring courtship display when the male circles round the female as she glides in smaller circles and when she tires of this and settles on a telegraph pole or high branch, the male continues to show off his aerial skills before flying down to join her.

Breeding sites are extremely varied, with a rocky ledge in a suitable habitat being one of the most common. But old crow nests, as well as those of other large birds in the country, and window ledges in high buildings, derelict or otherwise, in urban areas are all accepted. In some habitats, such as recently planted forestry ground, nest boxes are used successfully.

The eggs are laid in late April or May and incubated mainly by the female. For the first two weeks after hatching the young are brooded and tended by her alone while the male catches and carries the prey to the nest site. At times he will approach the area with prey in his talons and settle on a post or other vantage point, calling softly to attract his mate, who then flies out to retrieve the victim, carrying it back to feed her chicks.

Kestrel eggs are laid at two-day intervals, with incubation commencing with the laying of the first egg. For the first two weeks the difference in size and development is not apparent, but when the oldest youngster in a family of four is 28 days old the difference is more obvious, as the oldest bird is almost on the wing while the youngest is not much more than a downy chick.

Motorways are not the best places to stop in order to watch a hovering Kestrel, for obvious reasons, but on our minor roads you can pull in, as I often do, to watch the expertise with which this falcon secures its prey, since no other bird uses the wind or its hovering ability to such perfection. With head bent slightly downwards and keen eyes scanning the ground below, the Kestrel can remain on quivering wings for minutes at a time, this being its best identifying feature. When prey is sighted, it drops feet first to secure its victim, before carrying it off for its meal.

On one such occasion I watched a Kestrel land on a fence post with a shrew firmly clasped in its talons and, as I watched with my binoculars, the falcon cast a pellet before devouring the shrew. A few minutes later I approached the fence line to retrieve the pellet in order to examine it, and found not one pellet but many: in fact, there were several at the base of about six posts in all. I collected a number for examination and found that beetles played a large part in furnishing the Kestrel with nourishment, but there was no evidence whatsoever of small birds being taken, sparrows featuring strongly on the menu of our urban Kestrels.

'Pellets', although associated mainly with hawks and owls, are cast by a variety of birds including Rooks, Herons and Kingfishers.

Ejected from the mouth, they contain the indigestible parts of the bird's diet such as fur, feather, bone and beetle husks, and they can be

KESTREL
Comparative size Well known, smaller than Pigeon.
Status Resident.
Habitat Found almost everywhere.
Nest Scrape on ledge, old nest.
Eggs White blotched with reddish, clutch 3-6.
Food Small mammals, small birds, beetles.

The hovering Kestrel is a familiar sight above motorway verges and open ground.

collected from a roosting place and then dissected to reveal what the bird has been feeding on.

Some species have more efficient digestive systems than others and a pellet slightly smaller than a golf ball cast by a Heron, even after eating fish, contains no bones at all, only vegetable matter with a distinct fishy odour.

Red Grouse

Lagopus lagopus

Ptarmagin

Lagopus mutus

The grouse moor is as much a Scottish tradition as whisky, and it is essential that this type of habitat be preserved as it supports an impressive list of breeding species, all of which are lost when the area is planted with conifers.

The **Red Grouse** is entirely dependent on heather for its existence: young shoots for food and older, deeper heather for concealing it's nests.

The birdwatcher looking over an expanse of grouse moor sees a habitat that in his or her estimation supports many favourite species, and accepts as a matter of course that the Red Grouse are there. But this is not so, as a successful grouse moor requires careful management, one of the main tasks being controlled burning which ensures that there are always areas of heather at different stages of development to suit the grouse population.

In appearance the Red Grouse is reddish-brown from head to tail, heavily marked with a darker shade.

The wing tips and outer tail feathers are almost black, and the legs and feet are feathered to the toes with greyish-white, almost hair-like feathers. The short stubby beak is black and there are red wattles above the eyes. Hens are more lightly marked and have less prominent wattles.

Red Grouse have much in common in their

behaviour and movements with the Partridge, rising from the heather with a whirr of wings and flying close to the ground with rapid wingbeats, before dropping once more into cover a few hundred metres further out.

As with other Grouse, the spring courtship display of the male includes some curious antics, particularly one where he leaps straight up into the air, rapidly beating his wings and leaping from stance to stance uttering a loud crowing call.

The best known and most characteristic call of the Red Grouse is his rather 'cheeky' 'go-back-go-back-go-back', heard as he drops into cover after having been disturbed. To me, this call, like that of the Curlew, symbolises our hill moors.

RED GROUSE

Comparative size Larger than Patridge.
Status Resident.
Habitat Heather moors.
Nest Scrape among heather.
Eggs Off white, blotched, dark brown, clutch 7-10.
Food Mainly heather.

Sitting tight on her eggs in a nest among stunted heather, the Red Grouse becomes almost invisible, demonstrating to perfection her natural camouflage.

While incubating her eggs, the hen Red Grouse demonstrates one of the finest examples of cryptic colouration throughout the avian world, for among the heather, sitting tight, she is extremely difficult to locate. This camouflage serves her well, since vermin such as Carrion and Hooded Crows are greatly underestimated, with thousands of groundnesting species losing their eggs or young each spring to these raiders.

Young Grouse, like other gamebirds develop quickly. At two weeks old they are able to flutter two or three metres, and about a week later they are capable of scattering in all directions when threatened by a predator appearing overhead.

As any grouse moor can only support a certain number of birds, in late autumn the cocks select their territories for the following spring and it is these cocks, and their prospective, hens that generally survive the winter, as older birds and birds without territories are the ones which are usually predated or die of starvation, thus ensuring 'survival of the fittest.'

If snow covers the ground in winter, the

Grouse dig down to reach the heather shoots, and also dig small trenches in which to roost, congregating in small numbers for company and safety.

A bird of our highest Scottish mountains, the **Ptarmigan** is at home where very few birds could survive, and to thrive in such hostile terrain it blends with the surroundings at all times by changing its coat three times a year.

This helps the bird to avoid being seen by its main predator, the Golden Eagle, and when humans approach Ptarmigan in such places as ski slopes among the Cairngorms they find them quite tame and reluctant to fly, preferring to crouch among the short vegetation or lichen-covered rocks to avoid detection when alarmed.

In late summer plumage, the Ptarmigan is greyish mottled with dark markings, with white wings and large red wattles, the hen being much browner. In early winter the classic Ptarmigan emerges, pure white body and leg feathers, which are thick and downy, with the black tail and eyestripe.

In spring, a third moult dresses the birds in colours blending with the sparse vegetation, somewhat yellower and more heavily marked than the summer dress. This, of course, is the time when the hens depend on perfect camouflage while incubating eggs or brooding young, as the Golden Eagle is ever quartering the high tops hunting for a meal.

Both parents tend the chicks when hatched and are absolutely fearless in their defence, running around with much wing beating and croaking, and feigning injury to distract from their brood. But not for long – the young can fly 12 days after hatching.

Only in the severest of winter conditions do Ptarmigan leave the high peaks and visit the haunts of their close cousins the Red Grouse, where conditions are slightly less harsh.

PTARMIGAN

Comparative size Larger than Partridge.
Status Resident.
Habitat Mountain tops with sparse vegetation.
Nest Mossy scrape in stunted heather.
Eggs Creamy, with blackish blotches:
Clutch 5-9
Food Vegetation, some insects.

Black Grouse
Tetrao tetrix

Over the past 25 years many of the Blackcock 'leks' in the south of Scotland have been lost under the dark green canopy of conifer plantations, but fortunately where the forest edge borders the open moor the habitat suits the **Black Grouse,** as he has a fondness for pine and larch buds as well as blaeberries and bog myrtle.

The Black Grouse or Blackcock is unmistakable – or rather he should be. Often he is mistaken for a Capercaillie by those seeing him for the first time, especially when he displays his unique lyre-shaped tail with pure white undertail coverts, which can be held upright in a fan-like position. The rest of his plumage is predominantly glossy black, with a conspicuous white wing bar and large red wattles.

The female, or Greyhen, does not resemble him in the least, for her plumage is barred brown and black, with a white wing bar and a tail that is distinctly forked. She is also much smaller, being 41cm in length compared to her mate's 53cm.

In flight, blackgame are typical of the Grouse clan – low, fast and direct – and on the ground they walk with a slow, deliberate step. The most extraordinary characteristic of the Blackcock is the display which takes place at dawn and at dusk, when the cocks gather on an open piece of ground called – a 'LEK' – and literally show off to one another, in due course attracting the Greyhens who stand around the perimeter of the lek, becoming bolder as the spring progresses until they eventually succumb, allowing mating to take place as they wander from one territory to another, usually in small parties. While indulging in this polygamous act, the cocks continue to display, guarding their territories vigourously as they jump in the air, twisting and turning and, with head lowered, rushing at their neighbour, wings and tail outspread, occasionally buffeting one another, but seldom do any feathers fly. During this display much 'roo-cooing', the Blackcock's bubbling call, is heard.

The Greyhen meanwhile wander off to seek a nest site, perhaps among dead bracken, and it is here that her cryptic colouring is as necessary as the prominent display colouring of the cocks as she incubates the eggs alone, relying on her camouflage to avoid detection.

Returning home one spring evening along a hill track, I came across a party of half a dozen

The Blackcock's communal display area is called a 'lek'.
This individual displayed to his own reflection in the wheel
disc of a parked car.

Blackcock displaying at a lek by the verge. The light was fading, but I managed to take a few photographs. The following evening I was in position about an hour earlier than my previous encounter, with the car conveniently parked overlooking the lek. Before the sun had set the Blackcocks appeared right on cue, and I was treated to a firstclass performance, managing to photograph some of their antics. To end a perfect day, or rather evening, one individual approached the car while displaying to his reflection in the wheel disc, allowing me to 'shoot' him in profile. On a few occasions in the autumn I have come across the odd Blackcock wandering about as if dazed, but later discovered that the condition was one more suited to a true Scot – the bird was tipsy, possibly from fermenting blaeberries in his crop, perhaps with a 'dash' of bog myrtle, as this plant was used to flavour beer in the old days.

BLACK GROUSE

Comparative size Larger than Partridge.
Status Resident.
Habitat Forest edges, hill moors.
Nest Depression among bracken etc.
Eggs Creamy, spotted reddish brown.
Clutch 5-8.
Food Pine and larch buds, blaeberries, other wild plants.

Capercaillie

Tetrao urogallus

The **Capercaillie** cock, the bird for which the Blackcock is at times mistaken, is our largest member of the Grouse clan, being a massive 86cm in length. The hen, measuring 62cm is also much larger than the Greyhen.

The Capercaillie disappeared from the Scottish scene over 200 years ago, but by Queen Victoria's reign they were once more established in the Caledonian Pine forests, where they remain.

As large as a turkey, the cock Capercaillie appears black at a distance, but closer to he is seen to be dressed in browns, greys, bluish green and white. His tail is rounded and he has red wattles above the eyes. The hen is dressed in reddish brown and grey, mottled and barred in black – ideal camouflage when she is incubating eggs in her nest, a scrape among the fallen needles at the base of a pine tree.

The Capercaillie walks heavily on the ground and, although it is such a large bird, once disturbed from the low branches of a tree, where it has a fondness for perching, the initial explosive fluttering is followed by rapid flight.

In spring the cocks display to each other and to the hens at a lek in the forest, starting with a series of clicking notes which end in a loud pop as the birds puff out their neck and breast feathers, fan their tails, lower their heads and wings and approach one another in mock battle. Occasionally a real fight will ensue, but this is usually brief as the main purpose of the display is to discourage other cocks from intruding on the territorial stamping ground. At times, in an area where there are few cock, a Capercaillie will defend his territory against all comers, humans, animals and even motor cars, but these rogues are few and the most one can hope for when birdwatching is to see a disturbed bird disappearing among the trees.

CAPERCAILLIE

Comparative size Larger than Blackcock.
Status Resident.
Habitat Pine forests, also conifer forests.
Nest Scrape at base of pine tree.
Eggs Creamy, reddish-brown markings. Clutch 5-8.
Food Pine shoots, flowers, leaves, berries.

Grey Partridge

Perdix perdix

Red Legged Partridge or French Partridge

Alectoris rufa

Once common and widespread throughout the country, the **Grey** or **Common Partridge** is now decreasing at an alarming rate. A few years ago large coveys could be seen in autumn as one walked the river banks bordering the fields, and in spring pairs could be regularly seen, picking their way through the short grass, one feeding while the other remained alert.

Easily recognised with his brown plumage, streaked with light and dark markings, and round-shaped body, the male also has a distinctive horseshoe-shaped chestnut patch on his breast. This is almost lacking in the female, but her chestnut head and tail are similar to those of her mate.

In habitats that still support Partridge, early spring finds the males extremely aggressive towards one another, with many squabbles taking place while the female runs around, flapping her wings in excitement.

This spring courtship forms a very strong bond between the pair and by the beginning of May, when the female lays her eggs in a nest concealed among the vegetation of the hedgerow, the male becomes more attentive, never being far away. When the eggs are hatching some males become so involved that they make constant visits to the female, and at one such nest I witnessed the male become so excited that he ran around in circles, oblivious of his surroundings and ran full tilt into the base of a tree, winding himself momentarily. Needless to say, when the chicks leave the nest both parents tend them, even after they take to the wing.

For the first three weeks of their lives the chicks feed mainly on insects which are injurious to crops, such as aphids and sawfly larvae, and unfortunately in intensely farmed areas this source of food is strictly controlled by the use of pesticides. Severe hedge cropping and the cutting of roadside verges in farming country also pile the odds against a secure future for these appealing little birds.

Through the winter months the family stay

Unfortunately owing to modern farming methods the appealing little Grey Partridge is becoming a less familiar sight throughout the countryside.

together as a covey, at times being joined by others of their kin. January, however, finds the covey being disbanded, with pairing taking place for the new season. Should the original pair survive the guns and hardships of winter they will remain together through the new season and hopefully rear another family.

Throughout the country today there are as many **Red-Legged Partridge** as there are Grey, but in Scotland breeding is confined mainly to the south and along the east coast almost to the Moray

Firth. Introduced about 200 years ago to supplement the gamebird population, they have thrived in some areas while in others, even with extensive breeding programmes on some estates, they have yet to gain a foothold.

The Red-Legged Partridge is easily recognised by its colourful appearance, the sexes being similar in colouring with rich chestnut-brown upperparts, and grey and orange underparts. The flanks are barred with black, white and chestnut and the face is white, broken by a black eyestripe. The beak, legs and feet are blood red, features from which the bird gets its name.

The Red-Leg is less shy than the Grey, wandering about on open ground, and keeping

---

GREY PARTRIDGE

Comparative size Smaller than Pigeon.
Status Resident.
Habitat Mixed farmland.
Nest Scrape in undergrowth, lined with grasses, leaves.
Eggs Glossy, pale brown. Clutch 8-16.
Food Seeds, leaves, grain. Chicks eat insects.

RED-LEGGED PARTRIDGE

Comparative size Larger than Grey Partridge.
Status Resident.
Habitat Farmland and rough ground.
Nest Grass-lined scrape on ground.
Eggs Buffish, speckled with brown.
Clutch 10-12.
Food Mainly seeds, leaves, some insects.

---

on the move while feeding. It is more reluctant to fly than the Grey, preferring to crouch in hollows on the ground when threatened, but once airborne the flight, low and direct, is difficult to distinguish from that of the Grey Partridge.

The nest is a scrape on the ground, lined with dead grass and leaves, and usually well hidden among the vegetation of a hedgerow or on rough ground.

A clutch may contain about a dozen eggs which in some cases, and for some unknown reason are apparently abandoned while the female lays another clutch in another nest. The two clutches are then incubated simultaneously, one by the female and the other by the male, and when the chicks hatch each parent tends its own brood.

Pheasant

Phasianus colchicus

Quail

Coturnix coturnix

It was probably during Roman times that the first **Pheasants** were introduced into Britain, but as recent as 250 years ago when the Chinese variety was added to the then existing stocks. Everyone is acquainted with the multi-coloured cock Pheasant, bronze, purple, chestnut and greens combining together to produce a most attractive result. Bright red wattles and an exceptionally long tail round off the characteristics of this popular gamebird. The 'Old English', as the original Pheasant came to be known, and the Chinese are similar in colouring, except for a thin white collar sported by the latter – Hence we find birds throughout the country with collars of various sizes produced through interbreeding.

The ideal sporting bird is one of a fair size which at the same time is not too reluctant to fly, as some birds prefer to run and conceal themselves in thick undergrowth when intruders appear in their territory, incurring the need for an army of 'beaters'.

Working on those ideals, over the years a melanistic (darker) mutant has evolved, slightly smaller in size but more flighty and this variety is favoured by some gamekeepers.

The cock is a glossy, dark, greenish-black bird, which when seen from a distance appears totally black, and the hens of this type are much darker than the pale brown, mottled hens of other Pheasants, although they are similarly patterned.

Woodlands set aside for sporting Pheasant support many other bird species and as vermin are more strictly controlled here these same species have a much better chance of survival than they do in woodlands which are not 'keepered. Recently I have found that predation by Carrion Crows is beyond the tolerance level of some species, a riverside walk on a particular afternoon producing destroyed and eaten eggs of Pheasant, Oyster Catcher, Lapwing, Redshank and even Willow Warbler, with nest and contents torn out.

Early spring finds resident cocks becoming aggressive, when their territorial rights are challenged by other males with much displaying which is more visual than brutal, as disputes are usually settled without coming to blows.

A cock Pheasant will stand on some elevated piece of ground and utter a harsh double syllabled crow, this having the effect of warning other cocks in the vicinity not to venture too close, while at the same time inviting all the hens to come and join him. This results in his acquiring a harem, and often a proud cock can be seen, head held high, on guard, while half a dozen or so hens feed close by, picking the ground for seeds and insects.

His harem is not too loyal though for these fickle females have a habit of wandering from one territory to another indulging in polygamy.

Egg laying starts in April in a simple scrape among bramble or heavy undergrowth, very often close to a wall or tree root, and this gives the sitting hen a feeling of security. As she is perfectly coloured to match her surroundings, she often goes undetected.

Her clutch can contain many eggs, but about 12 is average, and the downy chicks hatch following a 24 day incubation period. They are active at once and soon leave the nest with the

PHEASANT

Comparative size Very long, 75cm.
Status Resident.
Habitat Woodland, farmland.
Nest Scrape among dense vegetation.
Eggs Pale olive to darker. Clutch 10-20.
Foods Seeds, grain, worms, berries, insects.

A cock Pheasant forages among dead leaves in search of a morsel.

hen, who is constantly on the lookout for predators while helping her brood to find insects on which they thrive until they are old enough to feed on seeds and plants.

During the winter months cocks and hens can be found together roaming the woodlands and farms, but when winter gives way to spring, comradeship is soon forgotten, as once again the proud cock Pheasant takes up his stance and crows loudly.

The tiny **Quail** is only 17cm in length, making it smaller than a Starling, though much dumpier.

A summer resident, it is a pity that this scarce little gamebird is so persecuted as it makes the perilous journey to and from its winter quarters in South Africa. Hunters, both in southern Europe and north Africa, take a terrible toll of the migrating birds, making it almost miraculous when a pair turn up in a barley field in the south of Scotland and successfully rear a brood, as has happened over the past few years.

In appearance the Quail is sandy-brown, streaked with buff and darker brown, and the male has a dark head with a white eyestripe which is lacking in the female.

When seen in flight the wings are noticeably longer in comparison with those of our other gamebirds, which is necessary for a migratory species. However, Quail are difficult birds to put to flight, usually giving away their presence by uttering their characteristic 'wet-my-lips' call which hopefully, will resound among the barley for many years to come.

QUAIL

Comparative size Much smaller than Grey Partridge.
Status Summer resident.
Habitat Cereal farmland.
Nest Grass-lined scrape on ground among vegetation.
Eggs Yellowish-brown, spotted with dark brown. Clutch, 7-14.
Foods Vegetable matter and insects.

Water Rail

Rallus aquaticus

Find a stretch of dense, boggy reedbed, preferably with overgrown ditches, and you will find yourself in a habitat capable of supporting one of our most elusive birds, the **Water Rail.**

Fortunately, Water Rail do not require a large area in order successfully to rear a family, but, unfortunately, these same areas can be drained by modern methods in a very short space of time, as many of them are, and the Water Rail is becoming increasingly difficult to locate.

From its head to its back end, the Water Rail is rather slenderly cone-shaped, which is extremely handy for poking its way through the dense reeds and close-knit vegetation of overgrown ditches. As if skulking habits and a small size of 25cm were not enough to pose problems for the birdwatcher, the cryptic colouration of the species adds yet another dimension. The upperparts are olive-brown boldly streaked with black, and the underparts are blue-grey, with black-and-white bars on the flanks. The undertail coverts are conspicuously white, the longish downcurved bill is red, being duller in winter, and the legs and feet are greenish.

At times, the Water Rail's presence is announced by its call, either in the nesting season, or during winter when several birds find themselves sharing a limited food supply.

The nest is built of sedges and reeds concealed amongst the dense aquatic vegetation and the first clutch of eggs is laid in April or May, sometimes followed by a second clutch in June or July. The chicks leave the nest as soon as they are hatched and they are tended by both parents.

In severe winters constant low temperatures freeze much of the marshy habitat, and it is at this time that shyness is forgotten as the birds struggle to survive. During the severe winter of 1962-3, it was brought to my attention that a number of Water Rail were feeding at our municipal rubbish tip. The tip was bordered on one side by a burn, which for some reason or other remained ice-free, at the other side of which was thick, reedy vegetation. A hasty visit verified that the birds were indeed Water Rail, about half a dozen in all, and it did not take long to ascertain that certain points were favoured for crossing the burn to and from the tip, where I soon discovered that the fare in favour was offal from local butchers' shops.

Normally shy and secretive the Water Rail is seldom seen in the open for more than a few moments at a time.

As I had only recently taken up photography I had not as yet acquired any telephoto lenses, but by using an air-pressurised remote release I could operate a camera from a distance of about 15 metres, taking one shot at a time.

Selecting the most frequently used crossing place, I waded into the burn and positioned the tripod with the camera, which was focussed on a twig in the shallow water near the far bank. The Water Rail crept past this twig when they crossed the burn, so with the camera and flash bulb set, and the remote release leading back to the parked van, I sat and waited.

It was fully an hour later when I eventually squeezed the bulb, the flash momentarily piercing the shadows – and the Water Rail scurried away. On opening the van door I discovered that one of my waders had frozen to such an extent that when I stepped forward it actually cracked and, on stepping into the burn, water flowed freely through the hole. Camera and flash were hastily stowed away and minutes later I was soaking in a hot bath.

The resulting photograph was not as good as I had hoped for, but it was a fair record, and during the next two weeks I succeeded in taking a few presentable shots by concentrating on the 'runs' through the vegetation leading to the burnside. My attention was drawn to these 'runs' by the noise when two birds met head – on, the sound being reminiscent of the squealing of a young pig – as the birds disputed right of way.

During the following few winters Water Rail frequented the tip in varying numbers, but as tip and marshy area have long since gone one can but hazard a guess as to their present status. Fortunately, though, there are still boggy places throughout the country where the elusive Water Rail survive, let us hope for many years to come.

WATER RAIL

Comparative size Smaller than Moorhen.
Status Resident.
Habitat Densely reeded areas, overgrown ditches.
Nest Platform of reeds, lined with dead leaves etc.
Eggs Light buff, lightly spotted with dark brown. Clutch 7-11.
Food Mainly freshwater animal life.

Corncrake
Crex crex

Spotted Crake
Porzana porzana

It was almost 25 years ago, in 1966, when I last recorded three pairs of **Corncrake** in arable fields in Upper Annandale. Since then they have been totally absent, and to find the Corncrake in breeding habitat in Scotland one must visit the Hebrides.

The characteristic 'crek-crek', 'crek-crek', of the brown-mottled, chicken-like Corncrake could in the past be something of an annoyance on summer nights, but as farming became increasingly mechanised the Corncrake population crashed, and the previous breeding haunts of this summer resident became barren.

A very rare breeder in the British Isles, the **Spotted Crake** appears as a summer resident, and on a few occasions has turned up in the south of Scotland. The habitat frequented by this species is similar to that of the Water Rail, a bird it closely resembles both in size and colour, though the beak of the Spotted Crake is both shorter and stubbier, and when a good view is obtained the orangey-coloured undertail coverts are noticeable.

CORNCRAKE

Comparative size Smaller than Grey Partridge.
Status Summer resident.
Habitat Farmland grass and hay fields.
Nest Sparsely-lined depression in grass tussock.
Eggs Yellowish-buff with reddish spots. Clutch 7-12.
Food Insects, worms, slugs and snails.

Moorhen
Gallinula chloropus

From reedy ditches to our largest rivers, from the marshy corner of a field to our largest lochs – the **Moorhen** finds a habitat as long as there is adequate edging of aquatic vegetation for cover. A bird that would appear to be wrongly named, the Moorhen would be better suited with one of its local names, 'Waterhen', as water rather than moorland is a more appropriate connection.

The Moorhen's plumage is mainly brownish-black with a white streak along the flanks. It has a curious red, waxy frontal shield at the base of the yellow-tipped red beak, and the legs and feet are greenish. The toes are unusually long, ideal for walking over soft mud and lily pads.

The undertail coverts are conspicuously white, being used to warn others when an intruder approaches, at which point the Moorhen retreats, flicking upright white feathers while uttering its 'kek-kek', alarm call. When the birds are in their breeding territories, these same white undertail coverts are displayed as a warning to other males, but sometimes a visual warning is not enough and the birds engage in a noisy struggle in which the large feet can be interlocked while wings thrash the water.

The Moorhen swims high in the water with a rhythmic jerking of the head and tail, and it propels itself at a fair pace by closing its long toes into a ball which makes a convenient paddle. When rising from the surface of the water, the Moorhen has a bit of a struggle, running and flapping to get airborne, but once in the air the flight is strong and well sustained.

Nesting begins early in the spring with most nests being located among reeds, but other sites are also used such as a heap of branches, sticks and various other bits and pieces left high and dry at the riverside by an earlier spate. The nest is cleverly concealed, but always in danger of being washed away.

Most Moorhens raise two broods in a season which, even with a high mortality rate among the chicks, maintains an abundant population and to see such a population reduced to less than 20 per cent in a single season, as happened in 1980, is indeed a major problem. At that time escapees from mink farms invaded all our rivers and tributaries with the result that fish stocks plummeted, and I found numerous headless Moorhens in backwaters and along drainage ditches. What was even more worrying was the fact that this catastrophe was nationwide.

In Upper Annandale the local angling club was fortunate in having among its members an extremely capable trapper, who was duly elected to deal with the problem being ably assisted by one of our constables who also had a vested interest, and who has since carried on controlling

A Moorhen cautiously approaches her nest situated among the debris (cast up by a previous spate) by the burn side.

these vermin. The following results speak for themselves:

Year	Mink trapped
From 1980-1	120
From 1981-2	20
From 1982-3	35
From 1983-4	16
From 1984-5	21

From 1985 to the present day (1991), the average is only about a dozen per year, and we are enjoying a restored Moorhen population. It's a pity the trout stocks haven't followed suit.

Moorhen nests, unlike those of the grebe family, do not rise and fall with the water level but are fixed structures, and if built by the side of a small pond, a sudden rise in the level of the water can cause problems for the pair. On a Saturday evening in late April, I found a Moorhen nest containing seven eggs at the base of a small willow bush by the edge of a pond near the village of Wamphray, in Dumfriesshire. The position of the nest was ideal for photography, and with this in mind I decided to keep my eye on the situation, hoping to be on hand when the chicks were hatching.

Later the same evening it started to rain and as there is no outlet to the pond the level rose steadily. About 24 hours later, on the Sunday evening, I visited the pond to assess the situation and was absolutely amazed at what I found. Firstly, the willow bush instead of being at the water's edge was at least four metres from it, and secondly, what was even more surprising was the fact that the nest was still intact, steadily climbing higher as the Moorhen constantly added more material.

At this point they had added about 40cm of reeds resembling a small haystack, and on closer examination it became clear that only one egg had gone astray during the construction. I was fascinated by this conversion as I had never seen anything like it before, so I parked the car at a position overlooking the pond and waited. Almost immediately the female was at the nest, somehow managing to clamber up to her eggs and I thought that would be the end of it – but no, for the male headed towards the nest through the water, carrying in his beak a large piece of reed stem. The female took the stem and added it to the rim of the nest, while the male set off to bring another. He headed towards the bank by the shortest route to the place where I assumed he would collect more material, but once again,

no – he ran along the bank fully fifteen metres before stopping to pick up another stem, having passed (in my estimation) hundreds of stems that would have served the same purpose. Then he returned to the point on the bank from which he swam to the nest, and this proceedure was repeated for fully half an hour before I finally left for home.

By Monday morning the drizzle had stopped and at 11.am I was seated in a hide overlooking a most unusual Moorhen nest which in due course produced the desired photographs. There is no doubt that further happenings at this nest plus situations both humourous and tragic at other

Moorhen nests all bear narrating but space is limited until perhaps a future date.

MOORHEN

Comparative size Smaller than Mallard.
Status Resident.
Habitat Ponds, lochs, waterways, ditches.
Nest Platform of reeds, sedges.
Eggs Buff, blotched and spotted with brown, clutch 5-12.
Food Weeds, water insects.

Coot
Fulica Atra

Lochs and ponds with a good reedy margin are the favoured habitats of the **Coot**, which is one of our more easily recognised waterbirds.

Its plumage is all black with a white bill and forehead, and the legs and feet are greenish, the sexes being similar in colouring. The Coot is the only member of the Rail family with 'lobed' feet,

Coots abandon their quarrelsome nature outside the breeding season and become more tolerant towards one another.

each toe being fringed with a layer of skin, which makes an extremely effective paddle and is also handy for walking over soft mud. Coots are excellent swimmers and divers, constantly disappearing from view, diving under the surface to search for food among weeds on the bottom.

They rise from the pond with some difficulty, fluttering along the surface before taking off, but once airborne the flight is similar to that of the Moorhen, neck extended and feet stretched straight out behind. Noted for their quarrelsome behaviour, Coot are extremely territory conscious, with odd birds defending their area all year round, and on ponds with large populations a number of birds without territories must be content to mingle with others in a neutral area.

Nesting begins as early as March and the nest, a bulky affair built of reeds, sedges and other aquatic vegetation, is usually concealed in a reedbed, though at times nests are built in more open sites based on some submerged object.

Incubation is shared by both parents for about 21 days, and when hatched, the chicks are extremely comical with their bald foreheads, orangey side whiskers and bright red faces. They are brooded for a few days by the female while the male brings food to the nest, and at about four weeks old they are capable of diving for food themselves.

As with the Moorhen, the Coot's nest is a fixed structure so flooding is a major factor in nest failure, but an even bigger menace is the threat of the Carrion Crow, with as many as two thirds of eggs laid being taken by these predators in some areas.

Although mainly a diving species when feeding Coots will feed on shore, where they are noticeably less at home than Moorhens, never venturing far from the water's edge. In winter large numbers of Coots can be seen on the ice-free areas of ponds and lochs and it takes really severe frost to force them onto estuaries.

COOT

Comparative size Larger than Moorhen.
Status Resident.
Habitat Reservoirs, lochs, ponds – with cover.
Nest Bulky, sedges, reeds, vegetation.
Eggs Stone coloured, with blackish spots, clutch 4-10.
Food mainly aquatic vegetation, insects.

Oyster Catcher
Haematopus ostralegus

It is less than 100 years ago that the first **Oyster Catchers** moved inland to the central regions of the south of Scotland to establish themselves as a breeding species.

For a long time their nesting habitat was entirely on gravel beds along river courses, but within the last 20 years cultivated fields have also been favoured, being less vulnerable to flooding and providing better cover.

A most attractive and welcome bird, they leave their coastal wintering quarters and return to their breeding haunts as early as February, and by late March territories are well established. Male and female are similar in colouring, having blackish heads and upperparts with the bill bright orange. The wings have white bars which are conspicuous in flight, and there is a black band at the top of the white tail. The underparts and rump are also white and the sturdy legs and feet and pinkish.

The name Oyster Catcher is perhaps a bit misleading, as oysters are not their main food – in fact, mussels are much in favour, carried to the point where they are attacked with the chisel-tipped bill. Molluscs also form much of the diet, but these are quietly stalked and, once in their open position, a quick jab and the Oyster Catcher devours another juicy titbit. Individuals normally favour one or the other of these feeding methods.

In their breeding haunts two or three pairs can have territories on the same large gravel bed, and as it takes about four years before young birds reach maturity there are always some of these younger birds close by. Early in the season when the weather suddenly turns cold and windy, old and young birds will roost together in groups for warmth and safety. The nest is merely a depression among the gravel, or on the bare soil in a cultivated field, at times lined with small pebbles or even tiny pieces of stick or straw, and when laid in such surroundings the eggs are extremely difficult to see.

The three or four eggs are laid at intervals of about 36 hours and are left exposed until the clutch is complete – perhaps this is another reason why cultivated fields are now producing a higher percentage of successful nests, as there are always Carrion or Hooded Crows strolling over the gravel beds, ever on the scrounge for easy

Oyster Catchers spend the winter in large numbers on esturial coastal waters but most return inland to breed.

pickings. Unlike most waders, young Oyster Catchers have food taken to them by their parents for the early part of their lives, possibly due to the fact that they have such a specialised way of feeding, and also because, inland, earthworms and caterpillars form a major part of the youngster's diet.

Approach a gravel bed from a high vantage point such as a hillside and by using binoculars, sitting birds can be pinpointed, allowing an assessment of the breeding population to be made. Even with the most careful method of marking the sitting birds, however, once they are in the air their eggs, blending so well with the stones, are difficult to spot. It can be even more difficult if the young are hatched, as they too blend perfectly with the stones in their grey-black mottled down.

Watch an Oyster Catcher on her nest as an angler moves cautiously downstream, and you will note that her neck is stretched to its limit as she adopts an alert position. She remains like this until she feels threatened, then slinks away from her eggs towards the edge of the river – if the

intruder gets too close, she will take flight. At this point she is joined by her mate and both birds will pipe in annoyance above the intruder's head until he has passed through their territory. Then the hen alights some distance away from the nest and cautiously makes her way back to her eggs.

It is estimated that there are about 30,000 breeding pairs of Oyster Catchers in the British Isles, with by far the largest proportion in Scotland. In autumn, when our breeding population heads for coastal waters to spend the winter, they are joined by many thousands more from northern countries when numbers can rise to anything between 100,000 and 200,000, with estuaries like the Solway Firth being one of the main wintering areas.

OYSTER CATCHER

Comparative size Larger than Lapwing.
Status Resident, winters in estuaries.
Habitat Coastal, fresh waterways, rivers.
Nest Depression on gravel or soil.
Eggs Buff, marked with blackish spots, clutch 3-4.
Food Mussels, molluscs, worms, caterpillars.

Lapwing

Vanellus vanellus

Both the plumage and the voice of the **Lapwing** are characteristic and distinctive, and the 'peewit' call over meadows and fields in spring is a familiar and welcome sound.

Males arrive back in their breeding territories shortly before the females, staking their claim on a certain area that suits their purpose, and when the females arrive the males perform their courtship display, flying to and fro, sweeping one way, then another, their wings producing a 'whooshing' sound as their wheezy 'peewit' calls resound over the fields.

When the male is eventually joined by a female he begins courtship in earnest, forming 'scrapes' on the ground and displaying with fanned-out tail while bowing before her. On being accepted, he will then display at many different sites, gyrating his body to form a series of scrapes before the female finally accepts one and egg-laying begins. The accepted scrape is lined with varying amounts of material, sometimes a few wisps of hay, sometimes a substantial amount, and the four eggs are usually laid in April. Both parents take part in incubating the eggs, with the female taking by far the larger share, and it is during this time that the watcher

The characteristic sight and sound of the Lapwing is welcomed by both farmer and birdwatcher as the birds return each spring to arable fields.

is fortunate enough to be able to study the pair from a hide can note the subtle differences in the bird's appearance.

Observe Lapwings in flight or at a distance in a field and we register a black and white bird, observe the same Lapwing from a distance of about four metres from a hide and how wrong we are, for on closer observation the upperparts prove to be dark, glossy green with purplish highlights, the blackish throat has a greenish tinge and the underparts are white, with bright orange undertail coverts. In close up the observer soon sees that the breast patterns differ slightly from bird to bird and the wispy crest feathers of the male are about twice the length of the female's.

Defensive in protecting their nests, the males will rise, 'peewitting' loudly to mob a passing crow or other large bird, and domestic animals wandering too close by will receive similar treatment until they vacate the nesting area.

The chicks of the Lapwing are 'nidifugous', that is to say that, like many other ground-nesting species, the young leave the nest as soon as they are dry. They are extremely vulnerable at this time, crouching low at the first sign of danger, which is usually conveyed to them by the 'peewitting' of their parents, and when they take cover in a grassy tuft or the imprint of a hoof they are very difficult to see.

In early spring, flocks of many hundreds of Lapwing can be found in the flat low-lying fields of the Annan valley feeding vigorously, at times interspersed with a few Golden Plover, and making one ever hopeful that a fair percentage will stay to breed. But these birds are on their way northwards – possibly they are of Icelandic or Scandinavian origin – and a few weeks later the same fields are completely cleared of these attractive and useful waders.

Sadly, but surely, the Lapwing has been evicted from many of its former breeding grounds, and as severe winters also decimate their numbers, increasingly we will have to accept the Lapwing as mainly a passing migrant.

Following the severe winter of 1962-3 the numbers of breeding Lapwing in Scotland fell by almost 50 per cent. Five years later former numbers were practically restored, but since then, especially in the south, a steady and more worrying decline has taken place.

The main reason for the drastic fall in numbers is loss of habitat. Many water meadows that supported Snipe and Redshank as well as Lapwings have been drained, and within a fortnight of dry weather in spring the ground is rock hard, depriving the birds of their food source.

Two areas in particular that I have monitored over the past decade, three miles apart, support this theory, as both locations contained breeding pairs of all three species, and the gradual desertion of the areas were similar in both cases. Firstly the Snipe disappeared, followed closely by the Redshank, but still two or three pairs of Lapwing persisted in their attempts to rear their broods. But starvation and predation by crows proved too much, and the later years found only one pair attempting to nest.

I am ever hopeful that Mother Nature will revert a few fields to water meadow once again, to provide a habitat for our familiar and well-loved 'Peewits', but only time will tell.

Ringed Plover
Charadrius hiaticula

Like the Oyster Catcher, the **Ringed Plover** has moved inland, following river courses to colonise new breeding territories as more and more of its coastal habitat has been lost through industrial and leisure development.

Ringed Plover appear along Scottish rivers early in the spring, probably having wintered on an estuary only 50-100 miles distant. They are attractive little waders, somewhat smaller than Blackbirds being only 19cm in length, and on gravel beds, one of their favoured nesting sites, they can be elusive until you recognise the plaintive call and are able to trace the sound to the spot where the Ringed Plover is standing.

The sexes are similiar in colouring, the light

LAPWING

Comparative size Smaller than pigeon.
Status Resident, wintering in estuaries and coastal fields.
Habitat Water meadows, arable farmland, moorland.
Nest Scrape in ground, lined in varying degrees.
Eggs Pear-shaped, buff, heavily marked with black blotches, clutch 4.
Food Earthworms, slugs, snails, insects.

Another example of nature's camouflage can be seen as the Ringed Plover approaches her three eggs laid in a slight depression among the pebbles.

brown upperparts having a white wingbar, while the underparts are unbroken white. The Ringed Plover gets its name partly from the white ring round its neck and partly from the black collar, which is broad at the front and narrower at the back. The blackish cheeks and crown contrast with a white forehead, and the bill and legs are orangey, the former tipped with black.

Appearing to have much in common with the Oyster Catcher, the Ringed Plover has moved into cultivated fields bordering rivers to nest. Like that of the Oyster Catcher, the nest is a very scant affair, a mere scrape in the soil or, if found on a gravel bed, a slight depression among tiny pebbles.

Four eggs is a normal clutch, and the similarity to the Oyster Catcher is again apparent as the eggs, though much smaller, are very similar in colouring. Ringed Plover eggs appear too large for the size of the bird, but on observing the parent from the close proximity of a hide it is surprising to see just how easily they are covered. When the eggs hatch, the necessity for such a

---

RINGED PLOVER

Comparative size Smaller then Lapwing.
Status Resident, winters in estuaries.
Habitat Shingle shores, gravel beds.
Nest Shallow scrape on gravel or soil.
Eggs Buff with browny-black spots, clutch 4.
Food Molluscs, crustaceans.

---

large egg soon becomes apparent – smaller chicks would certainly have difficulty in surviving for, once again, we have a 'nidifugous' species, the chicks leaving the nest as soon as they are dry.

The Ringed Plover is a sturdy little wader, active and lively, running to and fro and pausing frequently, as if listening for the movement of a small shrimp or worm.

In flight it is fast and direct, and on landing it runs a short distance with its wings raised before settling. An expert at the 'broken wing trick', the Ringed Plover will stumble over the gravel trailing a wing, at times even rolling over in an attempt to lure you away from the nest, and if the intruder be fox or stoat this ruse must surely be effective.

Although Ringed Plover are a regular breeding species on some of our gravel beds, they are by no means abundant, and if for some reason both birds vacate the gravel at the same time, possibly to avoid passing anglers, on returning the male always makes his presence more obvious while the female is extremely cautious, moving only a few metres at a time as she returns to her well camouflaged eggs or young.

Ringed Plover are perhaps best seen in winter when they frequent coastal estuaries where they can be seen pattering with their feet in the soft mud, attempting to bring worms to the surface.

They also feed on small shrimps and snails, picked up and not probed for as they are by most other waders.

If by chance a small flock of Ringed Plover are suddenly alarmed, perhaps by an overhead predator, they will take to the air with incredible speed, wheel and turn, and then land close to the spot from which they took off, busying themselves once again in the never-ending search for food.

Grey Plover
Pluvialis squatarola

The **Grey Plover** is a passage migrant to Scotland, and then only to coastal regions mainly on the eastern seaboard, but they can also be seen on the Solway where they appear mainly in winter dress: uniform brownish-grey upperparts with lighter underparts. However, in summer dress the plumage is most striking, silver-grey spangled upperparts, black cheeks, throat and underparts, with the white of the forehead extending behind the eye, down both sides of the neck and becoming broader and very conspicuous down each side of the dark breast.

Coastal Wintering Waders

I have always found the term 'Winter Visitor' somewhat misleading, especially when compared with 'Summer Resident'. Some of our summer residents arrive in the spring, raise their families, then migrate back to Africa all within the space of five months, and yet birds spending over seven months of the year in the British Isles are termed merely as 'visitors'.

Among these winter visitors are our coastal waders, with Scottish estuaries such as the Moray Firth, The Firth of Forth and the Solway Firth supporting many thousands that arrive from the Arctic and north-eastern and central Europe, where winters are much more severe.

Birdwatching on estuaries can be a daunting task for the novice, suddenly confronted with a mass of 'greyish' coloured waders either in the flesh, or contained within the pages of a 'Field Guide'. But there is no need for despair, as they all have their own characteristics which make them as obvious as road signs, and by knowing the 'old faithfuls', our resident waders, the simple process of elimination can be brought into play. Our resident waders are most helpful by dressing the same in winter and summer, making them readily recognisable, and as there are always 'locals' among the visitors, relative size can at once be noted.

The familiar resident species required for comparative measuring are:

Ringed Plover
Lapwing
Oyster Catcher

The Ringed Plover is l9cm in length, helping us identify one of our most familiar little shoreline waders the **Dunlin.** *Calidris Alpina* at l8cm.

The Dunlin is a dumpy little bird which feeds in groups by systematically probing in the soft mud. It has greyish upperparts, a dark breast and lighter underparts, and the bill, a fraction longer than the length of the head, is slightly downcurved. Most of our wintering Dunlin arrive from the Arctic regions but we have a regular breeding population in Scotland.

A Dunlin pauses for a short break by the riverside while heading inland from the coast.

A less abundant, but more characteristic little wader is the **Sanderling.** *Calidris Alba*, at 20cm in length. Paler than the Dunlin, it has a shorter, straight beak, white breast and black shoulders. This little wader frequents sandy beaches in small groups where it runs the tide line with amazing speed, catching and feeding on sand hoppers and other small items of food while it avoids the incoming waves.

At 25cm in length, the **Knot**, *Calidris Canutus* is larger than the Ringed Plover, but smaller than the Lapwing. It is a more uniform grey and

white, with black wing tips and a short, black bill, but by far its best identification feature is the large flocks in which it congregates above the estuary, flashing white, then various shades of grey, according to the light, as a thousand pairs of wings twist and turn. Knot probe in the estuarine mud for insects and small crustaceans.

At 23cm, the **Turnstone,** *Arenaria Interpres* is larger than the Ringed Plover, but this little wader is one of the easier ones to recognise in its black and chestnut upperparts with black throat, orange legs and short, stout bill, which it uses on shingly beaches to turn over the stones to find the insects and invertebrates on which it feeds – it does therefore not compete with other species for food. The Turnstone's appearance reminds one of a small Oyster Catcher.

The **Black-tailed Godwit** *Limosa Limosa* at 4lcm is smaller than the Oyster Catcher, but it has longer legs and a longer, straight bill. The upperparts are a uniform pale brownish grey, and the underparts are lighter. Godwits use their long, black legs to advantage to wade in deeper water, probing the soft mud for worms and shellfish.

The **Bar-tailed Godwit** *Limosa Lapponica* at 38cm is smaller than the Black-tail, but have similar long legs and the bill, also long, is slightly upcurved. The plumage, similar in colour to the Black-tail, is mottled in dark brown.

Although these six common waders are described as we in Scotland see them in their winter dress, a good 'Field Guide' will also depict them in their summer plumage and describe and illustrate our rarer wintering waders.

Golden Plover

Pluvialis apricaria

In early March the large flocks of **Golden Plover** wintering in fields round our coasts start to disperse, and it is then that small flocks of a dozen or so can be found inland at locations that are almost traditional.

Certain low lying fields in the Annan valley are regular 'stopping off' places for these beautiful golden spangled little waders, where they can be seen feeding with larger flocks of migratory Lapwing and smaller numbers of Curlew.

From there it is only a short 'hop' to the heathery peaks of the Southern Uplands where, Golden Plover reside throughout the summer months, as they do throughout the Scottish hills. Stunted heather is the favoured habitat of the Golden Plover – an area of hilltop which has been burned the previous season, resulting in patchy growth, will almost certainly attract breeding pairs.

In its summer dress the Golden Plover truly lives up to its name, for when seen in different degrees of light the black and gold spangled upperparts reflect accordingly, as I found when I took a series of photographs of a bird at her nest early one morning. The first photographs depicted her as almost greyish, but an hour later, illuminated by the early morning sun, the

As the Golden Plover settles on her eggs in the early morning sunlight she presents an almost 'oil-painted' picture.

resulting photographs of the bird had an oil-painted effect which is most attractive.

Golden Plover have the typical round head and slender bill of the family, though in the Scottish race the black breast and dark cheeks are not so clearly defined as in the Northern; the white band separating the dark breast from golden upperparts is also quite vague.

The nest is a depression amongst short vegetation, scantily lined with stalks and grasses, and the four pear-shaped eggs blend perfectly with their surroundings. The birds too, depend strongly on cryptic colouring to remain unnoticed when a predator passes overhead, scarcely blinking as they draw their heads down into their bodies, closely resembling a tuft of vegetation.

When the chicks hatch they are born with their eyes open and with the well-developed legs, necessary for young nidifugous birds that leave the nest as soon as they are dry, but at the first sign of danger the alarm call of the parents induces the chicks to 'freeze' on the spot, thus becoming almost invisible.

During the winter months, Golden Plover provide birdwatchers with a marvellous display of syncronised flight as the large flock turns and banks in the air, shimmering gold, then black, then white, all in the space of a few seconds, before finally peeling off in a continuous line to settle once more in the fields.

undertakes the domestic duties which are usually undertaken by females of other species.

Dotterels are colourful little waders, the mantle and breast being greyish-brown and separated from the chestnut underparts by a white line. The chestnut underparts then merge into a black belly, and the undertail coverts are white. The dark head has a broad white stripe over each eye which meets in a 'V' shape at the nape of the neck. Once again we have an exception to the rule with the male being less colourful than the female.

Dotterels pass through the south of Scotland on migration, *en route* to their breeding haunts on the peaks of the Cairngorms and other ranges where they can be found sitting on eggs in June, but they are difficult to spot as they sit very tight, allowing one to approach almost to within stroking distance. The eggs are also marked in such a way as to render them almost invisible.

Confined to such a specialised environment, Dotterels are constantly disturbed by the many people with various interests who visit the Cairngorms, and to such an extent that some areas which previously were strongholds are now deserted.

Fortunately some of our southern peaks, although not as high, are less well known and virtually undisturbed, and are offering sanctuary to these unusual little summer residents.

GOLDEN PLOVER
Comparative size Smaller than Lapwing.
Status Resident, winters in coastal fields.
Habitat Hill moors, heathery tops.
Nest Scrape among short vegetation, scantily lined.
Eggs Pear-shaped, yellowish-buff, blotched with blackish-brown, clutch 4.
Food Animal and vegetable matter.

DOTTEREL
Comparative size Smaller than Lapwing.
Status Summer resident.
Habitat Lichen and heathery-covered mountains.
Nest Shallow scrape on ground.
Eggs Olive-grey with dark-brown blotches, clutch 3.
Food Mainly insects.

Dotterel
Charadrius morinellus

The **Dotterel** is such an attractive little wader of the Plover family that it is a pity its name is associated with being foolish. Perhaps this has come about because, being so tame, they can be easily caught, or perhaps it is because the male

Common Snipe
Gallinago gallinago

The 'drumming' of the **Snipe** high above its breeding territory is very characteristic, and for many years there has been much speculation as to how the sound is produced – is it vocal, or is it produced by the wings or the tail?

From a height of about 150 metres the Snipe dives at an angle of about 45 degrees, during which time the tail is fanned out, with the two outer tail feathers twisted at an angle to the others, and it is the resulting vibration which produces the sound. After each dive, the bird rapidly regains height to repeat the performance, which can continue for several minutes, and though both birds display in this way, it is more often the male who performs while the female is incubating.

The Snipe's upperparts are rich brown, mottled with buff in such a way as to give the bird a streaky appearance. The breast is buffish as are the undertail coverts, with the remainder of the underparts white. The legs and toes are greenish and the long bill is pale brown.

Far out on the moors a Snipe settles on her eggs while high above her mate performs his 'drumming' display flight.

The Snipe is 27cm in length with the bill accounting for 7cm, and it is indeed a specialised tool, used to extract worms and grubs from under the surface of moist earth. The tip is extremely sensitive, being able to locate an earthworm simply by touch. Once it is located, the tip of the upper mandible functions independently, and is opened sufficiently to grasp and extract the meal.

The nest of the Snipe is a deep cup-shaped structure, built from rushes and lined with finer grasses, and well concealed amongst marsh or moorland vegetation. The four eggs, though quite variable in their background colouring, are always marked in such a way as to make them difficult to see; the sitting bird is also endowed with perfect cryptic colouring being rendered almost invisible from a short distance.

The female undertakes the incubation alone, the young leaving the nest as soon as they are dry, and the male then lends a hand by taking and tending half the brood while the female looks after the other two. In this way there is more chance of some of the brood avoiding predation by crows or stoats.

The camouflage of the species serves them well while resting or feeding, and they can be almost trodden on before breaking cover and zig-zagging away with an erratic flight that has fooled many a hunter.

The Snipe is the only moorland wader to remain inland throughout the winter and as long as the weather is not too severe they can eke out a living in boggy areas and along marshy ditches, where at time they are joined by their smaller cousin, the Jack Snipe.

COMMON SNIPE

Comparative size Smaller than Lapwing.
Status Resident.
Habitat Marshy places, moorlands.
Nest Cup shaped, on ground, rushes, grasses.
Eggs Background variable, olive to grey with dark markings, clutch 4.
Food Earthworms, insects, crustaceans.

Jack Snipe
Lymnocryptes minimus

The **Jack Snipe** appears in Scotland mainly as a passing migrant and it is distinguished from the Common Snipe by its small 19cm size.

It has a distinct black stripe running lengthways over its crown, and there are four buffish stripes down the back. The underparts are off-white streaked with dark brown, and the bill is noticeably shorter being only 3.5cm long. Usually a difficult bird to observe, I feel that a passage from my 'Field Notes' is worth narrating at this point:

'On the 16 February 1970, I pulled in by the roadside at Gateside Farm Wamphray, to watch birds bathing in and drinking from the burn. After watching for a few moments, a movement on the other side of the burn caught my eye, as a Common Snipe stood preening only ten metres from the car. A minute or two later a weasel made its way down the bank, drawing my attention to another Snipe standing by the burnside, a few metres from the other.

This bird was noticeably smaller than the first and, on training my binoculars onto it, I saw that its bill was much shorter and that it had a double eyestripe. The markings on the back were also heavier, and the legs were shorter. The second bird was a Jack Snipe and when it walked it bobbed up and down, its whole body dipping, not just its tail.

On being disturbed by a dog the Common Snipe rose with a typical Snipe 'squak' but the Jack Snipe rose without uttering any sound.'

Fortunately, before the dog appeared I had photographed both birds – a little distant, but a good record.

Woodcock
Scolopax rusticola

The **Woodcock**, as its name suggests, is the wader of the woodlands, remaining under cover during the daylight hours and feeding in late evening.

In early spring, one can be standing by the edge of a wood as darkness begins to fall when a bird, somewhat owl-like, passes overhead at a height of about thirty metres. From some distance away, a peculiar sound can be heard as the Woodcock utters his two distinct calls, a double croak followed by a high-pitched 'tsi-tsi', whistle, which is particularly audible as the bird passes directly above. This evening flight is called 'roding' and is undertaken every evening and at dawn from late February to July as part of the territorial display before and during nesting, the male flying in a circuit around the perimeter of his territory. This 'roding' flight lasts for about an hour each evening and at times he will make contact with a neighbouring male, when a short, noisy, mid-air scuffle takes place.

The Woodcock is a stoutly built, round-winged bird of 34cm, which includes the 7cm long bill. The plumage is mainly brown in colouring, with its mantle marbled in tints of rusty brown, buff and black. The lighter brown underparts are finely barred in dark brown, and the head and neck have dark bands running across from side to side. The long, probing bill, about three times the length of the head, has a sensitive tip for locating earthworms and grubs under the damp vegetation of marshy places, with the tip of the upper mandible being flexible enough to be opened and closed under the surface, securing and extracting the meal.

The eyes of the Woodcock are unique, for they are located in such a position on the sides of the head as to give the bird full 360° degree vision without moving its head. This avoids any unnecessary movement when an intruder approaches while the bird is incubating, and it will sit very still, relying on the perfect camouflage of their colouring to remain undetected, thus protecting its eggs.

The eggs are laid on a bed of dead leaves in a slight depression, well concealed among the bracken or bramble undergrowth of the birchwood, or by a branch lying among the needles of the conifer wood floor, and they are incubated for about three weeks by the female.

Unless disturbed, the Woodcock remains under cover by day and, being 'crepuscular' (active around twilight) in its habits, as evening falls it leaves its hiding place and, on silent and steady wings, heads for its feeding grounds, usually a marshy place which can be some distance away.

Sought after as a game bird, the Woodcock is seldom seen as a target for more than a fleeting glance, as it rises suddenly from the undergrowth with a rapid, twisting flight, producing a swishing sound with its wings as it dodges among the branches.

A number of reliable observers have seen Woodcock carry their young away from danger by clasping them between their legs, but the closest I have been to witnessing this for myself was while in the course of photographing a Woodcock at her nest in a small copse by a country road.

Following a session in the hide late one April afternoon, I examined the eggs and found that they were 'chipping'. Knowing that the chicks would be hatched early next morning and that I would not have time to photograph the family, I informed a friend who, in due course, was in the hide by daybreak. Shortly after this, telephone engineers parked their van only five metres from the nest, agitating the mother to such an extent that she led her chicks to a small bramble patch about two metres away before settling down to brood them. At this point the telephone engineers were joined by several roadmen and, with the

The distraction display of the waders can take some peculiar forms, as demonstrated by this Woodcock.

ensuing activity proving too much for the mother Woodcock, she stood up, lifted one of her chicks between her legs and flew off with it to a wood about a hundred metres across a field. She broke her journey about halfway, either to rest or to adjust her load, and then immediately returned to her remaining three chicks and flew off with another, the remaining two being airlifted in the same manner soon afterwards. On each flight, the mother paused briefly in the middle of the field.

It had been an overcast morning, without a single photograph being taken, but the observations are well and truly documented in my field notes.

WOODCOCK

Comparative size Larger than Lapwing.
Status Resident.
Habitat Woodlands with bracken, bramble undergrowth.
Nest A slight hollow on ground, well hidden, lined with dead leaves.
Eggs Greyish-buff, marked with chestnut, clutch 4-5.
Food Earthworms, grubs, insects, some vegetable matter.

Curlew

Numenius arquata

The **Curlew** is our largest and most familiar wader, a real favourite on our hill moors, its distinctive call conjuring up in our minds the romance and mystery of the Scottish moorlands, and it is a pity that its breeding visit is over in such a short space of time. Although Curlews disperse from their wintering grounds on the estuaries to their inland breeding haunts by mid-March, they generally start making their way back to the coast by mid-July, and by August, the hill moors hold only a few stragglers.

Birds are usually paired up before they arrive in their breeding haunts, where the male can be seen standing guard on some vantage point while the female is close by. The male then indulges in some wonderful aerial displays, flying low over the moor, then suddenly rising to a height with rapidly beating wings, hanging momentarily as if hovering before planing down again, while calling to his mate.

The plumage is a uniform, streaky brown, beautifully patterned on the upperparts, while the head, breast and underparts, also streaked, are much paler. The tail is barred with light and dark brown, and the white rump is conspicuous in flight.

The bill is long and downcurved, the male's being 13cm in length while the female's is longer at 17cm. Like other waders with deep-probing bills, the tip of the upper mandible is sensitive and flexible while under the surface of damp mud or earth, allowing detection of earthworms and insect larvae which are caught and pulled clear before being eaten. On the shore small crabs and molluscs are extracted and swallowed whole, the Curlew being unable to deal with them in such an efficient manner as the Oyster Catcher, but one advantage that the Curlew has in this type of habitat is the ability to probe deeper than the other waders in search of a morsel.

Areas of grass with patches of heather are the favoured upland breeding haunts of the Curlew, while lower down, reedy meadows and rough pasture provide the necessary cover, and in all locations the nest is never far from some water logged place.

The nest is a depression in a clump of grass or reeds, lined with grasses, and the eggs can be quite variable both in size and colour, being incubated by both parents for a period of about 28 days.

The chicks are fluffy balls of dark-streaked, buff-coloured down with short, straight beaks and large feet, and they thrive on a mainly insectivorous diet for about six weeks before mastering the probing technique. Though shy and wary towards humans, the Curlew likes the company of other birds, especially on the shore where it wades into the water, probing for food

---

CURLEW

Comparative size Larger than Oyster Catcher.
Status Resident, winters on coast.
Habitat Moorlands, tidal shores.
Nest Large scrape on ground, lined fine grasses.
Eggs Greenish or olive, spotted with grey and brown, clutch 4.
Food Molluscs, crustaceans, earthworms, insects and larvae.

In the hot June sun, Curlew chicks emerge into a world fraught with danger for ground nesting species.

with its remarkable beak, and parties flying to and from the estuaries often fly in 'V' formation.

The Curlew is known as the 'Whaup' in Scotland, where in some districts it certainly is much less common than it was quarter of a century ago, extensive land drainage and the planting of conifers depriving it of suitable breeding habitat and to make matters worse, disturbance at the nest site is followed, more often than not, by predation by Carrion Crows.

Whimbrel

Numenius phaeopus

The **Whimbrel**, ranging from 40-46cm in length, is larger than most of our waders but also 10cm shorter than its more familiar cousin, the Curlew.

The Whimbrel resembles the Curlew very much in its colouring, being a uniform streaky brown on the upperparts, with the paler edging to the feathers producing a diamond-shaped effect. The head is different, having two broad dark stripes above the eyes which are separated by a pale stripe running over the crown. The legs are greenish-grey, and the bill long and downcurved – though slightly heavier than that of the Curlew, is only twice the length of the head, whereas the Curlew's is three times the length of its head.

In the south of the country the Whimbrel is known only as a bird of passage, *en route* to and from its winter quarters in Africa in spring and autumn, but birdwatchers on the coast have a fair chance of spotting small parties near the marshy areas of river mouths on the estuaries where they can be seen probing for molluscs and worms and picking insects from among the vegetation.

Away from the coast, it is the characteristic call that attracts the watcher's attention as the birds fly overhead, usually at a considerable height. The call has given rise to its colloquial name of 'Seven Whistler' and consists of a series of seven shrill whistles.

In the far north of Scotland the Whimbrel can be found in its breeding territory, where, at closer

range, the distinctive white of the rump is seen to extend further along the back of the bird, ending in a 'V' shape behind the shoulders, and the underwing is also paler than that of the Curlew.

The nest is built in a grassy hummock scantily lined with moss and grasses, and the eggs, usually laid in June, are incubated for about four weeks. When hatched, the chicks feed on an insect and berry diet until they are able to probe in a similar manner to their parents.

In early autumn the birds once again leave their breeding territories and head south, pausing at intervals to excite the birdwatcher, then on again towards their wintering quarters in Africa.

WHIMBREL

Comparative size Smaller than Curlew.
Status Summer resident.
Habitat Moors, bogs and marshes.
Nest Scrape on ground, lined heather, grasses.
Eggs Olive-brown, black and grey markings, clutch 4.
Food Worms, molluscs, insects and their larvae, berries.

During the spring migration Whimbrels can be seen on esturial mud flats as they pause briefly before flying northwards to their breeding haunts.

Red-necked Phalarope

Phalaropus lobatus

The **Red-necked Phalarope** is an extremely scarce little breeding wader, being found only in the most northerly regions of Scotland where they prefer the seclusion of well vegetated little lochans as a summer habitat.

A delightful little bird the Red-necked Phalarope shows little or no fear of man as it swims buoyantly on the surface, spinning in tiny circles to bring minute aquatic organisms to the surface from where they can be picked and eaten.

As with the Dotterel, the roles of the sexes are reversed, and to aid this purpose the male is much less colourful than the female. The female in summer plumage has greyish-brown upperparts and head with orange patches on the cheeks and neck, while the throat and underparts are white. The small, pointed bill is black, and the toes of the blue-grey feet are 'lobed' as in the Coot. The male is rather smaller and less colourful, with buffish streaks on the upperparts and less obvious orange cheeks.

Arriving in their breeding haunts in early June, a courtship ceremony takes place in which the female rises from the water with rapidly beating wings producing a humming sound, and her mating calls can be heard as she chases the male, which at times can be pursued by two or three females at once.

The nest is a hollow, 'scraped' in a grassy tussock by both male and female and lined with fine grasses. On completion of the clutch, which is usually four eggs, the male undertakes the incubation alone for about 21 days; he then tends for the chicks for about the same period.

Occasionally in autumn, especially following stormy weather, a solitary Red-necked Phalarope turns up on some wet place in the south of Scotland, but any that I have known of were in their more sombre immature plumage.

The male Common Sandpiper stands guard on a vantage point while his mate tends their small chicks.

RED-NECKED PHALAROPE
Comparative size Smaller than Ringed Plover.
Status Summer resident.
Habitat Moors, bogs, marshes.
Nest Scrape on ground, lined with fine grasses.
Eggs Olive brown with chocolate brown markings, clutch 4.
Food Small crustaceans, insects and larvae.

Common Sandpiper

Actitis hypoleucos

By the shores of lochs and reservoirs, and from the lower river valleys to the high hill burns, the **Common Sandpiper** is a summer resident throughout Scotland.

Arriving in April, his three-part whistling call soon becomes familiar to the angler plying his skills against the wary trout, and by mid-May the Common Sandpiper is well established in his territory.

A small bird of around 20cm, the Common Sandpiper is easily recognised by having brown upperparts and white underparts. The wings have a white bar and there is a brownish tinge on either side of the breast. It has a slender bill, about the same length as its head, a short tail, and greenish-grey legs.

The sexes are similar in colouring and when they are seen probing among the shingle at the riverside, a constant bobbing action is characteristic. The flight is also distinctive, a few sharp flicks of the wings, then a glide with the wing tips held slightly downwards below the level of the body as the birds fly up or downstream.

Although often found nesting on a gravel bed where a pair of Ringed Plover have their territory, the two nests are very different – where the Ringed Plover chooses to lay her eggs in the open, the Common Sandpiper always builds her

COMMON SANDPIPER
Comparative size Smaller than Redshank.
Status Summer resident.
Habitat Loch sides, river courses.
Nest Grass-lined depression, among herbage.
Eggs Buff, with dark brown spots, clutch 4.
Food Small invertebrates, vegetable matter.

nest, a deep cup-shaped structure lined with grasses and leaves under some form of herbage such as a dock or other broadleaved plant. Both sexes share the incubation period of about 21 days, and when the chicks hatch they are tended by both parents.

If by chance an intruder comes in close proximity to the young family by the riverside, the parents indulge in a well planned manoeuvre. The female crouches, hiding among the herbage with her chicks, while the male makes his presence obvious by selecting a vantage point close to the intruder, calling and constantly bobbing up and down. This ruse usually has the desired effect, by drawing the intruder away from the brood as the male moves further and further away, until finally the danger has passed. He then flies in a semi-circle back to the exact spot where his family is concealed.

In autumn the birds make their way south, most of them spending the winter in the southern half of Africa, but exceptions do occur and odd birds can be found on the south coast of England throughout the winter months.

Wood Sandpiper
Tringa glareola

The **Wood Sandpiper** is mainly a bird of passage in the British Isles, occasionally being seen on the east coast in small numbers, usually in August and September following strong easterly gales which coincide with their migration from Scandinavian breeding grounds.

During the return spring migration a few pairs linger in northern Scotland, finding the habitat to their liking. Here they nest in damp, open woodland, but are extremely difficult to locate.

Similar in size to the Common Sandpiper, though somewhat slimmer, the Wood Sandpiper is darker brown on the upperparts, with the

---

WOOD SANDPIPER

Comparative size Smaller than Redshank.
Status Summer resident.
Habitat Marshy woodlands.
Nest Hollow lined with grass, old nest of other birds.
Eggs Olive green, blotched with brown.
Food Mainly aquatic insects and their larvae.

---

feathers having paler edges. There is also a prominent white eyestripe, and the legs are slightly longer than those of the Common Sandpiper.

Green Sandpiper
Tringa ochropus

Like the Wood Sandpiper, the **Green Sandpiper,** can be found breeding in Scandinavia, but as its full breeding range is more widespread than that of the Wood, the nesting period varies accordingly, with migrating Green Sandpipers turning up in the British Isles from mid-June onwards.

Inland marshy pools and sewage farms are favoured stopping places, where the feeding bird may be quite inconspicuous, but most are seen in flight as they follow the course of a river. On a number of occasions in the autumn while fishing a stretch of the River Annan, I have heard a Sandpiper-like call, and looked up to see a Green Sandpiper flying downstream with its typical jerky flight. Passing only a few metres from where I was standing, the dark plumage and distinctive white rump were obvious, as were the dark underwings. On one occasion I saw a pair in a similar situation spend an afternoon in a waterlogged field by the river. The birds were very flighty, taking to the wing often, circling and landing repeatedly before finally flying south.

Purple Sandpiper
Calidris maritima

The **Purple Sandpiper** is an Arctic breeding species found in Britain as a passage migrant and winter visitor, and is a bird of the rocky sea coasts.

It is a dumpy little bird about 20cm in length, with dark greyish-brown upperparts, a dark grey breast and paler underparts. The bill, about the same length as the head, is yellowish at the base and slightly downcurved, and the short, yellowish legs are characteristic. Early experiences with Purple Sandpipers, prompt me to draw attention to the fact that they are extremely approachable, often being missed on nearing a rocky point from which first the Oyster Catchers took flight, followed by the Turnstones, leaving the rocks apparently deserted. Walking a few metres further on and examining the seaward side, however, you will find a small party of Purple Sandpipers on the rocky ledges.

Like the Wood Sandpiper, a few pairs nest annually in the far north of Scotland.

Redshank

Tringa totanus

The **Redshank** is a familiar bird of the tidal estuaries from autumn to spring, where it thrives by exploiting more of the waterline than most of our other small waders through being equipped with long legs and a longish bill and thus being able to wade and probe in deeper water for marine insects, small molluscs and crustaceans.

The Redshank is an elegant bird, distinguishable from other waders by its long, reddish legs. The upperparts are greyish-brown with darker markings and the neck and breast are paler, boldly streaked with black. The underparts, rump and tail are white, the latter having dark barring, and there is also a broad white band on the hind wing which is noticeable in flight.

Moving inland from the coast in March to a variety of habitats such as a marsh, a meadow near a river, or even rough pasture, the Redshank occupy their breeding territories where they have the delightful habit of perching on fenceposts and the like, alighting delicately with wings held high for a few moments before adopting an 'on guard' position.

Redshank and Lapwings can be found nesting in the same meadow, where it may be noted that the nests are somewhat different, that of the Lapwing being placed in the open while the Redshank's is always concealed under a canopy of reeds or long grass, having a much neater cup lined with fine grasses.

Like the Lapwing, The Redshank generally lay

The long, red legs are a characteristic feature of the Redshank.

four eggs, but although similar in size those of the Redshank have a lighter background colour, and paler markings. Redshank chicks hatch after an incubation period of about 24 days in which both parents take part, and for the next month or so the young are accompanied by the parents as they pick insects and seedlings from the meadow grasses, until their bills are sufficiently developed to allow them to probe for earthworms.

At the first sign of danger the parents take to the air, flying in wide circles above the spot where the chicks are feeding and calling in alarm as the tiny, fluffy chicks 'freeze' to avoid being seen, but as they grow older a similar situation will find the young running for cover among the denser vegetation. Autumn finds the family moving to the coast, where once again they become birds of our tidal estuaries.

REDSHANK

Comparative size Smaller than oyster catcher.
Status Resident, winters on coast.
Habitat Meadows, waterlogged fields, mudflats.
Nest Scrape on ground, lined with fine grasses.
Eggs Yellowish-brown, blotched dark brown, clutch 4.
Foods Small molluscs, crustaceans, earthworms.

Greenshank

Tringa nebularia

The Flow Country of Caithness and Sutherland in the extreme north of Scotland is an open expanse of peat, pools, moss and rare flowers, and a habitat for many of our rarer birds. It is the only area of its kind left in Europe, recognised by the international scientific community as being one of the world's outstanding ecosystems, so hopefully the recent encroachment of afforestation will be controlled sufficiently to ensure a future for birds like the **Greenshank.**

The Greenshank is slightly larger and taller than the Redshank, with long, green legs and a longish bill which is slightly upturned. The mantle and wings are mottled greyish-brown, the latter showing no white, but the underparts and rump are white and in summer the breast is marked with dark spots.

Greenshank arrive back in their moorland breeding territories in March, and by May nests can be found containing eggs. The nest is a mere hollow in the ground lined with heather, bits of wood, and leaves, and usually placed close to some marker like a piece of rotting wood and never far from water. Both parents incubate the eggs for 25 days, and when sitting the bird's colouring blends perfectly with the surroundings, so much so that they can almost be touched by a watcher approaching the nest. The chicks are striped buff and black and are tended by both parents for roughly 30 days, by which time the young can fly and fend for themselves.

Greenshank migrate south in autumn to winter on the Mediterranean, with a few from further north wintering on our western shores Here they favour small, muddy estuaries and can be seen feeding in typical wader fashion, by picking and probing, and occasionally running madly about through the shallow water in pursuit of a small fish.

GREENSHANK

Comparative size Smaller than oyster catcher.
Status Summer resident, part migrant.
Habitat Open heather moorland with pools.
Nest Scrape on ground, lined heather, grasses.
Eggs Pale yellowish-brown, blotched rusty colour, clutch 4.
Food Aquatic insects and their larvae, small molluscs.

Dunlin

Calidris alpina

Already mentioned as one of our little 'grey' wintering waders of the mud flats and estuaries, in summer plumage the **Dunlin** is a different bird indeed.

It is estimated that there are 500,000 Dunlin around our shores throughout the winter, but only 8,000 pairs breed in Scotland, mostly in northern parts.

Scottish Dunlin move inland in April, following river courses and hill burns until they arrive in their selected breeding territories, usually heathery or reedy areas bordering hill lochs or reservoirs.

They are very approachable little birds, and

most attractive with their bright chestnut upperparts flecked with black, and greyish-brown wings bearing a slim white bar. There is a conspicuous black patch on the breast contrasting with white undertail coverts, and the short legs are jet black.

The nest is nearly always near water, a compact little bowl of grass; the eggs, which are laid in late May or June, hatch in about 21 days. Both parents tend the young, leading them to the lochside to feed, but at times the mother loses interest in her brood and starts migrating before the young can fly, leaving the male to care for them until they, too, are capable of flying south. Despite this strange behaviour, the Dunlin are the most abundant waders on our coasts in winter.

DUNLIN

Comparative size Smaller than Ringed Plover.
Status Resident and winter visitor.
Habitat Moorland in summer, tidal shores in winter.
Nest Scrape on ground among low vegetation.
Eggs Buffish, variable, spotted with browns, clutch 4.
Food Insects, small molluscs and crustaceans.

Great Skua

Stercorarius skua

It is difficult to imagine that the **Great Skua** was almost extinct in Scotland only 150 years ago, when one realises that today the breeding population of the Shetlands alone amounts to over 4,000 pairs.

The Great Skua is a large, fierce and powerful

GREAT SKUA

Comparative size Slightly larger than Herring Gull.
Status Summer resident, oceanic in winter.
Habitat Coasts and islands, moorlands.
Nest Depression on ground, lined heather, grass, moss.
Eggs Olive, spotted with browns and grey, clutch 1-2.
Food Omnivorous.

---

bird, 58cm in length, capable of catching and killing smaller birds such as young Kittiwake, which it snatches from their nests in its powerful beak, although more often the Skua will pursue and harass birds like Guillemot off the sea coast until it drops its catch of fish which is immediately retrieved by the Skua. Even birds as large as Gannets are not entirely safe from this pirate who will catch the Gannet by the wing tip, forcing it to crash dive into the sea, and hang on until the Gannet disgorges its catch, which is then devoured by the Skua.

The 'Bonxie', the name by which the Great Skua is known in the Shetlands, is slightly larger than a Herring Gull, predominantly dark brown in colour, with paler streaks and conspicuous white patches on the outer part of the wings. It has a fierce looking beak, slightly hooked, and the legs and feet are black.

Great Skuas nest in loose colonies, with each pair having a well-defined territory which is defended against all intruders, bird or animal, and anyone venturing too close to the nest is sure to be dive-bombed from a great height, the birds swooping steeply, levelling out at the last moment, skimming the intruder's head, and even on occasion making contact with the webbed feet.

The nest is a depression on the ground among the stunted growth, lined with heather and grasses. Only one or two eggs are laid and incubation takes about 30 days, the young fledging about seven weeks later and leaving the nesting area soon afterwards.

For six months the Great Skuas roam the open sea, then two months before nesting they are back in their breeding territories again, displaying in their raucous fashion and staking their claim.

Arctic Skua

Stercorarius parasiticus

If it were not for the two long, straight feathers projecting from the middle of the wedge-shaped tail, the **Arctic Skua** would more often be mistaken for a gull, especially in poor light.

The Arctic Skua is peculiar in being 'dimorphic', ie there are two distinct forms of the same species. The light and dark phases occur in varying proportions throughout their range, with the higher proportion of the light phase being found further north. In Scotland about 75 per

The Arctic Skua incubates eggs in her nest on a remote Scottish Isle.

cent of the breeding population are dark-phased specimens whose plumage is a uniform dark brown with paler colouring to the cheeks, and the light phase birds have pure white underparts, nape and cheeks.

The Arctic Skua flies with buoyancy and grace, the regular, easy wingbeats resembling the flight of a hawk, until a fish-laden tern or puffin is singled out to provide the Skua's next meal. Then despite the Skua being much larger, the chase is on, and no matter how the victim twists, turns and dives, the pursuit is relentless, only ceasing when the fish is dropped, being caught and eaten in mid-air by the piratical Skua.

Arctic Skuas return to their breeding haunts in April where they nest in small colonies on the barren moorland. The colony is organised in such a way that there is always a 'guard duty', two or three birds at strategic points keeping watch for any intrusion and immediately giving alarm signals at the first sight of danger. Though not as large and fierce as the Great Skua, the

Arctic Skua will almost certainly 'have a go' at the intruder.

Another tactic of the Arctic Skua when the young are threatened is for one of the birds to feign injury and, being a master of the 'broken wing' act, it leads the intruder in one direction, while the other parent takes the young to safety in thicker cover.

Arctic Skuas winter on the open seas of the southern oceans, and during migration the light-phased birds can be confused with two other 'tailed' Skua of similar size. The first is the **Long-tailed Skua** *Stercorarius Longicaudus*, which is slightly smaller in body length but with longer

---

ARCTIC SKUA

Comparative size Smaller than Herring Gull.
Status Summer resident, winter oceanic.
Habitat Depression in grass or heather.
Nest Depression in grass or heather.
Eggs Olive brown, spotted brown and greys, clutch 2.
Food Omnivorous, but mainly fish.

central tail feathers, making it 55cm overall As the nearest breeding grounds to Scotland are in southern Norway, the Long-tailed Skua is a scarce bird of passage, best seen off our western coasts in autumn.

The Pomarine Skua (Stercorarius Pomarinus) or 'Twist tail' is also an Arctic breeding species, with two long, spoon-shaped central tail feathers, twisted at an angle to give the bird a length of 5lcm.

They are best seen off our coasts in autumn when strong winds force them inshore, and on one such occasion a juvenile was found with a broken wing in a waterlogged field near overhead pylon cables, 25 miles inland (For a full account of this bird, see the journal of the Scottish Ornithologists Club, *Scottish Birds*, Vol 2, page 42).

Greater Black-backed Gull
Larus marinus

Glaucous Gull
Larus hyperboreus

Equally as bad as the Carrion Crow, whose plundering of eggs and young birds can devastate whole areas frequented by inland ground nesting species, the **Greater Black-backed Gull** is a menace among the coastal nesting birds, for not only do Greater Blackbacks take the contents of nests, but also kill and devour thousands of Puffin and Manx Shearwater each nesting season.

A noble-looking bird, the Greater Black-back will scrounge alongside his smaller cousin the Herring Gull in fishing ports when the catches are being landed, waiting for the fish to be cleaned and filleted. Although it is not quite so brazen as the Herring Gull among people, at any source of food away from human presence the dominancy of the larger bird prevails.

The Greater Black-backed Gull is unmistakable, for it is a massive 65-80cm in length with a wingspan of slightly over l.5m. It has a large head, a formidable beak, black upperparts and pink legs.

Although they can be found nesting in loose colonies, even among the smaller Lesser Black-backed Gull and Herring Gull, the Greater Blackback shows a preference for solitary nesting, choosing some rock stack or ridge where its large construction of sticks, seaweed and mosses can be built. The eggs are laid in April or May, both parents taking a share in incubation, and when one bird is on the nest the mate spends much of its time on guard, perched on a vantage point close by. When the chicks hatch they are fed by regurgitation, pecking at the red mark near the tip of the parent's yellow beak, inducing it to 'cough-up' the main course.

Greater Black-backs appear inland singly or in pairs, where they select a point on a river that appeals to them as a fishing territory, and if the fishing is good they will linger for a few weeks.

Birdwatching, like any other pastime, has its humorous moments, and when spectacle is added to the humour then that is entertainment indeed. Leaning on the metal railings on the White Sands beside the River Nith in Dumfries idly watching salmon leaping at the Caul Dam, I spotted a small island of gravel which was occupied by a few Black-headed Gulls and a solitary Greater Black-backed Gull. The Greater Blackback pounced into the shallow water near the island, emerging with an eel about 40cm in length which it laid on the stones before grasping it by the head and swallowing it in two or three hefty gulps. Eventually the entire eel was inside the Greater Blackback's crop, causing it to bulge and heave in wobbly rhythm, and as I watched the eel's head appeared, dangling from the large bird's beak, and wriggling vigorously till more and more of it could be seen. Finally, the eel was completely free and snaked off towards the water's edge, but it was seized once again by a rather surprised-looking Greater Black-back, and beaten savagely on the stones before being devoured for a second and final time. There were hundreds of people milling about the White Sands on that particular morning, but I wonder if any one of them witnessed this curious and amusing event?

GREATER BLACK-BACKED GULL

Comparative size Larger than Herring Gull.
Status Resident.
Habitat Coasts, islands, rivers.
Nest A bulky construction of grass, roots etc.
Eggs Buffish-brown, blotched and spotted darker, clutch usually 3.
Food Seabirds and their young, fish offal.

The **Glaucous Gull** is the size of the Greater Black-backed Gull, an Arctic species regularly seen at some fishing harbours, with a few spending the summer in northern Scotland. The Glaucous Gull is altogether a lighter coloured bird, being pearl-grey on the back instead of black.

Lesser Black-backed Gull

Larus fuscus

The **Lesser Black-backed Gull** is a smaller and slimmer version of the Greater Blackback, and 50 years ago it was classed as a summer resident in the British Isles.

Since the mid-1950s Lesser Black-backs, have increasingly been wintering in the southern part of the country, but these birds are from northern territories, with much of the Scottish population still moving further south as far as the Iberian Peninsula.

As well as being smaller than the Greater Black-back at 55cm, the Lesser Black-back is

The Lesser Black Backed Gull makes an attractive subject as it stands in shallow water rushing over a caul dam.

lighter coloured, slatey-grey on the upperparts, with bright yellow legs.

Lesser Black-backed Gulls are catholic in their choice of nest sites, nesting on buildings as well as more conventional rocky or grassy sites, and the nest itself is built of stalks, seaweed, mosses and any other local vegetation. The nest and its contents are guarded fiercely against intruding predators, and one pair giving the alarm is soon joined by others from the colony, driving off the invader.

LESSER BLACK-BACKED GULL

Comparative size Similar to Herring Gull.
Status Summer resident, some winter on south coast.
Habitat Coasts, islands, lochs, rivers.
Nest On ground, local vegetation.
Eggs Olive-grey, with brown and grey spots. clutch 3.
Food Largely fish - omnivorous.

Both male and female take part in the incubation period, which lasts about four weeks. The chicks are clad in grey down spotted with dark brown, exactly like those of the Herring Gull. They are fed in the nest for a few days, and then wander off among the rocks and herbage to find cover. When a parent arrives with food the young appear, seemingly from nowhere, making straight for the red 'target' spot on the lower mandible of the parent's beak and prodding at it vigorously before being fed on regurgitated fish.

Some gull colonies are enormous, consisting of a population of some thousands of pairs made up of equal proportions of Lesser Black-backs and Herring Gulls. Such enormous numbers of Lesser Black-backs give cause for concern, as they roost on reservoirs following a day's scavenging on city rubbish dumps.

Herring Gull

Larus argentatus

The **Herring Gull** is 60cm in length, some 20cm longer than the Common Gull, but being similarly coloured the two birds are often confused with one another.

The plumage of the Herring Gull is snowy-white with silver-grey upperparts and wings, the latter having black tips with white 'mirrors'. The legs and feet are a pinkish-flesh colour and the heavy, hooked beak is yellow, bearing a red spot near the tip of the lower mandible in the breeding season.

The Herring Gull is most successful in exploiting man's waste products – from following fishing boats, where they demonstrate the art of using the air currents to allow them to glide on motionless wings, sharp-eyed, ready to drop on the tiniest morsels thrown overboard, to raiding massive city rubbish dumps where thousands of Gulls forage for anything edible, and often swallow objects that are not. At fishmarkets some birds gorge themselves to such an extent that they are unable to fly, while others are so familiar with the routine that they walk among the feet of the fishwives, picking up fish heads and other titbits.

Herring Gulls have also developed the knack of dropping crustaceans and molluscs from a height of about seven metres onto the stones below in order to crack the shells open, allowing them to get at the soft centres.

The Herring Gull's nest is a substantial untidy structure, built with any available material such as grass, heather, seaweed and moss, and though both parents share in the nest building, the hen undertakes most of the incubation. The chicks take about four weeks to hatch, after which both parents tend them for a following six weeks. Soon afterwards they are on the wing. At this time they are mottled in browns and greys and almost impossible to tell apart from immature Lesser Black-backed Gull.

Common Gull

Larus canus

The **Common Gull** is similar in colouring to the Herring Gull, having silver-grey upperparts and white underparts, but the legs of the Common Gull are yellowish-green, not pinkish as in the Herring Gull. The Common Gull also has a less formidable beak, giving it a much softer look – in fact, singled out as an individual it is a truly attractive bird.

Accompanying Black headed Gulls as they 'follow the plough', Common Gulls can be seen devouring all manner of snails, slugs and grubs, thus benefitting the farmer.

On the coast, unlike the Herring Gull the Common Gull has not completely mastered the

---

HERRING GULLS

Comparative size Larger than Black-headed Gull.
Status Resident.
Habitat Summer - coasts, islands, winter - coastal, urban, agricultural areas.
Nest Built of local vegetation.
Eggs Olive with dark-brown markings, clutch 2-4.
Food Omnivorous.

COMMON GULL

Comparative size Smaller than Herring Gull.
Status Resident.
Habitat Coastal and inland waters.
Nest Heather, seaweed, grasses.
Eggs Greenish-blue, with dark-brown blotches and spots, clutch 2-3.
Food Varied, mainly animal matter.

---

art of opening shellfish by dropping them onto stones from seven metres up – the shellfish more often falls on sand, and the Gull has to retrieve it many times before either it is successful or gives up.

The Common Gull is plentiful as a breeding species in Scotland, with their numbers greatly increased by the influx of wintering birds from Scandinavia and eastern Europe, when large roosts can be found on coastal estuaries and inland lochs and reservoirs.

In the breeding season, colonies of various sizes are established on moorland or coastal sites, the nests being lined with appropriate local material – heather and grasses in moorland sites, with seaweed the main material in coastal nests. Although the majority of nests are built on the ground, occasionally a more unusual site is chosen. I can recall two of these, the first in an old Carrion Crow nest, and the second built on top of a straining post, with a cup-like depression fashioned by the wood rotting in the centre.

The eggs are usually laid in May, with both parents sharing the 21 day incubation period, the chicks are tended for a further twenty-one days, after which they soon find their wings and become independent.

A Common Gull sitting tight on her eggs in a nest by a small hillock.

Black-headed Gull

Larus ridibundus

The **Black-headed Gull** is our most familiar inland breeding gull, and on closer inspection it is not difficult to see that instead of being black, the head is actually coloured chocolate-brown. In mid-winter, though, when the bird is seen in city parks or standing in groups in playing fields, one has to be slightly more observant, for at this time of year the head is completely white except for a dark smudge behind each eye, and from a distance Black-headed Gulls bear a similarity to Common Gulls.

Both in summer and winter, the main plumage of the Black-headed Gull is white with a pearl-grey mantle. The bill and legs are reddish, and in the breeding season the brown head has a white circle round the eye.

Breeding colonies can contain anything from a few pairs to many hundreds, with the birds quick to exploit any new manmade water sources. Ponds created in recently planted forestry as an attraction for wildlife, doubling as a source of water for firefighting, are readily occupied as long as there is suitable reedy vegetation round the edges in which the Gull can build their nests.

Three eggs generally constitute a full clutch, being laid in April and incubated by both parents

for about 21 days. Then the downy chicks, which can take to the water soon after hatching, are tended by their parents for about seven weeks, during which time they are fed on whatever happens to be available near the colony – insect larvae, worms, 'leather-jackets' and many other farmland pests feature in the diet.

As this Black Headed Gull stands at its nest it can be seen that the heads of these gulls are not black but chocolate-brown.

BLACK-HEADED GULL

Comparative size Smaller than Herring Gull.
Status Resident.
Habitat Estuaries, marshes, moorland.
Nest Depression on ground, lined reed and grasses.
Eggs Variable, usually olive/brown, dark markings, clutch usually 3.
Food Fish, crustaceans, worms, scavenges at rubbish tips.

Some years ago, the founding of a colony of about 170 pairs of Black-headed Gulls, near my home town of Moffat found chimney perches, which are normally occupied by Jackdaws, being disputed by the Black-headed Gulls as they hung about, ready to pounce on kitchen scraps or any other morsel picked up from the streets to supplement their chicks' diet.

Black-headed Gulls tend to feed in large groups with 'following the plough' being the method with which they are usually associated. At times the Gulls follow the blades too closely when the furrows are being cut, resulting in some of the delving birds being entombed by the cut turf falling back into the furrow.

At other times, especially after rain, large

numbers can at times be seen in fields not grouped together, but each bird in its own 'stamping-ground' of about one metre square, looking extremely regimental. Row upon row of white sentinals turn first one way, then another while 'marking time', the rhythm bringing earthworms to the surface, from where they are picked and eaten.

The most fascinating method of feeding I have witnessed, however, happened on a stretch of the River Annan. At first it appeared that the Gulls were playing, for they landed in the water at the head of a 'glide' about a hundred metres in length, allowing themselves to be carried downstream in single file to a point where the water tumbled into a lower stretch. From here they would take flight landing again at the start of the 'glide'. Watching for some time with my binoculars, I noticed that during their journey downstream the Gulls were continually picking at the surface of the water. Curiosity took me to the reeds lining the bank, where I noticed that thousands of small, winged insects were being carried in the breeze onto the surface of the water providing a novel way for the Black-headed Gull to enjoy their meal.

Kittiwake

Rissa tridactyla

Like most of our seabirds, the **Kittiwake** is oceanic in winter, returning to its sea-cliff nesting sites around our shores as early as mid-January, but it is usually April before the colonies are at full strength.

The Kittiwake is our smallest breeding gull, 41cm in length, and in form and build like a smaller version of the Common Gull with a slightly darker grey mantle. The head, breast and underparts are snowy-white, and the black wing

KITTIWAKE
Comparative size Smaller than Herring Gull.
Status Resident, winters at sea.
Habitat Oceanic, coastal in summer.
Nest Built on ledge, grass and mud on seaweed base.
Eggs Pale buff, spotted with brown and black, clutch 1-3.
Food Mainly fish, crustaceans.

tips are void of any white markings. The bill is yellowish-green and the legs are black.

Kittiwakes build on the narrowest ledges of inaccessible sea cliffs, with the base of the nest constructed from gooey green algae which sets very hard, the nest is then completed with seaweed, mud and grass. The finished product is quite bulky, often overhanging the ledge, but as it is solidly constructed the young, which hatch in June, are safer there than the chicks of any other member of the gull clan as no land predators such as the fox can approach the nest.

As it is a sheer drop from the nest to the sea below, the young birds linger at the nest for longer than may be necessary, adopting a 'better safe than sorry' attitude. They are able to fly at about 36 days old, but prefer to 'stay put' for fully a further seven days. Along the east coast Kittiwakes have taken to nesting on the windowsills of high harbourside buildings, with some colonies having now been in existence for a number of years.

The flight of the Kittiwake is graceful and buoyant, with the wing beats noticeably faster than those of its larger cousins. The mournful but pleasant 'kittiwaking' call is more characteristic than any of the other gull calls, constantly sounding through the colonies in the breeding season, though seldom heard at other times. Kittiwakes feed chiefly on fish obtained from just under the surface of the sea, diving somewhat more heavily and shallower than the Terns and, unlike other Gulls they never scavenge at rubbish dumps or fish markets.

After the young have left the nest, the parents occasionally linger at the colony for a few days before eventually heading seawards, possibly wintering off the west coast of Greenland where there are rich pickings among the plentiful fish stocks.

Common Tern

Sterna mirundo

The Common and Arctic Terns are so very alike that even experienced birdwatchers have to look very closely to tell them apart, in fact in winter plumage they resemble each other so much that observers note them as 'Commic' Terns.

In summer the **Common Tern** is an attractive bird in its pearl-grey mantle, with dark wing tips and white underparts. The head and nape are black, the tail is white and forked, and the bright red bill has a black tip.

The Tern's flight is graceful and buoyant, a pleasure to watch on a summer visit to the coast, but on land it has an awkward walk which contrasts strongly with its mastery of the air.

Common Tern usually return year after year to the same location, and a colony during the breeding season is a fascinating place, with the adult birds visiting their mates or young in a constant stream, bringing food in the shape of sandeels. Intruders to the colony usually find there are a few individuals who are extremely aggressive in defence of their eggs or young, dive-bombing and, on occasion, drawing blood as the unsuspecting individual fails to take evasive action quickly enough.

The nest is a mere scrape in the sand or turf, and while the birds are incubating eggs or brooding young one of the most curious aspects of Tern behaviour occurs. From time to time, and for no apparent reason, the clamouring colony falls silent and all the adult birds peel off in low flight, heading out to sea and leaving the area ominously quiet. This 'dread' period, as it is known, has baffled experts for years, one suggestion being that it forecasts the visit of an avian predator, but as most 'dread' occurrences are unaccompanied by raiding predators it would appear that the cause is more deep rooted.

Terns feed mainly on sandeels and crustaceans from the surface layers of the water. This food source can at times be affected by a bloom of *Dinoflagellates*, tiny marine organisms which are always present but occasionally, in freak conditions, multiply to such an extent that the mass gives the sea a reddish tinge. The toxins contained in these organisms build up in marine species such as the sandeels and this build-up is then passed on to the birds which feed on them, sometimes causing fatal illnesses.

Arctic Tern
Sterna paradisaea

The **Arctic Tern's** habits and behaviour follow closely those of the Common Tern as does its appearance. The face, breast and underparts are white with the wings pearl-grey, the latter having dark tips. The head and nape are black and the legs and pointed bill are deep red, this being the best identification feature, for the red bill lacks the black tip of the Common Tern.

The Arctic Tern is the most seagoing of the terns, spending more of its life in daylight than any other living creature. Breeding in the summers of high northern latitudes, it then flies south to spend another summer just north of the Antarctic pack ice.

Arctic Terns have the typical graceful flight of the Tern family, and it is a pleasure to watch them in the air, or while feeding, as they fly low over the surface of the sea, ever on the alert for a shoal of sandeels, their favourite fare.

The breeding season is in May and June, the nest a mere scrape in the sand, in sparse vegetation, or on bare rock, and for 21 days both parents take a share in the incubation. The chicks remain in the nest for about three days after hatching and then toddle off among the pebbles and scant vegetation, flying about three weeks later, but they are still fairly dependent on their parents.

Arctic Tern colonies are prone to the same 'dread' periods that affect the Common Tern colonies, when the clamouring activity is suddenly silenced as the adult birds leave *en masse*, flying out to sea and returning some time later to continue their domestic duties.

The toxins that affect the sandeels, when there is a dramatic increase in the tiny *Dinoflagellates* organisms, can in turn affect the terns, but a much greater threat to the Arctic Tern is over-fishing of the sandeel. From the mid-1980s

COMMON TERN
Comparative size Smaller than Black Headed Gull. **Status** Summer resident. **Habitat** Shingle bars, small coastal islands. **Nest** Scrape in shingle or sand. **Eggs** Buff or brown, dark markings, clutch usually 3. **Food** Small fish, crustaceans, molluscs.

ARCTIC TERN
Comparative size Similar to Common Tern. **Status** Summer resident. **Habitat** Shingle bars, small coastal islands. **Nest** Scrape on shingle, turf, sand. **Eggs** Grey or brown, dark markings, clutch 2-3. **Food** Small fish, crustaceans, molluscs, sandeels.

The blood red bleak of the Arctic Tern helps to distinguish it from the Common Tern.

sandeel harvesting around the Shetland Isles coasts has been so efficient that stocks are now dangerously low. This low level has resulted in Arctic Tern, as well as Puffin and Kittiwake, colonies almost disappearing. Areas like Ronas Voe, which previously held many hundreds of breeding pairs could be totally void of Terns in a few years.

Roseate Tern

Sterna dougallii

In the early 1800s the **Roseate Tern** was discovered nesting on some islands in the Firth of Clyde. Accepted as a separate species, it soon became a trophy for egg and skin collectors and by the end of the century, even though further colonies had been discovered, it was almost extinct in the British Isles.

It took protective legislation to save the few surviving birds, which steadily increased their numbers over the following years, and a census in 1970 showed a healthy population of some 2,500 pairs. Unfortunately, a similar count in 1988 showed that a dramatic decline had taken place, with only 470 pairs being recorded. No one knows for certain why there has been such a crash in numbers, but many hundreds of young chicks are known to have died of starvation in their nests.

The streamers of the forked tail of the Roseate Tern are slightly longer than those of the Common and Arctic Terns, making it 3cm longer and fully 38cm in length. The Roseate Tern also has a much whiter appearance, longer red legs, a black bill with a red base, and in summer a rosy tinge to its breast, hence its name.

In habits and spring display the Roseate Tern differs little from the other Terns, but in flight the longer tail streamers give the bird a more 'swallow-like' appearance – a true 'sea swallow'.

ROSEATE TERN

Comparative size Larger than Common Tern.
Status Summer resident.
Habitat Coastal estuaries, small islands.
Nest Slightly hollow on rock or sand.
Eggs Creamy buff, dark markings, clutch 1-2.
Food Small fish, sand-eels.

During National Service in the mid-1950s, I couldn't have wished for a better posting, spending two summers among the breeding Terns of the Moray Firth, at times watching five different species in the air at the same time.

Sandwich Tern

Sterna sandvicensis

The breeding habitats of the **Sandwich Tern** are more restricted than those of our other Terns and in Scotland it is the Ayrshire, Fife and the Moray Firth regions where our main colonies are located.

The Sandwich is our largest and most distinguished-looking Tern, easily identified by its larger 41cm length. The mantle is pearl-grey, the underparts white, the dark grey wings are long and narrow and the tail is less deeply forked than those of other Terns. The legs are black, as is the bill, the latter having a yellow tip, and in summer the forehead, crown and nape are black with a shaggy crest, while in winter the forehead is white and the crown and nape are speckled with grey.

Although the flight of the Sandwich Tern retains much of the attraction of the Tern family, it is heavier and more gull-like, and when plunging into the sea in pursuit of prey the dive is undertaken from a greater height, taking the bird wholly under the surface.

Sandwich Tern return to their breeding haunts earlier than other Terns, some arriving in March, and by the second week in April colonies are usually established. Sandy and shingle seashores, as well as low-lying rocky islands provide the nesting sites for these Terns, which are by nature less aggressive than the Common or Arctic Terns, so at times the Sandwich Terns will colonise among nesting Black-headed Gulls, benefitting from the pugnacity of the Gulls against predators.

Nevertheless, stoats, rats, hedgehogs and foxes can create havoc in the close-knit colony.

The eggs are laid in a slight hollow on the ground, with the shared incubation taking about 25 days. A few days after hatching the chicks take cover amongst nearby vegetation, being able to pick out their parents arriving with food among the noisy clamouring of the colony.

When the food supply is scarce close to the breeding colony, Sandwich Terns will fly over 25 miles to where the fishing is more productive, with sprats, sandeels and small herrings providing the source of nourishment.

Little Tern

Sterna albifrons

Of our five breeding species of Terns, the **Little Tern,** at 24cm, is the smallest and one of the most vulnerable, as it chooses to nest on sandy beaches frequented by people indulging in various pastimes, or on shingly beaches only a metre or so above the high-tide line, where many nests are destroyed in stormy weather.

The upperparts of the Little Tern, like those of our other Terns are pearl-grey, the underparts are white, and the black head has a heart-shaped, white mark on the forehead. It is our only Tern with a yellow bill, which has a black tip, and the legs and feet are orange-yellow.

Little Terns are less gregarious than other Terns, and their colonies are smaller with the nests more widely scattered, mere scrapes in the sand or shingle. The eggs are incubated for about 21 days by both parents, and as soon as the chicks hatch they leave the nest to hide among the pebbles or grassy tussocks, where they are fed by the parents on small sandeels, and annelid worms. The fledging period lasts for about four weeks, and by the end of July the birds start congregating for their southward journey.

SANDWICH TERN
Comparative size Larger than Black-Headed Gull.
Status Summer resident.
Habitat Sandy estuaries, coastal islands.
Nest Scrape among scant vegetation.
Eggs Pale buff, blotched with brown, clutch 1-2.
Food Sprats, small herrings, sand-eels.

LITTLE TERN
Comparative size Smaller than Common Tern.
Status Summer resident.
Habitat Mainly sandy coastal estuaries.
Nest Scrape in sand or shingle.
Eggs Pale buff to brown, darker blotches, clutch 2-3.
Food Small fish, sand-eels, annelid worms.

The Little Tern is extremely vulnerable in its breeding territory with the increase of coastal leisure pursuits.

Razorbill

Alca torda

The **Razorbill** is a typical member of the Auk family, and a descendant of the extinct Great Auk. It has a heavier and more thick-set body than the other Auk and a larger head, emphasised by the curious beak. In summer the head, neck and upperparts are glossy black, with a narrow white line running from the top of the heavy bill to the eye. The underparts are white, and the white-tipped secondaries form a white wing bar.

An oceanic species, the Razorbill can be found back at their sea-cliff nest sites in February, but it is well into April or even May before the clamouring colony reaches its peak, the single eggs being laid on the bare rock, either under an overhang or deep in a crevice.

The incubation period of about 35 days is shared by both parents, the male spending his off-duty time at sea, while the female chooses to spend her off-duty period close to her sitting mate – perhaps she doesn't trust his domesticity.

About two or three weeks after hatching the solitary chick is plump and buoyant, and one evening at dusk the parents encourage their offspring to leave the relative safety of its crevice for the uncertainty of the open sea.

In the gloaming, safe from aerial predators, the chick bounces its way downwards and, following what can be a very arduous journey, eventually plops into the water and swims to some calm spot, soon to be joined by its parents who constantly present it with a variety of fish until it can fend for itself.

By August the cliffs are deserted once more as the birds make their way to their Atlantic and Mediterranean wintering grounds, hopefully avoiding contact with the modern-day menace of the oil spill, as Razorbills are one of the species to suffer most from this type of disaster.

RAZORBILL

Comparative Size Slightly smaller than Guillemot.
Status Resident, winters at sea.
Habitat Sea cliffs.
Nest Egg laid under rock, or in crevice.
Eggs Whitish, brown and black streaks, clutch I.
Food Fish.

Puffins in breeding plumage are attractive birds with their curious, multi-coloured bills.

Little Auk

Alle alle

The **Little Auk** is the smallest member of the Auk family, a dumpy little bird only 21cm in length with a short stubby bill and short grey legs.

It is a truly oceanic species of the high Arctic Zone, which at times is driven to our shores in stormy conditions, mainly on the east coast, but also turning up further inland.

On occasion Little Auks occur in the extreme south of Scotland in mid-winter, and at this time the contrasting black upperparts and white underparts are less defined, with the black throat tinged with white, and white smudges on the black cheeks. Few of these individuals return successfully to their Arctic habitat as they are generally in an exhausted condition.

Puffin

Fratercula arctica

One of our most attractive and amusing seabirds is the **Puffin,** instantly recognised by its pied plumage and massive, multi-coloured bill.

The upperparts are glossy black, the underparts white, and the short legs and feet bright red. In summer the bill is adorned with a horny sheath, blue-grey at the base, then striped yellow and red to the tip, and each corner of the mouth is decorated with a yellow wart-like rosette. In winter the horny sheath is lost and the bill becomes smaller and duller.

The Puffin at 30cm in length is smaller than other members of the Auk family such as the Guillemot and Razorbill. It has the same 'whirring' flight and rises from the surface of the water with difficulty, but it is an excellent swimmer and diver.

PUFFIN

Comparative size Smaller than Guillemot.
Status Resident, winters at sea.
Habitat Coastal cliff tops, islands.
Nest Usually burrow, rabbit hole.
Eggs White, occasionally pale-grey markings, clutch I.
Food Small fish, sand-eels.

Most of our suitable sea cliffs and islands provide breeding territories for the Puffins, which, after wintering at sea, form rafts just offshore, landing for a short time and then returning to the sea, repeating this procedure a few times before eventually settling to nest.

Although the birds return during March it is into April before the nesting activity begins, the pairs either jointly excavating a nesting burrow or taking over an existing rabbit hole, which is meagrely lined with a few beakfuls of grass, on which the single egg is laid.

Following a fairly lengthy incubation period of about six weeks, during which time the off-duty birds mostly bob about on the sea. The solitary chick grows rapidly on the huge beakfuls of sandeels brought in by the parents, and at this time one realises that the unusual bill, as well as looking somewhat comical, is also a highly efficient fishing and carrying implement, brought into use as the birds catch fish underwater, using their wings for propulsion and feet as rudders. Up to, and often more than, six sandeels are caught and held criss-cross in the uniquely adapted bill, and it is while carrying their catch back to the nesting burrows that they are often harassed by piratical Skua.

About six weeks after hatching the chicks are so fat that they completely outweigh their parents. The reserve of fat is necessary for the chick's survival, as they are ruthlessly abandoned by the parents in their musty cavelets. Six or seven days later the fat reserve, as well as keeping the youngster alive, has also assisted in the growth of the feathers so, with considerable loss of bodyweight and tormented by pangs of hunger, the young forsake the burrows.

In late July and August the young Puffins venture forth, heading towards the sea, but *en route* they are extremely vulnerable, some being predated by Greater Black-backed Gulls as they stumble over rocks penguin-fashion – and reaching the sea is no guarantee against predation as Great Skuas continue the slaughter, having the nasty habit of killing more than fulfils their needs.

Following dispersal from the breeding colonies, the adult birds assume duller winter dress, similar in fact to the plumage of the young birds. Then adults and young together begin their journey towards North Atlantic and Mediteranean winter quarters.

Common Guillemot

Uria aalge

Most seabirds nest in colonies, some crowded, some noisy, but the pinnacle of seabird colonies is that of the **Common Guillemot,** overcrowded and clamorous.

The Common Guillemot is typical of the Auk family, an oceanic species of pied plumage and short wings, in fact, in proportion to its size, those of the Common Guillemot are smaller than those of all our other seabirds.

The upperparts are dark greyish-brown with a white wing bar, the underparts pure white, and the black bill is long and pointed. Some birds have a distinct white ring around each eye with, a white line extending back from it – these are known as Bridled Guillemots and, while not a separate species, this type increases percentage-wise the further north one travels.

Outside the breeding season, Common Guillemots spend their lives at sea, but in late autumn they visit the nesting sea cliffs of the Scottish mainland and islands, to 'stake their claim' to the few centimetre square patch that will serve as a nursery for their solitary chick some months later.

During the autumnal visit much squabbling and jostling takes place, each pair getting acquainted with the prospective neighbours, so that when they return in April to lay their eggs, – which are laid on the bare rock surface – there will be less chance of their being knocked over the edge as the birds will be on friendly terms with one another.

For an egg that is laid on bare rock in a crowded situation, little is left to chance. It is pear-shaped in the extreme, pointed at one end and broad at the other, so that if it is moved it rolls in a tight circle. It is also very large for the size of the bird, producing a big, well-developed chick covered in thick down and, with open eyes, able to dodge the bustling birds, thus lessening the chance of it being pushed over the edge.

Guillemots are expert swimmers and divers, diving to depths of about twelve metres to catch fish for their young. The chick shows little sign of

Laying and hatching a single egg in such crowded conditions it is a marvel that so many eggs and young Guillemots survive.

rapid growth: instead the intake of food is directed towards developing a fully waterproof plumage, necessary for the next stage in their young lives.

When the chicks are only two or three weeks old, only one-third the size of their parents' 42cm and still flightless, they are encouraged by their parents to plunge from their rocky ledges into the foaming sea far below. As there are thousands of Guillemots on the sea at the bottom of the cliffs, barking encouragement to the youngsters, one would expect many of the young birds to be lost in the mass – but this is not so, for as soon as the young bird plunges downwards one of its parents joins it immediately, forming a family bond by their calling to one another. The pair then swim seawards, not returning to land for some months, by which time the youngster is identical to its parents.

COMMON GUILLEMONT

Comparative size Larger than Pigeon.
Status Resident, winters at sea.
Habitat Oceanic, breeds on sea cliffs.
Nest Egg laid on bare rock.
Eggs Variable, white to deep blue-green-brown-spotted and streaked with black clutch l.
Food Fish.

Black Guillemot
Cepphus grylle

The least known of our breeding Auk is the **Black Guillemot,** and unlike the other members of the Auk family it is not a sociable bird, being usually seen alone or in small parties of threes or fours.

As its name implies, the Black Guillemot is

BLACK GUILLLEMOT

Comparative size Smaller than Common Guillemot.
Status Resident, winters at sea.
Habitat Oceanic, breeding among rocks, cliffs.
Nest Eggs laid in crevice.
Eggs Pale buff to greenish, blotched/spotted purple-grey, brown, clutch 2.
Food Fish, molluscs, crustaceans.

---

predominantly black with conspicuous large, white wing patches and red legs and feet. In winter the plumage is very different, when the head, neck and underparts are white with black markings, and the back is barred with black and white.

Although several nests can be located quite close together, the Black Guillemot is not as colony-minded as are the other Auk.

They begin to arrive on the rocky coasts and islands around the end of February, but it is into May before they finally occupy their nest sites, laying their eggs in a crevice in the rocks or under a boulder, close to the level of the sea.

Both parents share the incubation period of about 28 days, and when the young take to the sea about 38 days later their plumage is fully developed, resembling the winter plumage of their parents.

Wood Pigeon
Columba palumbus

Collared Dove
Streptopelia decaocto

One of the most familiar sounds of the countryside throughout the spring and summer months is the cooing of the **Wood Pigeon,** but these soothing sounds, plus the gentle appearance of the bird itself are deceptive, for the Wood Pigeon is a pest on arable farms, especially among cereal crops and peas.

The largest of our native Doves, the Wood Pigeon or 'Ring Dove' is 41cm in length, and is distinguished from our other species by a broad white band across the wing, which is conspicuous in flight, and small white patches on the sides of the neck. The rest of the plumage consists of pale blue, brown and grey, with the breasts of mature birds showing iridescent green and purple highlights.

The Wood Pigeon is widely distributed throughout Scotland, though it is somewhat scarce in the far north, and in autumn large numbers arrive from Western Europe to spend the winter here.

Nesting sites vary considerably, from nests built on the ground with the eggs laid on a handful of twigs, to others placed at various levels in bushes and trees, some being bulky affairs, while others

The white patches on the neck and wings of the Wood Pigeon are good identification features.

are so scant that the two eggs can be seen from underneath. With laying beginning in April three broods are not an unusual occurence, each clutch being incubated by both parents for about 17 days. The young are fed on a peculiar substance called 'pigeon's milk', which is formed in the crop of the adult birds and regurgitated for the young.

As the first two youngsters can be in the process of being fed in April, many a garden is paid an unwanted visit by Wood Pigeon, which can create havoc among the young shoots of produce, but since the mid 1950s gardens have encountered a new and even more daring pest,

the Wood Pigeon's close relative, the **Collared Dove.**

The spread of the Collared Dove from its origins in Asia is nothing short of remarkable. During the late 1950s, birdwatchers were thrilled to add this appealing little Dove to their 'list' – a few short years later it was listed as a pest.

A successful opportunist, the Collared Dove also raises at least three broods in a season, frequenting urban as well as rural habitats, where it can be found nesting in anything from laurel bushes and yews in gardens to hybrid limes on main streets in towns.

The Collared Dove is somewhat smaller than the Wood Pigeon, being 32cm in length, and its upperparts are greyish-brown with dark primaries on the wings. The underparts are pale pinkish-grey, with conspicuous black and white markings

---

COLLARED DOVE

Comparative size Smaller than Wood Pigeon.
Status Resident.
Habitat Mainly suburban or urban.
Nest Flimsy twiggy platform in dark tree.
Eggs White, clutch 2.
Food Grain, seeds, young shoots of garden produce.

WOOD PIGEON

Comparative size Larger than Feral Pigeon.
Status Resident.
Habitat Woodlands, farmlands.
Nest Platform of twigs, in tree or thick bush.
Eggs White, clutch 2.
Food Grain, cereals, vegetable shoots, acorns.

on the tail, and around the sides of the neck is a black half-collar, hence its name.

The Collared Dove was so successfully in its spread throughout Scotland that by the early 1960s it had colonised the Outer Hebrides, and by 1970 it had also appeared on St Kilda, fully 50 miles further west.

Stock Dove
Columba oenas

Rock Dove
Columba livia

Like the Wood Pigeon, the **Stock Dove** is widespread throughout Scotland except for the far north.

Again we have one of the smaller Dove at 33cm in length, and the absence of any white on the grey-blue plumage is one of its best identification features, as the Wood Pigeon has white patches on its wings and neck, the Rock Dove a white rump. The throat and breast of the Stock Dove are tinged with purple, with patches of iridescent green on the sides of the neck. The underparts are pale grey, the wings have two broken black bars and black tips, and the tail is also tipped with black.

Stock Dove are usually hole-nesters, with any tree-hole offering security being accepted, as are holes in old buildings and bridges. The two white eggs, typical of the Dove family, are laid as early as March, with as many as three broods reared in a season. Each clutch is incubated for about 18 days by both parents, the chicks being fed for the following 28 days on 'pigeons milk', a substance formed in the crops of the adult birds and on which the young are fed until they leave the nest.

Stock Doves frequent woodlands and open country, where it may be noted that the flight is faster and more dashing than that of the Wood Pigeon, but very similar to that of the **Rock Dove**.

The general colouring of the Rock Dove is similar to that of its close relative the Stock Dove but three main differences help separate the two – the Rock Dove has a conspicuous white rump, more defined black wing bars, and no black on the wing tip. All our domestic and feral pigeons originate from the Rock Dove.

Inland nest sites are scarce, as true Rock Doves prefer sea-cliff habitats. Fortunately, small colonies exist in some steep wooded glens in southern Scotland, one which I visit regularly rearing enough young to ensure the future of the species in this area. Apart from preferring to nest in clefts in the rocks, the behaviour and habits of the Rock Dove resemble those of the Stock Dove.

STOCK DOVE
Comparative size Smaller than Wood Pigeon.
Status Resident.
Habitat Agricultural land, open woodland.
Nest In tree hole, or other, twigs, leaves.
Eggs White, clutch 2.
Food Seeds, grain.

ROCK DOVE
Comparative size Smaller than Wood Pigeon.
Status Resident.
Habitat Sea or inland cliffs, rock faces.
Nest On ledge, twigs, stems.
Eggs White, clutch 2.
Food Mainly seeds.

Turtle Dove
Streptopelia turtur

At only 32cm in length, the Turtle Dove, is one of the smallest members of the Dove family, which breeds in the British Isles, and though I have half a dozen personal records of the bird appearing in the south of Scotland, as yet I have no proof of breeding success.

A summer resident, the Turtle Dove is the most colourful of the Doves, recognised by its brown and black marbled mantle and black and white patches on the sides of the neck, but the best identification feature is the long, fan-shaped tail with its broad band of white at the tip.

Cuckoo
Cuculus canorus

Identifying the **Cuckoo** by sound is as easy as recognising the Robin by sight, but recognising

The adult Cuckoo is hawk-like in appearance hence it is often mobbed by small birds wherever it settles.

the Cuckoo by sight can, because of its hawk-like appearance, cause a few problems, especially in open woodland where it may be seen gliding through the trees in similar fashion to the Sparrow Hawk.

On more open ground, the Cuckoo has the habit of perching on telegraph poles and the topmost branches of stunted hawthorns, where it is more readily observed and recognised.

The Cuckoo is 33cm long, and at first glance appears completely grey. However, a closer look shows that there are dark grey and white bars on its underparts, from its breast to its undertail coverts, and there is no mistaking the long, graduated, white-spotted tail. The sexes are similar in colouring, or at least they are for most of the time, but in nature there is always an exception to the rule and in this category the Cuckoo is the 'Blue Riband' bird, for it is the exception no less than four times.

The female, on rare occasions, can resemble a female Kestrel, having the same reddish-brown colouring and barring, a much brighter shade than that of the young Cuckoo. For the second

exception we focus on the feet, which differ from those of all other British birds. Of the four slender toes, the middle two, which are the longest, point forwards and the outer two point backwards.

During the month of May the female Cuckoo, who is extremely polygamous, lays her eggs not, as is the rule, in her own nest, but in the nest of a pair of small birds that she chooses to rear her offspring. The host parents are, in most cases, the same species that reared her, with Meadow Pipits, Dunnocks and Sedge Warblers being most often chosen as Scottish foster parents.

The female Cuckoo keeps her victim under observation for some time then when the time is right, she approaches the nest and in a matter of seconds removes one of the eggs with her beak, which she swallows or carries off after laying her own egg among those remaining. Not only is the egg exceptionally well matched in colour to the existing eggs in the nest, but it is also very close to the size, and here the fourth exception is introduced. If the female Cuckoo laid an egg in comparison to those of other birds, it would resemble in size the egg of a Mistle Thrush, which lays an egg one ninth of its own bodyweight. In reality, the Cuckoo's egg which weighs a mere 3gm, is only ONE FORTIETH of its bodyweight, and this is essential in order to deceive the chosen foster parents, as they would almost certainly forsake their nest on finding an egg as large as that of the Mistle Thrush, which weighs about 8gm, in their clutch.

In all, the female Cuckoo lays about twelve eggs in twelve different nests in her territory, leaving the foster parents to cope with what will eventually be a very large chick. The incubation period of the Cuckoo's egg is slightly shorter than that of the foster parents eggs, so that on hatching, the young Cuckoo finds itself in a nest with unhatched eggs or newly-hatched young. The young Cuckoo finds this situation so much of an irritation that it positions itself in such a way as to cradle an egg or chick between its shoulders

CUCKOO

Comparative size Slightly smaller than Kestrel.
Status Summer resident.
Habitat Open moor, to woodlands.
Nest None, parasitic on small songbirds.
Eggs Variable, matching those of host species, laying about 12, I in each nest.
Food Insects and invertebrates.

and, with its back to the wall of the nest, the specially adapted toes are brought into use, grasping and heaving until finally the load is bundled over the edge of the nest. Apparently exhausted, the young Cuckoo stumbles back into the bowl of the nest, where it repeats the process of removing the contents until finally it is the sole occupant, and from that moment on all the food that would normally be brought to a brood of four or five young Pipit, ends up inside a young changeling with an insatiable appetite.

The young Cuckoo develops quickly, soon outgrowing the nest which it flattens with its huge bulk, and after a fledging period about twice that of young Pipits, another hawk-like bird flits off among the woodland trees, or over the moors, always accompanied by one or two small birds, keeping their 'eye' on this strange hawk.

In Scotland, Meadow Pipits are most often chosen as the host species, and long before the Pipits leave the hill moors to winter on the coast the Cuckoos will be back in their winter quarters in Africa or India, leaving us looking forward to hearing once again the familiar 'cuckoo-cuckoo' which tells us that, spring is here.

Barn Owl

Tyto alba

In order to raise a family successfully, a pair of **Barn Owls** not only require a habitat which can provide them with the necessary food, but also a nest site capable of providing shelter for the young for about 12 weeks, as this is the period of time required by them to reach the free-flying stage.

One of the main reasons for the drastic fall in Barn Owl numbers over the past few years is that practically all the derelict roadside cottages in rural areas which previously held Barn Owls have either been rebuilt or demolished completely.

Another site frequently chosen was on top of old hay bales which had lain in a dark corner of the hayloft from a previous haymaking, but modern farming methods have seen the decline of hay stored in this way. Losing the two main nest sites means that tree holes, already under pressure from Jackdaws and Tawny Owls are sometimes used, but these have to be large enough to hold up to six young Owls, as this number is not an unusual brood.

The Barn Owl has always been a favourite of the birdwatcher with its golden-brown plumage flecked with grey contrasting with the snow-white underparts which give rise to one of its other names 'Ghost Owl', and as it does not hoot but utters blood-curdling shrieks when encountered on a dark night, this name is most fitting. The typical owl face of the Barn Owl is covered with white feathers fringed with orange, and the powerful feet have strong talons with which to grasp its prey.

The Barn Owl is a solitary and nocturnal bird, roosting away the daylight hours in some dark nook in a barn, derelict building or hole in a tree. Only in winter, when hard pressed for food, can it be seen hunting during the day when, if you are in a position to witness the owl in its plight, the noiseless, buoyant flight as it quarters the open ground can be observed.

Some years ago it was brought to my attention that a pair of Barn Owls had taken up residence in the loft of an old roadside cottage which at the time was used as a grain store. It was late April, and on checking the site late one evening I found that the nest contained six eggs. It was one of the most perfectly sited that I have ever worked at as the loft was completely empty, so a hide was installed in due course from which both the nest and skylight could be covered, and by the middle of June all six eggs had hatched.

The plumage of the Barn Owl is soft and downy, which is ideal for silent flight as the bird searches for prey, but in damp weather the feathers become sodden and matted, forcing the Barn Owl to take shelter until the next dry spell. On the night of 18 June, I spent a two hour session in the hide, during which time a fine drizzle steadily increased until the pitter-patter on the slates inches above my head announced the beginning of what turned out to be a very wet night.

During the first hour of my vigil three voles were brought to the young, and I noted that the male became more and more bedraggled on each

---

BARN OWL

Comparative size Smaller than Tawny Owl.
Status Resident.
Habitat Open areas and farmland.
Nest In barn or suchlike, tree hole.
Eggs White, clutch 4-10.
Food Small mammals, birds.

The Barn Owl does not hoot, but utters a blood-curdling eerie shriek. This, plus its ghostly white appearance and preference for old churchyards has led to the origin of many a ghost story.

visit. It was fully 45 minutes later before he returned in a really wet state carrying a Tree Pipit, possibly disturbed and caught among the branches of a large beech tree as the Barn Owl took shelter on the opposite side of the road, and oddly this was the only bird that I recorded in over 1 000 items of prey brought to the family in the course of 12 weeks.

Barn Owl eggs are laid at two-day intervals, incubation beginning with the first egg, which results in the oldest chick being about ten days older than the youngest in a family of six. Consequently, the first items of prey brought to the nest in the evening are taken by the older, stronger birds, and if rain forces the parents to give up hunting for the rest of the night, before the tiniest has been fed, then it is likely that this chick will perish. On the evening of 25 June, following a few partly wet nights, a brief visit to check the situation found that the youngest of the brood had perished, but the other five were thriving.

The evening of 29 June was fine, calm and dry, and at 10.35pm a vole was brought in, and taken and devoured by the oldest youngster. Within half an hour he had gobbled another TWO, having the audacity to tackle the fourth item of prey which happened to be a shrew, but as he was adjusting it in order to swallow it head first the second largest owlet grabbed it from him, swallowing it immediately.

I spent many hours in and around the cottage over four months, during which time not only did I achieve an excellent series of photographs, but I was able to imitate the curious 'shushing' sounds of the young and their parents (from my car which was parked by the roadside, covered in camouflaged netting) to such an extent that I could coax the young owls to appear at the skylight, and the parents to glide down from the beech trees and onto the skylight, from where they would peer inside to see what the family was up to.

Finally, on the evening of 6 August, I sat in

the car parked about seventy metres from the cottage and watched four young Barn Owl and their parents hawking, hovering and flying around the old cottage which had been their home, and which had provided me with an insight into the life of a family of Barn Owls for over four months.

The Tawny Owl is the owl of open deciduous woodland, at times nesting in suitable situations in large gardens.

Tawny Owl
Strix aluco

The characteristic hooting of the **Tawny Owl** is a common nocturnal sound in broadleaved woodland, especially from October to December when the male is laying claim to his territory, but it can also be heard to a lesser degree at other times of year, with the females answering call a shrill 'Kewick'.

The Tawny Owl, like the Barn Owl, is widespread throughout Scotland, becoming scarcer in the far north, but unlike the Barn Owl the Tawny is fairing well, finding its requirements for food and nest sites readily available in our mixed woodlands.

The Tawny Owl's plumage is quite variable, with the dominant colouring of most birds being a rich chestnut-brown. To a lesser degree, in others the dominant colouring is grey, with both colour varieties covered in markings of grey, buff and brown. The shape of the body is round and stout, with a head that always appears too large, and the wings are broad and round, barred with dark and light brown.

The Tawny Owl has the typical slow, silent flapping flight of its family and when it appears by day it is always 'mobbed' by a host of small birds, which continue to harass the owl until it settles, usually very close to the trunk of a tree where its mottled plumage serves as camouflage.

Sometimes as early as March the Tawny Owl lays her eggs, the most common site being a hole in a tree, but old crow and hawk nests are also used and occasionally they can be found nesting on the ground under a fallen tree stump.

The downy chicks only stay in the nest for about two weeks, but after this as they wander about they are kept in check by their parents for a much longer time, being fed by them for at least another eight weeks. It is while the young are in the nest, that one must be extremely vigilant when in Tawny Owl territory in the evenings, for the female will at times attack human intruders. The young are fed mainly on small mammals but birds, earthworms and beetles also form part of the diet, the indigestible material being ejected from the beak in the shape of a 'pellet' or 'casting' containing fur, feather, bone and beetle husks.

Tawny Owls can catch mice in almost total darkness by using hearing so extremely sensitive that the slightest rustle in the undergrowth or on the floor of a barn induces the owl to glide to the spot, where large eyes and strong talons are used to seal the victim's fate.

Little Owl
Athene noctua
Snowy Owl
Nyctea scandiaca

At 22cm in length, the **Little Owl** is the smallest Owl occuring in Scotland, where it has within the last few years gained a foothold as a breeding bird, though only in the south.

The account of my first personal record appeared in the journal of the 'Scottish Ornithologist's Club', **Scottish Birds,** Vol 2, page 248, which was the second authentic record for Dumfriesshire. Observed by my wife and I, part of the record, dated 26 April, 1962, reads as follows:

'On our way home we saw an owl sitting on the drystone dyke of a sheep pen and stopped to observe the bird. We were immediately struck by its small size and generally spotted appearance, and stayed in the car to view it. Although the bird was facing us, it frequently turned its head around, and when it did so it appeared to have a light collar.

The general colouring was greyish-brown, the breast spotted and barred with brownish, the face was greyish-white and the belly was also whitish, which proved conspicuous in flight.

After studying it for some time, I opened the car door to observe the flight. It flew with short, rapid wing-beats, very low, with a short glide after each flight, and settled on a large rock after flying only about forty metres.'

Since then I have seen Little Owls on a number of occasions, including a rather promising sighting in July 1969 when a pair were seen, but so far I have no record of breeding in Moffatdale.

TAWNY OWL

Comparative size Smaller than Wood Pigeon.
Status Resident.
Habitat Woodland, parkland.
Nest Tree hole, old crow/hawk nest.
Eggs White, clutch 2-4.
Food Small mammals, birds, beetles, earthworms, fish.

SNOWY OWL

Comparative size Larger than Buzzard.
Status Resident.
Habitat Northern isles.
Nest Depression in hummock.
Eggs White, clutch 4-8.
Food Rabbits, smaller rodents, birds.

At the other end of the scale, as far as size goes, and at the opposite end of the country, in the far north of Scotland is the huge **Snowy Owl,** 60cm in length with a wingspan of some 150cm.

Since the late 1960s a pair of these magnificent Arctic owl have bred with varying success on the island of Fetlar in the Shetlands. When seen this bird is ummistakable, the male being uniformly white, occasionally flecked with a few spots of brown, and the female again predominantly white but with narrow, dark brown barring on her breast and broader, darker, barring on her underparts and wings. The rapid flight of the Snowy Owl is more like that of the Buzzard than that of other owls, and as it hunts by day it can be seen pursuing and striking down its prey on the wing, falcon-fashion, or pouncing on wood mice and rabbits.

Long-eared Owl

Asio otus

One of the favourite nesting haunts of the **Long-eared Owl** the small, dark plantations of mature firs which have been in existence for many years, and which act as 'shelter belts' in hill sheep country. Because of this, the Long-eared is the least known of our owls, as it is also the most strictly nocturnal.

At 36cm tall, the Long-eared Owl is only 2cm shorter than the Tawny Owl, but when seen standing upright on a branch its slimmer build gives it the appearance of being somewhat longer and, unlike the Tawny which has large, black eyes, those of the Long-eared Owl are orange.

The upperparts of the Long-eared Owl are buffish, mottled in brown and grey, streaked with darker brown, and the underparts are also buff, streaked and barred in such a way as to form small cross and arrow-like shapes on the breast. The feature that gives the bird its name, the erectile 'ear-tufts', are not actually ears but tufts of feathers used in display and when the Owl is alarmed or angered. At other times the tufts are laid back along the head, making them almost invisible.

In March or April the Long-eared Owl lays her eggs in old nests, such as those of a crow, hawk or wood pigeon, and as the latter can be quite flimsy sometimes the nest disintegrates

Truly the most nocturnal owl the Longeared Owl prefers the darkest woodland as a breeding habitat.

completely following the activity of the young once they have hatched. This leaves the owlets either perched on a branch or huddled close to the trunk at the bottom of the tree, where if you come across such a youngster it adopts the most grotesque attitude, holding its wings and tail in such a position as to appear about three times as

---

LONG-EARED OWL

Comparative size Smaller than Tawny Owl.
Status Resident.
Habitat Mainly dense woodland, scrub in north.
Nest In old crow, hawk, pigeon nest.
Eggs White, clutch 3-5.
Food Small mammals, birds, beetles.

large and quite frightening, snapping its bill and 'spitting' at the intruder.

While the female is incubating the eggs the male is usually nearby, perched on the branch of a tree very close to the trunk, where the cryptic colouring of his plumage blends perfectly with the bark – another reason why he is seldom seen. Flying silently through the trees, if by chance he has been disturbed from his roost, it is amazing to see how quickly the small birds appear to 'mob' him, only leaving him in peace when he resettles, merging once more into the browns and greys of the tree bark.

The edge of the 'shelter belt' bordering open fields is one of the Long-eared Owl's favourite hunting grounds, where voles, mice and other small mammals are caught and brought to the family – on visiting one nest that I knew of in the midst of a bushy growth on the side of an oak tree, I found the solitary chick surrounded by 25 voles and mice.

Outside the breeding season Long-eared Owls can be found roosting communally on rough ground, and in the extreme north of their range they can also be found nesting on the ground, where they appear to be less nocturnal than they are in the south.

Short-eared Owl

Asio flammeus

As soon as an area of hill moor has been ploughed, planted with conifers and fertilised the luscious new growth of grass shoots provides food for voles, which in turn provide the staple diet of the **Short-eared Owl,** and this type of habitat will continue to suppport Short-eared Owl until the trees reach a height of about one metre.

Like the Long-eared Owl, the 'ear-tufts', which are positioned above the eyes, are not ears, but adornments raised during display, or when the bird is alarmed; unlike the Long-eared Owl, the eyes are yellow instead of orange. The general colouration of the plumage is buff, the mantle richly marbled in dark brown, the wings having an almost chequered effect, and the underparts showing long, dark streaks.

In early spring, the wonderful display of the Short-ear can be seen as, high in the air, he circles, glides and soars, with characteristic wing-flapping, then drops to the ground, uttering his low-pitched, vibrating hoot which, when heard on the moors, sounds like something mechanical.

Once the territory has been selected, egg-laying begins in April, the size of the clutch being a good indication as to the vole situation, for in 'poor vole years' three or four eggs will be the limit, while in good years I have seen as many as ten eggs in a clutch. It is also noticeable that there are more pairs of Short-ear in an area in a good vole year.

The nest is a depression, scantily lined with a few stems or stalks and concealed among rough grass, reeds or heather. The eggs are laid at two-day intervals, with incubation commencing with the first egg. A moorland ground nest, containing ten young owlets graduating in size, would certainly be extremely vulnerable to a marauding fox or stoat, so nature has endowed the owlets with a strong sense of self- preservation. As soon as they are capable of shuffling about, usually at about ten days old, they wander off in all directions, keeping in vocal contact with their parents, who ensure that the chicks are continually fed.

During the period that the young Owls are being cared for by the parents, the birdwatcher is provided with an entertaining and thrilling time for, unlike our other owls, the Short-eared Owl hunts regularly during daylight hours, peaking when the voles are most active, during the evening. It is then that the characteristic hunting flight can be observed.

Only two or three metres above the ground, the Short-eared Owl quarters the hillside, flapping noiselessly, then gliding and sometimes hovering briefly, before dropping into the vegetation having seen or heard a slight movement. After prey is secured, the male flies directly to the nest site and when he alights, a short distance from the sitting female, she bounces out to greet him, accepting the prey. When voles are plentiful, five or six birds can be seen quartering among the young trees at the same time.

SHORT-EARED OWL

Comparative size Smaller than Tawny Owl.
Status Resident, southerly movement in winter.
Habitat Open hill moorland.
Nest Scrape on ground, well hidden, lined grasses.
Eggs White, clutch 3-11.
Food Small mammals, birds, insects.

The Shorteared Owl is best seen in early evening as it quarters the moorland or young conifer plantation in search of voles.

At rest on a fence post, rock or telegraph pole, the horizontal stance of the Short-eared Owl can be seen to differ from the upright stance of other owls. On finding a favourite perching post, a search round the bottom will produce a number of 'pellets', the castings of indigestible fur, feather and bones of the Short-ear's victims.

Unlike those of the Tawny Owl, which contain few bones – possibly due to the fact that the Tawny has a stronger digestive system – the 'pellets' of the Short-ear are a good indication as to the Owl's diet.

In winter the Short-eared Owls leave the Scottish hill moors in favour of coastal or inland marshes in England.

Nightjar

Caprimulgus europaeus

The Woodcock's final 'croak-croak', tsi-tsi' call of his evening roding flight heard as he flies round the perimeter of his woodland territory, is a prelude to another crepuscular bird whose song,

delivered somewhat later is equally as characteristic and much more strident. The 'churring' of the **Nightjar** has been likened to the sound of a small two-stroke motorbike engine, with a gearchange-like dip as the bird turns his head while delivering the song from a favourite perch.

Unlike the Woodcock, the Nightjar is a summer resident, rarely appearing before May. It is therefore one of our latest summer arrivals but, like to the Woodcock, the Nightjar favours open mixed woodlands and heaths, with bramble and bracken undergrowth as a breeding territory where, again like the Woodcock, the cryptic colouring of the sitting female makes her almost invisible. The entire plumage is greyish-brown, spotted and barred in dark and light shades of brown, with a hint of chestnut on the head, back and shoulders, so that when the bird is incubating the entire shape merges into the surroundings. The male has white tips on his outer tail feathers, and three white spots on his outer primaries which are lacking in the female, and which are conspicuous as the male twists and turns in

pursuit of moths and the other night-flying insects which form his diet.

The nest, a slight scrape on the ground among bracken, bramble or cut fir branches, usually contains in June two beautifully marbled eggs, and while the female is incubating the male is always nearby, being the first to break cover if an intruder appears, but he does not fly far before landing again among dense cover.

During the day, while at rest the male remains silent, being even less noticeable as he prefers to rest on a branch lengthwise instead of crosswise, and as his chosen perch is often an old lichen-covered branch it renders him even more invisible. When the young are hatched they are fed on regurgitated insects, mostly taken on the wing by the male hawking in the dark, his large eyes and wide gape assisting him in his forays.

NIGHTJAR
Comparative size Smaller than Kestrel.
Status Summer resident.
Habitat Open woodlands, heaths.
Nest Scrape on ground in undergrowth.
Eggs White, blotched with brown and violet, clutch 2.
Food Night-flying insects.

The churring evening call of the Nightjar betrays its presence where otherwise it would go unnoticed.

Sometimes two broods are reared in a season, the male taking care of the first two youngsters while the female is incubating the second clutch, but by late August or September adults and young leave their Scottish breeding haunts for warmer climes in Africa.

Swift

Apus apus

In late April or early May, one of our fastest-flying birds arrives to spend the next four months in the skies above rural and urban habitats, announcing its arrival by its loud screaming call as it wheels and turns in the air.

The **Swift** is our most aerial species, and when watching a party of them high above as they sweep back and forth feeding on flying insects, you have to agree that this bird is aptly named. Aptly named, but often wrongly identified as a member of the Swallow family, the only relationship that the Swift has with the Swallow and Martin being the fact that they are all aerial feeders, while there are a number of differences between the species.

The visual characteristics that distinguish the Swift from the Swallow are most noticeable in the shorter forked tail and long scythe-shaped

while and the plumage is totally dark brown except for a tinge of white on the throat. The thin bill and short, feathered legs are black with all four toes pointing forwards, an adaptation necessary for a bird that has to cling to masonry before entering its nest hole.

In urban areas it can be well into June before the Swift lays her eggs, as many of the nests are built on to of walls under the slates on roofs of buildings where previously Starlings had nested, the only fresh material added being a few feathers or wisps of straw that the Swift collect on the wing.

When the eggs are being incubated, usually in June, the sitting bird is sometimes joined by her mate when the weather is inclement; otherwise their life is entirely aerial, feeding, drinking, sleeping and even mating in the air. Following a shared incubation period of about 18 days the eggs hatch, the naked chicks being fed on small pellets of compressed flying insects collected in

SWIFT
Comparative size Because of longer wings looks larger than Swallow.
Status Summer resident.
Habitat Aerial, above town and country.
Nest Atop wall head, old woodpecker hole, few feathers and wisps of straw.
Eggs White, clutch 2-3.
Food Flying insects.

The most aerial of summer residents Swifts are often seen but seldom really looked at.

the crop of the parent as he sweeps through the air, with his 'gape' wide open.

As the young birds develop, the 'foodball' of insects increases in size as the parents are compelled to collect more and more, until when they are almost ready to leave the nest the young Swift are presented with a 'foodball' the size of a marble, containing up to 1,000 flying insects.

When the young Swifts leave the nest it is likely they will not land again for months or even years, feeding and sleeping on the wing – wings that are designed for fast flight with a span of 33cm, twice the length of the bird's body. Within days of vacating the nest they will be on their way to South Africa, having to spend around four full aerial years before they are old enough to join the colonies of breeding birds, which could quite well still contain one, or even both, of their parents.

By mid-August the pre-migratory groups of Swifts reaches a peak, with much noisy screaming, flying at almost unbelievable speeds, dodging telephone wires, and skimming over rooftops, until a few mornings later one looks upwards to find that the sky is still and quiet.

Kingfisher
Alcedo atthis

Walk along the banks of a river that supports both Dippers and **Kingfisher** and you will find the two birds behaving in a very different manner towards humans.

A Dipper standing on a stone, or feeding along the waters' edge, will pay little or no heed whatsoever to a human observer, but even partly concealed anglers are given a wide berth by the Kingfisher which, on sighting the intruder, will immediately swerve, flying over bordering fields before rejoining the river course, or rising high in the air above the treetop level and then dropping again when safely out of sight.

This is the reason why some birdwatchers see the Kingfisher only as a flash of brilliant blue as he flies up or downstream, but for those prepared to remain inconspicuous, using the riverbank vegetation as cover, on a stretch frequented by Kingfishers, the resulting views of the bird can indeed be well worth the wait.

The upperparts of the Kingfisher are brilliant cobalt blue with a slight greenish tinge on the shoulders, and the underparts shade from warm chestnut on the breast to pale orange undertail coverts. An orange band runs through the eye, merging into a white patch on the side of the

The Kingfisher's method of excavating a nesting burrow in the bank of a river can at times result in a slight mishap.

neck, and there is also a white patch on the throat.

The small legs and feet are bright red, the long dagger-like beak, fully the length of the Kingfisher's head, is black, with that of the female having a reddish lower mandible, the only colour difference between the sexes.

The Kingfisher is only 16.5cm in length, 5cm shorter than a Starling, and as 4cm of the Kingfisher's total length is his beak one realises just how small a Kingfisher is, always appearing larger when seen in flight.

In late January or February, Kingfishers pair up, with much play taking place as the male chases his mate among the riverside willows and alders, and though he is no songster, at this time of the year he utters a pleasant series of repetitive musical whistles.

Later in the spring, the pair decide on a site for their nest, selecting a high sandy bank, usually fairly well concealed under an overhang, and there they excavate their tunnel, using their beaks and feet. On selecting the site for the nest,

the tunnel is started by the birds flying beak first into the bank, and this must at times hold a few surprises, for at one site at which I was photographing a small splinter of about half a centimetre of the horny sheath of the beak pointed almost at a right angle from the tip of the upper mandible.

The nest chamber is situated at the end of the tunnel, approximately one metre from the entrance; the eggs are laid on the bare soil, and incubated by both parents for about 21 days. At first the male fishes alone while the female broods the naked chicks, but a few days later when the young huddle together in mutual suppport, both birds fish and feed the family.

At this time, if you are fortunate enough to have a nest under observation, the male can be seen to fly in the opposite direction to the female – if one flies upstream, the other flies down – possible explanation being that before pairing each bird held its own territory, thereby knowing the best 'fishing' places on its stretch and ensuring a plentiful supply for the family.

As the nest may contain about six or seven young the parents are kept busy fishing, which they do by diving into the water and catching the fish between the mandibles, then carrying it to the nest site crosswise in the beak. At the nest site Kingfishers have a favourite perch a few metres from the tunnel where they settle to adjust the catch, before presenting it head first to the young. As there is not enough room in the tunnel to turn round the parent birds reappear backwards, immediately plopping into the water to rid themselves of any grit or debris that could foul their plumage.

As the young develop the tunnel becomes more foul smelling and messy, providing the observer with further entertainment as the parents, on emerging from the entrance, take two or three dips each time before flying off to bring yet more fish for the family.

By the 'back end' the Kingfishers could have raised two broods, the youngsters dispersed up and downstream, and this for me is a magical time for, crouching by the riverside at a favourite salmon pool anticipating my next catch, I invariably see and hear Kingfishers disputing their territorial boundaries.

During one of my fishing visits to the river, crouching in a trench-like depression on the bank I spotted a Kingfisher which settled in the lower branches of an Ash tree about twenty metres downstream. It obviously failed to notice me, and as I watched intently I was rewarded by a performance which I have only seen once in my birdwatching years. The Kingfisher left its perch and hovered for some seconds a few metres from the bank, head and beak pointing downwards then it plunged, re-emerged from the water, and settled once more on its perch to devour its catch. All my previous sightings of Kingfishers catching fish were from a standing position.

Over the past decade, the Kingfisher appears to have been on the increase slightly on Scottish rivers and hopefully this trend will continue, for a visit to the river when you fail to hear or see the Kingfisher is equally as disappointing as an empty creel.

KINGFISHER

COMPARATIVE SIZE- Smaller than starling.
Status Resident.
Habitat Clear streams and rivers.
Nest Small chamber at end of tunnel.
Eggs White, small, round, clutch 5-10.
Food Small fish, i.e. loach, minnow, stickleback.

Green Woodpecker
Picus viridis

In May 1960 I reported finding the occupied nest hole of a pair of **Green Woodpeckers** to the 'Scottish Ornithologist's Club', which was reported in their journal **Scottish Birds**, Vol 1, page 379. This was presented as the first breeding record for Dumfriesshire, but as I had known of their presence for fully ten years prior to this, I feel that a little perseverance could have brought to light an earlier record. However, since then, there has been a gradual spread throughout south-west Scotland, with a similar spread on the east coast.

The Green Woodpecker favours ancient woodlands, where it is more often heard than seen, its characteristic 'yaffle' call heralding its presence, but by no means guaranteeing that you will see the bird itself, as it is most elusive. When it is seen, it proves to be a very colourful bird, with olive-green upperparts, pale greenish underparts, and a bright red cap from the base of the bill to the nape. The eye has a surround of black, and there is a black moustacial stripe, the male's having a red centre. The rump is bright yellowish-green which is most obvious when the bird is seen in flight, and the stout chisel-like bill is capable of chipping its way, first inwards, then downwards into the heart of an alder, one of the Green Woodpecker's favoured nesting trees.

All Woodpeckers behave in much the same way, progressing up or down the trunks of trees by using their four strong, clawed toes, two in front and two behind, with stiff tail feathers pressed against the trunk for support. This combination serves them well when they excavate their nest holes which can take as long as a week, and when complete, the eggs are laid on some loose chippings on the floor of the nest chamber. When feeding young, especially when they are well grown, Green Woodpeckers are kept busy tapping and boring into soft, rotting timber for the grubs of wood-boring insects, or searching for ants and other insects on the ground, where the birds move about in clumsy hops. When an anthill is located, a unique aid is brought into use to extract the ants and their pupae: the Woodpecker's 20cm sticky tongue long is probed down the tunnels into the chambers and then withdrawn, the ants being sucked into the bird's crop.

Photographing from a hide about six metres

In the south of Scotland, Green Woodpeckers show a strong preference for alders in which they excavate their nest chambers.

Great Spotted Woodpecker
Dendrocopos major

The name **Greater Spotted Woodpecker** can be somewhat misleading, causing one to imagine a much larger bird, but at 23cm in length this Woodpecker is only slightly larger than a Starling.

It is a very attractive bird in its pied plumage, and is sometimes referred to as the Pied Woodpecker. The upperparts are mostly black with large white patches on each of the wings, which also have white barring on the primaries. The underparts from the chin to the prominent red undertail coverts are white, and there are white patches on the sides of the head. The central tail feathers are black, the others showing white dots and bars, and the male's nape displays a prominent red patch which is lacking in his mate, but apart from this the sexes are similar in colouring.

The Great Spotted Woodpecker is more of a woodland loving species than the Green, being less inclined to feed on the ground, and this is the Woodpecker heard 'drumming' throughout the spring from late February to early May. Drumming on the dead wood of trees with its powerful bill produces an extraordinary sound which echoes through the woods, and can be heard from a considerable distance.

Having secured their territory, the Woodpeckers then excavate their nest chamber, and for this they choose a tree which is somewhat less of a challenge than that of the Green Woodpecker, usually a birch which has signs of a 'soft centre', with razor strop fungi growing outwards from the trunk. Often the nest hole is excavated immediately under this fungus, which forms a canopy against driving rain or strong sun, but it is likely that this is purely coincidental.

In some mixed woodlands, the Woodpecker holes excavated in previous years are occupied by Starlings, and each spring when the Starlings return to the wood to nest, nest sites become scarcer, so there is a danger of Woodpeckers being evicted from newly-excavated holes by the more aggressive Starlings.

Once a pair of Great Spotted Woodpeckers are firmly established in their nest, the eggs are laid on the wood chips on the floor of the chamber

from a Green Woodpecker's nest hole is a good way to observe the birds, and the first thing you notice besides the bright colours is the size, which at 32cm is almost as big as Jackdaw. Then there is the sound as the Woodpecker climbs up or down the trunk towards the hole, like someone screwing up a piece of greaseproof paper. Finally, when the young are being fed at the nest-hole by regurgitation, the parents' convulsive movements sound like the contents of a milk carton being vigorously shaken.

When the young leave the nest hole their plumage is duller and more uniform than that of their parents, with brownish-grey bars and streaks, and the family stay together for some time while the young are taught to fend for themselves.

GREEN WOODPECKER

Comparative size Slightly smaller than Jackdaw.
Status Resident.
Habitat Woodlands and parklands.
Nest Hole and chamber, excavated in tree.
Eggs White, clutch 5-8.
Food Wood boring insects, larvae, ants.

Great Spotted Woodpeckers prefer to excavate their nest chamber in a dead or dying birch.

however, when the young Great Spotted Woodpeckers poke their heads out of the hole they display a reddish crown which is totally lacking in both parents.

When the young leave the nest their peculiar rasping noise is silenced and, the wood becomes empty of woodpecker sounds, so we must wait until the following spring to hear once again the sound that tells us that the Great Spotted Woodpecker is back in his territory.

Wryneck
Jynx torquilla

The **Wryneck** is a summer resident, a peculiar little bird related to the Woodpeckers, but only slightly larger than a Sparrow.

It has a slim appearance and is dressed in greyish-brown streaked in darker shadings, with paler underparts which are slightly barred. It has the strange and unique habit of twisting and turning its head, hence its name, and chooses to nest in small natural holes in trees.

On 3 June 1970, positioned in a hide at the site of a Buzzard's nest in a wooded glen in Upper Annandale, I peered out of one of the side peepholes, and was amazed to see a Wryneck examining a small hole in an oak tree only six metres from where I sat. I watched it for a few minutes before it finally moved on. This was my first record of this rare bird.

where they are incubated by both parents, who also share in the rearing of the young. For the first ten days or so, the parent birds enter the nest hole to feed the chicks but later, as the young fledge, they climb up the interior of the chamber to meet their parents at the entrance hole.

It is at this time that the watcher is presented with a special treat, for these normally shy Woodpeckers will carry on with their domestic duties, allowing you to observe them as long as you remain inconspicuous by sitting at the base of a tree about fifty metres distant.

This is also the time when the photographer takes advantage of the situation, as both male and female can be portrayed in similar positions and the slight plumage difference can be recorded. As if trying to confuse the issue,

Skylark
Alauda arvensis

High above the meadow, pasture and golf course the **Skylark** soars in the air, hovers and descends, singing continuously, for as sure as the Blackbird marks his territory from a favoured song post, the Skylark with his aerial song is marking his boundaries, as well-defined as those of any other bird.

To many, the Skylark is just another of those 'little brown birds', about the size of a Sparrow. Possibly this is because Larks are often in the company of Meadow Pipits, both in their breeding haunts and in winter when they roam the countryside together as they flock in their search for food, but the Skylark is about 4cm

---

GREAT SPOTTED WOODPECKER

Comparative size Slightly larger than Starling.
Status Resident.
Habitat Mainly mixed woodlands.
Nest Hole and chamber, excavated in tree.
Eggs White, clutch 5-6.
Food Wood-boring insects and larvae.

*Often seen and heard high above golf courses, is the
Skylark – whose song is unmistakable.*

larger than the Meadow Pipit, making him fully
18cm long, so he is in fact a 'larger' small bird.

The plumage of the Skylark is brown, with
light and dark mottling on the head and mantle,
and the underparts are paler with a few dark
streaks on the breast. There is a buffish eyestripe,
which shows against the darker colour of the
face, and the outer tail feathers are white. The
birds also sport a short crest which is not always
obvious.

The Skylark's nest is always well concealed in
tussocky growth on the ground, either in grass
or in growing crops, and when in the latter the
compact structure, which is built in a slight
depression, soon disappears among the growing
shoots.

As the Skylark normally approaches its nest
from a short distance away a small tunnel, at
times about a metre long, is soon formed, leading
to the nest through the vegetation. With
sometimes as many as three broods being reared
in a season and the female laying her first clutch

in the latter half of April, and with incubation
taking eleven days and a further ten days'
fledging period, it can be well into July before the
last of her young are in the air.

When the eggs are in the nest the sitting bird
blends perfectly with its surroundings, and you
can get very close before the bird takes flight.
When the newly-hatched young are in the nest,
their hair-like feathers look exactly like young
shoots, and later, when fledged, the cryptic
colouring renders them almost invisible.

Skylarks walk easily on the ground, and

SKYLARK

Comparative size Slightly smaller than
Starling.
Status Resident.
Habitat Open fields, meadows, moors,
pastures.
Nest Grassy cup on ground among low
vegetation.
Eggs Greyish, speckled with brown, clutch 3-6.
Food Grain, seeds, greenstuff, invertebrates.

---

though they can be seen perched on a fencepost or wall, they seldom if ever perch in trees.

An example of the Skylark's ability to merge into its surroundings was demonstrated on a January morning when I pulled in by the roadside to observe a flock of finches feeding among stubble. Scanning the finches with my binoculars, I discovered a flock of about fifty Skylarks mingling with them. Then a lorry rumbled past, and as the finches took to the trees the Larks just seemed to disappear. It took a careful examination to pick out one or two of the crouching birds, but as soon as some of the finches flew down to continue feeding the Larks appeared as if from nowhere.

The Skylark is widespread throughout Scotland where in some districts it is known as the 'Laverock'.

Shorelark

Eremophila alpestris

The **Shorelark** is mainly a winter visitor to our coasts where it frequents salt marshes, usually in the company of Snow Bunting.

A northern European species, the male Shorelark is a strikingly coloured bird in his brown plumage, in which the upperparts are slightly tinged and streaked with pink and the underparts are whitish. His crown, cheeks and throat are black, the rest of the head being bright yellow, and he sports a pair of black erectile 'horns'.

Numbers of these birds visiting British coasts, can vary considerably from year to year, but over the past decade a few pairs are known to have nested on some of our Scottish mountains.

Swallow

Hirundo rustica

Swallows arrive in the south of England about mid-March, but it is fully a month later before they return to the south of Scotland, their arrival usually coinciding with the 'popping' of the beech buds.

To most people they are even more welcome as the harbinger of summer than the Cuckoo, as they are more graceful and friendly towards humans who look forward to their return,

whether it be a solitary pair to take up residence in a garage or outhouse, or many pairs which nest in a variety of sites on a farm.

Farms are the obvious choice of habitat for the Swallow, as they provide nest sites, material and a constant food source in the shape of flying insects, and on their return Swallows are sometimes quite content to refurbish a nest which has survived from a previous season. The nest, which could be built on a beam or rafter in an outhouse, byre or stable, is saucer-shaped, cleverly put together with mud, straw and feathers which both birds collect and use in the construction.

Swallows are distinguished from other aerial-feeding, long-winged birds, such as the House and Sand Martins, by their much longer 'tail streamers' and glossy, blue-black upperparts. They also have a similar coloured breast band, and a chestnut throat and forehead, with whitish underparts tinged in pink, and dark, long outer tail feathers patterned in white.

The breeding season extends from May to September, during which time a pair can rear three broods although two are more commonplace, with the four or five young from the first brood being fed and tended by the male while the female incubates her second clutch.

Swallows are constantly on the wing with an elegant and easy flight as they sweep low over fields, ponds and rivers in their search for flying insects which are caught in the wide 'gape' of the bill. Even quenching their thirst is achieved in flight, the Swallow skimming low over the surface of the water, then merely touching it with its lower mandible in such a way that a few drops are scooped into the open bill.

Seldom seen on the ground, except when gathering mud, straw or other material for its nest, the Swallow waddles in a clumsy, awkward manner as its legs, like those of other aerial species, are very short.

SWALLOW

Comparative size 19 cm, including long tail streamers.
Status Summer resident.
Habitat Rural, farmland.
Nest Saucer-shaped mud construction in barn, shed etc.
Eggs White with chestnut spots, clutch 4-6.
Food Flying insects.

The Swallow is at home around farms where out-buildings provide nest sites and where an abundance of flying insects provide a food source.

Swallows gather on telegraph wires in preparation for their long journey south in September. Then they soar, and glide at varying heights, sometimes almost disappearing from view as they turn towards the south.

House Martin

Delichon urbica

No other bird has been misnamed by the layman as often as the **House Martin** as, summer after summer, the colonies on public buildings constantly provoke remarks referring to the 'Swallows' and their nests, and again in the autumn one often hears, 'I see the Swallows are getting ready to leave,' when in reality the party consists entirely of House Martins. In all fairness, however, the Martins are members of the Swallow family, unlike the Swift which is in a family of its own.

The House Martin is noticeably smaller than the Swallow, being 12.5cm in length, and its tail is shorter and less forked. The upperparts are dark bluish-black and the underparts white, the white feathering extending down the legs to the toes, and the rump is also conspicuously white.

The nest, although built of the same mud base as that of the Swallow, is an entirely different structure, with many being built together under the eaves of buildings and under bridges and flyovers.

If one is fortunate enough to observe Swallows and House Martins collecting mud for their nests from the same source, which is usually a muddy puddle in a farmyard or track, or by the side of a shallow, muddy stream, one notices that the Swallows bring one or two wisps of hay in their beaks which they poke into the mud before flying off. The House Martins, on the other hand, collect mud in the shape of small pellets which they take back to their nests, cementing them together with saliva.

It can take anything between 2,000 and 2,500 mud pellets to construct one complete House Martin nest, so the mud supply has to be constant or the birds will run into difficulty, resulting in some very odd structures indeed, such as one that I photographed which resembled a patchwork quilt in design. The different mud sources must have dried up about eight times, thus allowing me to study the construction, the various muds used ranging from a very pale plaster-like substance to very dark, almost black mud.

Another two differences between the nests of the Swallow and the House Martin are that the Swallows are usually indoors while the House Martins' are outside, and the saucer-shaped base of the Swallows' nest is continued to the roof by the House Martins, with only a small entrance hole at the top.

Egg laying usually takes place in late May or June, the eggs being incubated by both parents for 14 days. After hatching the young are fed by both parents by regurgitation, and as soon as the first brood leave the nest the female lays again, the second brood often being fed by their older brothers and sisters as well as their parents.

Unlike the Swallow, the House Martin chooses to build a more substantial nest under the eaves of buildings outdoors.

HOUSE MARTIN

Comparative size Smaller than Swallow.
Status Summer resident.
Habitat Urban or rural.
Nest Mud and saliva cup, under eaves - bridges.
Eggs White, clutch 4-6.
Food Flying insects.

On occasion a third brood is attempted, the young being fed in a frenzy by about half a dozen different birds, but at times this mass feeding is to no avail as the migratory pull is too strong for the older birds, and the young are left to perish.

Although House Martins feed in the same manner as Swallows, they feed at greater heights, and can often be seen wheeling high in the air among the Swifts.

In autumn, the migratory preparation is similar to that of the Swallows, with large numbers congregating on telegraph wires prior to their journey south.

Sand Martin

Riparia riparia

The **Sand Martin** is the smallest member of the Swallow family. Only 12cm in length, it is a little, dark brown bird with white underparts and a brown breastband, and it is the first member of its family to return to Scotland for the breeding season.

Sometimes, Sand Martins arrive a little too early and are caught by the cold weather, for not only does the cold of an early April snowfall affect the birds themselves, but it reduces their chances of finding flying insects. As a result, a few individuals may perish as they huddle together for warmth in one of their nesting holes. Fortunately, this does not happen often and later when the birds congregate at the sandy face of a high riverbank it soon becomes a hive of activity, when as if at a word of command, the excavating operations begin.

Nesting burrows of the previous season are obviously the first choice, as these require little in the way of excavation, but when a new burrow is required the pair select a site and, sharing the effort, burrow inwards and slightly upwards with their feet for a distance on average of about a metre, ending in a small chamber to which a lining of straw and feathers is added.

In May or June the females lay their eggs, most of them laying at about the same time so that many chicks hatch together and the colony, whether consisting of only a few nests or many hundreds, becomes even more active as the parents continually fly to and fro with food for their young. Like the House Martin, the Sand Martin is an aerial feeder but tends to feed at a much lower level – similar, in fact, to the Swallow.

As soon as the first broods are free-flying the pairs nest again and, with more young birds than adults now in the colony it becomes even busier, with parents feeding chicks and immature birds

finding their wings, until the younger birds start moving south, followed some time later by the remainder of the colony.

Both the Sand Martin and the House Martin are widespread throughout Scotland, except for the extreme north.

Raven

Corvus corax

The western half and the far north of Scotland are the regions where the **Raven** is most numerous, and in the south, where it was a common bird only 25 years ago, it is now scarce. The Southern Uplands were once heavily populated with sheep, resulting in a steady stream of fatalities among the rocky linns, and in this way the Ravens were provided with a regular food source. But recently these areas have been planted with conifers, with the result that the decline in sheep numbers has brought a noticeable decline in the number of Ravens.

The Raven is a large black bird, 64cm in length, his stout, slightly curved beak, giving him a fearsome appearance, and his black mantle and wings shimmering with blue and purple gloss when seen in good light. Impressive as he is when seen standing on a rocky point in his rugged domain, those fortunate enough to find themselves in Raven territory in early spring will marvel at his mating display in which every manoeuvre out-perform the one preceding. On large, broad wings with a span of 1.3m, the Raven is most fascinating to watch as from a great height he performs magnificent aerial evolutions, wheeling, soaring, tumbling, diving and gliding upside down for short distances, displaying his well-separated primaries and long wedge-shaped tail.

Despite the biting winds and snow showers, Ravens nest early in the year, usually being found on eggs by the end of February and, with two or three traditional sites to choose from, the one most sheltered at that particular time is the one generally occupied.

The nests are huge constructions, solidly built of sticks, heather stalks, earth and moss, with the deep cup lined with hair and sheep's wool. The eggs are incubated by the female, while the male brings her food to the nest in his crop. The incubation period is about 21 days, and when the chicks hatch the female broods them while

---

SAND MARTIN

Comparative size Smaller than Swallow.
Status Summer resident.
Habitat Areas with sandy banks near water.
Nests Tunnel in vertical sandy bank.
Eggs White, clutch 4-6.
Food Flying insects.

This awesome Raven could have come straight from an Edgar Allan Poe novel, as it perches on a Celtic Cross on a dull, grey evening.

the male brings food for the entire family, but as soon as the young are feathered enough to keep warm both parents forage for food. Carrion such as dead sheep, are the predominant food source in open, hill country, but all types of carrion are taken, animal, bird or fish, while small mammals and some vegetable matter also feature in the diet.

RAVEN

Comparative size Larger than Rook.
Status Resident.
Habitat Mountainous, hilly moorland.
Nest Rocky ledge, tall tree, bulky, sticks, stalks, wool.
Eggs Bluish-green, spotted dark brown, grey, clutch 3-7.
Food Carrion, small mammals, vegetable matter.

Although the nests are usually situated on a sheltered, rocky ledge, some are built in trees, and more recently the odd nest has been found on a pylon, but no matter where they are built, they are durable and last for many years, providing nest sites for other birds such as Peregrines and Kestrels.

As Ravens and Peregrines can be found nesting on the same rocky crag the two birds often confront one another, with the Raven's deep 'pruk-pruk' call minglng with the screech of the Peregrine, and though much soaring, twisting and dodging takes place, seldom, if ever, is any real harm done.

Carrion Crow

Corvus corone

Hooded Crow

Corvus cornix

Some years ago, when every piece of woodland, scrub and copse was patrolled by gamekeepers at ome time or other during the year, you had to rudge well into the hills to find **Carrion Crows** – nowadays they can be seen on many main streets in towns.

The Carrion Crow, or 'Corbie', of the south east of Scotland becomes the **Hooded Crow,** or 'Hoodie' in the north west, and though there is a distinctive difference in the plumage of the two birds, their destructive behaviour is very similar. The Carrion Crow is slightly larger than a Rook, being 47cm in length, and it is a more dapper bird, lacking the Rook's 'baggy trousers'. Its plumage is all black with a blue-green gloss on the mantle, throat and wings, whereas the Hooded Crow has a distinct grey mantle, breast and underparts.

Carrion and Hooded Crows are sub-species of the European Crow, and though they have different breeding ranges and plumage they are regarded as the same species, because where their ranges overlap they interbreed freely, with the 'hybrid' offspring themselves supposedly being able to breed. While I agree that Carrion Crows and Hooded Crows interbreed and produce offspring, having witnessed this for myself, whether or not the hybrids are fertile is, I feel, debatable.

Throughout the part of the country populated

The Carrion Crow is the real menace on hill moors and river courses where the evidence of hundreds of eaten eggs can be found during the nesting season.

by Carrion Crows one finds that this species prefers to build its nest in a tree, from a dark canopied fir in woodlands, to a protective thorny hawthorn on the hill moors, and with a wide variety of trees being chosen between these two situations. The Hooded Crow, on the other hand, prefers to nest on a rocky ledge or on the ground among the heather in treeless country. Carrion and Hooded Crow nests are similarly constructed, being built of sticks, heather stalks, earth and moss, with a thick lining of sheeps' wool.

The eggs are laid in April, and incubated by the female alone for 21 days, while the male brings her food to the nest; after procuring the food from the male she, in turn, feeds the young for about 30 days after they have hatched.

Like the other members of the Crow family, the Carrion Crow feeds on the ground, and although it walks in an ungainly way with a curious sidling action, once in the air its flight is straight and direct with regular wing beats.

The Carrion Crow is a real menace towards all ground nesting species during the breeding season, destroying and eating many eggs. In fact I have seen the entire avian population on some riverside gravel beds lose their eggs to a single pair which were nesting in a solitary fir by the riverside, even Moorhens in backwaters of the river suffering the same fate.

It is a pity that these birds are so detrimental towards others as their intelligence has to be admired, the rate at which they exploit new situations being uncanny. A few years ago, a

---

CARRION/HOODED CROW

Comparative size Slightly larger than Rook.
Status Resident.
Habitat Woodland, moorland, farmland.
Nest In tree or on ground, sticks, twigs, earth, wool.
Eggs Bluish-green, spotted brown-grey, clutch 3-4.
Food Carrion, eggs, young birds, small mammals, seeds.

---

student arrived in the area, and after giving him a 'guided tour', he duly returned to work on a thesis on the Curlew. Approximately 20 nests were located and logged, while at the same time lidless bean cans were sunk into the earth as insect traps, in and around each Curlew territory.

Carrion Crows soon discovered the first nests with inevitable results, so it was decided that on visiting future nests a different approach route would be used each time. This ruse also failed, the Crows continuing to raid the nests, and, as if to add insult to injury, they were meanwhile pulling the 'insect traps' from the ground, and tipping them upside down to get at the beetles and other insects. Throughout the early summer, every single nest fell victim to the Crows – the study was abandoned but a lesson had been learned.

Ironically, the only successful Curlew nest that I knew of during that disastrous season was one in a patch of reeds close to a farm track, the young hatching and moving off with their parents during one of my photographic sessions.

Rook
Corvus frugilegus

In Scotland, the first Sunday in March is recognised as 'Crow Sunday', the day professed to be the start of activity in rookeries, and anyone visiting one on this particular day will not be disappointed, as many of the birds will be busily employed repairing nests which have survived the winter gales. Other **Rooks** will be carrying sticks to form the bases of the new nests, and in general, the rookery will have the appearance of just waking up.

In actual fact, some of the Rooks will have been active for some time, possibly for about a week or so, as Rooks are 'photo-periodic', which means that they are responsive to changes in the number of the daylight hours, the lengthening

The bare, grey skin patch at the base of the Rook's beak prevents the feathers from becoming soiled as the bird delves into the earth in search of worms and grubs.

days of February triggering their mating instincts.

In early spring, rookeries situated in deciduous trees are easily seen, with those in fir and pine woods, though more difficult to see, easily located by the clamouring activity, as the noise carries for some distance.

The reference to 'Crow Sunday' is doubly misleading, in fact, as the Rook is an entirely different bird from the Carrion Crow, having a very noticeable patch of rough, bare, grey skin on the face and base of the beak and, when on the ground, a pair of 'baggy trousers' are noticeable. The Carrion Crow, on the other hand, has a black face and beak, and his general appearance is much sleeker and tidier.

For many years distinguishing between Rooks and Crows was simplified in rather a humorous way: if you see a Rook alone, it is a Crow; if you see a crowd of Crows, they are Rooks – and although this is true for most of the time, lone Rooks can certainly be seen, with parties of Carrion Crows commonplace. Rooks are also often found feeding in the company of Jackdaws, where on the ground they walk in a sedate manner. In the air the flight is slow and laborious, the leisurely evening flight of Rooks wending their way home to the rookeries being a familiar sight in the country.

There can be many fatalities when young Rooks leave the rookery if the summer is hot and dry, as the ground becomes rock hard and the earthworms which are the predominant food source at this time will be far out of reach as they penetrate deeper into the earth.

There has always been much debate as to whether the Rook is a friend or foe of the farmer but, whichever way the balance tips, he certainly is not as much of a menace to the avian world as is his cousin, the Carrion Crow.

Jackdaw
Corvus monedula

Equally at home in town or country is the **Jackdaw,** one of the smaller members of the crow family, which is often seen in the company of Rooks since its Scottish range is similar to that of the Rook, being absent from the extreme north west.

In flight the Jackdaws' high-pitched 'caw' call, together with their smaller size of 34cm, helps distinguish the two species, and although the Jackdaws are also predominantly black, they are distinctly silver-grey on the nape and back of the head.

In spring the fantastic aerial displays of the mating birds take place, with great clamouring high above the rooftops, quarry faces or old oak woods, the sites where Jackdaws choose to build their nests. Nesting in holes of one type or another, both male and female carry masses of sticks, sometimes depositing them down chimneys, to form a base for the nest, which is then lined with grass, wool and bits of paper.

As Jackdaws have a distinct liking for bright objects, many nests have been found to contain some sort of glittering object, with 'ring-pulls' being one of the modern favourites, and a nest removed from a chimney on one occasion was found to have over 150 clothes pegs among the material used in its construction. In another nest that I recorded some years ago, in the chimney of an old roadside cottage, I found the eggs to be about two metres down from the top and, as the chimney was blocked solid from the fireplace upwards, the nest must have been built on about four metres of sticks, obviously the accumulation of some years.

The eggs are laid in April and incubated by the female alone, during which time the male brings her food to the nest; when the young hatch they are fed by both parents for about 30 days. They

---

ROOK

Comparative size Larger than Jackdaw.
Status Resident.
Habitat Farmland, woodland.
Nest Bulky, sticks, twigs, leaves, grasses.
Eggs Greyish-green, ashy-grey markings, clutch 3-5.
Food Earthworms, grain, insects.

JACKDAW

Comparative size Smaller than Rook.
Status Resident.
Habitat Urban, farmland, woodland.
Nest Tree hole, rocky crevice, chimney, lined paper, wool, mass of sticks.
Eggs Pale blue, spotted drk grey, clutch 3-5.
Food Insects, seeds, berries, kitchen scraps.

then follow their parents around, constantly calling and begging for food until they are able to fend for themselves.

The Jackdaw's walk is far less pompous that of either the Rook or the Crow, but it struts along with jerky movements, dashing the last half metre to grasp a piece of bread firmly in its beak before flying off to some chimney perch, usually with others in close pursuit.

Chough

Pyrrhocorax pyrrhocorax

In Scotland the **Chough,** the rarest member of the crow family, is confined to a small area of the south west, where the few remaining individuals choose to inhabit crevices and caves on the coast.

At 39cm in length Chough are slightly larger than Jackdaws and are very attractive and interesting birds in their purple-black, glossy plumage, with red legs and feet and red, longish, downcurved bills which are about 5cm in length. This specialised bill is useful in finding insects and larvae, for which they probe into the thin soil layer, but they will also feed on seeds, fruit and other vegetable matter on rocky ground.

At times, pairs or small parties perform fantastic aerial manoeuvres by wheeling around their cliff-top habitat, climbing to great heights and then dropping in a spectacular fashion on almost closed wings, and although these aerial displays are usually performed in conjunction with pairing they can, to a lesser degree, be seen at other times of the year. Nests are bulky affairs built of sticks, roots and other local material, the cup lined with wool or hair. When the eggs are laid in May the 18 day incubation period is undertaken by the female alone, with the pair sharing the responsibility of rearing the chicks for about five weeks till they fledge.

CHOUGH

Comparative size Larger than Jackdaw.
Status Resident.
Habitat Rocky coastline.
Nest Sticks, twigs, wool on rocky ledge.
Eggs Very pale blue, grey-brown markings, clutch 3-6.
Food Insects, spiders, seeds, vegetable matter.

Magpie

Pica pica

The strongholds of the **Magpie** in Scotland are the Central belt, the south east and an area south of the Moray Firth, with inexplicable pockets where these attractive members of the Crow family are totally absent, even though the habitat is suitable.

The Magpie is a familiar bird with its glossy, black head, mantle and breast, white underparts and conspicuous white wing patches. The rest of the wings have a blue and green glossy sheen, and the 23cm long tail which is fully half the length of the entire bird, is also glossy green with purplish highlights.

Magpies strongly favour the scrubby areas around disused pits, where they forage for food and build their nests in thick protective hawthorns, but they will also nest in much taller trees in other areas, where the large, domed structure is more easily seen.

The nest is conventional, with a strong well-defined cup of grass, mud and fine fibres, until the pair add a protective covering of sticks, usually hawthorn twigs. A formidable fortress indeed, which although built early in the spring, does not contain eggs until April.

The female incubates the eggs on her own while her mate brings her food to the nest, and when the chicks hatch he is still the sole provider for a few days, after which both parents forage for food. The Magpie's diet is extremely varied, with insects, small mammals, young birds and eggs sought after while the young are in the nest, but carrion, human foodstuffs and grain are also eaten.

Outside the protective cover of the hawthorn-dotted habitat Magpies can be very wary, and if

---

MAGPIE

Comparative size Larger than Jackdaw.
Status Resident.
Habitat Scrubland by woodland edge, farmland, suburban.
Nest Cup of roots and fibres, with large protective cover of hawthorn twigs.
Eggs Bluish-green, speckled with brown, clutch 4-7.
Food Invertebrates, grain seeds, fruit, carrion, eggs.

---

alarmed while feeding on the ground, they break into a quick side shuffle before taking flight, flying with rapid wing beats directly into cover.

Occasionally odd Magpies and even pairs occur in Upper Annandale, but as yet there is no sign of any breeding success.

Jay

Garrulus glandarius

Like the Magpie, the **Jay** is found in south-east Scotland and the Central belt, but it is absent further north. As it is one of our most colourful birds, people are often surprised to learn that the Jay is a member of the Crow family.

On most occasions when a Jay is seen it is in full flight, for it is a shy bird, but the white rump and contrasting black tail identify it immediately. When seen at rest, or on the ground, the full beauty can be appreciated. The predominant colour is pinkish-brown, with brown primaries on the wings, the remainder of which are attractively marked with black, white and blue. The chin and throat are white, contrasting with black moustacial stripes and on the crown there is a small, black and white striped erectile crest.

On the ground Jays move in clumsy hops with jerky body movements, and though the flight is weak, they move through the trees with tremendous agility.

In Scotland, forestry plantations are favoured by Jays as a nesting habitat. Nests are built in April, using sticks and roots with a lining of earth and fibres, both birds sharing in the building. Incubation of the eggs is undertaken by the female alone, during which time the male brings her food in his gullet, and when the chicks are old enough to keep themselves warm both parents bring food to the nest in this manner.

JAY
Comparative size Similar size to Jackdaw.   **Status** Resident.   **Habitat** Woodlands, parklands.   **Nest** In tree, sticks, rootlets, fine grass.   **Eggs** Greenish, brown speckled, black hair lines, clutch 3-7.   **Food** Varied, acorns, young birds, eggs.

The most colourful member of the crow family is the Jay whose habit of storing acorns in autumn has resulted in the birth of many a fine oak tree.

Jays predate other birds' eggs and young, but much of their food consists of injurious insects, and in autumn the Jays come into their own, when they collect and hide acorns. When the Jay has collected a gullet-full of acorns, he flies to a chosen spot and moves around, burying them one at a time as a winter and spring food supply. Although the Jay can return months later to the exact spot where acorns are hidden, at times a fatality means that some will not be located, thus assuring that oaks will grow for the future.

Great Tit

Parus major

Probably the most familiar family of birds throughout the country are the Tits, delighting thousands daily, especially in winter when they visit garden bird tables, performing acrobatic feats as they peck at nut feeders and other hanging feeding devices.

The largest and most colourful of these birds is the **Great Tit.** Although he is more apt to feed on the ground, he will dart to the nut feeder, take a peanut and immediately fly to the safety of some concealed perch to eat it.

In early spring, long before the leaves have grown, the woodlands and hedgerows ring out with his far-carrying 'teacher-teacher' call, allowing the watcher to associate the call with the bird and once this is achieved it is never forgotten. Early spring is the ideal time for those wishing to familiarise themselves with basic woodland and garden bird sounds, as the singing or calling birds can easily be seen amid the bare branches aiding identification. Then, when the summer residents arrive the familiar species can be eliminated, thus narrowing the field of possibilities.

The Great Tit is dressed in olive-green above and bright yellow underneath. The head and throat are black with a broad, black band

GREAT TIT
Comparative size Larger than Blue Tit.
Status Resident.
Habitat Woodland, parkland, large gardens.
Nest In hole, nest box, mossy cup, lined hair.
Eggs White, drk red spots, clutch 6-10.
Food Insects, caterpillars, seeds, nuts.

running from the throat to the undertail coverts; the rump, tail and wings are blue-grey, the latter having a white wing bar. The outer tail feathers are white and there are white patches on the cheeks, male and female being similarly coloured.

Great Tits often start prospecting for a nest site as early as March, examining a wide variety of holes in trees, walls, pipes and even flower pots, but they often decide on a nest box, where they build a moss-based nest, cosily lined with hair and feathers. As each egg is laid it is concealed among the feathers, until the clutch is complete. Then the female incubates alone for 14 days while the male brings her food to the nest, though later both parents feed the chicks. In normal years only one brood is reared.

All Tits have very similar habits and the Great Tit's only exception is that he tends to be more aggressive towards others. Although it cannot be denied that he has a fondness for spring buds and autumn fruit, it must also be said in his favour that the enormous amount of injurious insects eaten by his kind easily counterbalance the damage done.

Blue Tit

Parus caeruleus

The most familiar bird, of a familiar family of birds is the **Blue Tit,** one of the best loved birds that frequents garden bird tables throughout autumn and winter and even into spring, where they delight us with their bright, colourful plumage and acrobatic agility.

Almost cheeky in their attitude towards man, they are with us all the year round, with winter being the time when they almost come indoors if the nut feeder has been neglected, and to remind us if we haven't already done so in the autumn when it should be done) to remove the old material from the nest box in readiness for the new season.

Winter is also the time when Blue Tits are seen at their best, their plump little bodies having an azure blue cap, wings and tail, with a yellowish-green mantle and yellow underparts, and a white face with a dark blue stripe passing through the eye.

Natural holes in trees are favourite nest sites of the Blue Tit, but nest boxes are readily accepted, many thousands of chicks benefiting from these convenient and cosy homes each season. In fact, the Blue Tit population in mixed woodland can be greatly increased simply by erecting and maintaining standard type nest boxes.

In a small 13 acre wood in which the outer trees are mainly beech and oak, along with birch, rowan, ash and a few conifers, the installation of 24 nest boxes has proved most successful over the past few years. A visit to the wood in the early spring of 1990 found it sparsely inhabited by Wrens, Tree Creepers, Blackbirds and a few Finches, but by mid-May a transformation had taken place, as Blue Tits had occupied nine nest boxes which contained a total of 76 eggs.

By 22 May the eggs had hatched, the chicks being fed with a constant supply of nutritious caterpillars caught by the parents amid the succulent leaves of the oak trees, and by 9 June, hard-worked, scruffy little pairs of Blue Tits tended their families in the thick foliage of these food bearing trees. A pair of Great Tits and six pairs of Pied Flycatchers also benefited from the provision of the nest boxes, but we birdwatchers benefit even more by being able to observe these entertaining birds, constantly flitting among the branches at their nest sites as they collect caterpillars and flying insects to feed their young.

Following the autumnal harvest of fruit, berries and insects, the cold, bleak, bare trees and dropping temperatures find the Blue Tits moving closer to human habitation – where thousands will be helped to survive the winter months by those who delight in their presence – people like you and me.

BLUE TIT

Comparative size Smaller than Great Tit.
Status Resident.
Habitat Woodland, parklands, gardens.
Nest Hole in tree, nest box etc, moss, hair, feathers.
Eggs White, faint reddish spots, clutch 7-12.
Food Insects, caterpillars, buds, nuts.

The most common member of the tit family, the little Blue Tit is a favourite, regular visitor to feeding tables.

Coal Tit

Parus ater

A bird one would not normally associate with benefiting from afforestation is the **Coal Tit,** as one tends to think of the Tit family as preferring to inhabit deciduous woodlands, with even the Crested Tit of the Caledonian Pine Forests spending its life in a more open environment.

The Coal Tit, however, is well suited to its life among the firs where, by using its slightly longer and thinner beak than that of its close cousin the Blue Tit, it probes and among conifer needles and cones and into cracks in the bark of trees, to feed on insects, many of which are detrimental to the forest. Thus, it finds itself often in the company of Goldcrests.

The Coal Tit, at 11cm, is the smallest member of the Tit family. With greyish-green upperparts, dull-yellow underparts and it can be identified without question by the large white patch on the nape of its neck, which contrasts strongly with the black head. In addition, two faint wing bars help to distinguish it from the Willow Tit.

Because of the availability of insect life deep within the forest, even in winter Coal Tits are not as regular visitors to gardens as either the Blue or Great Tits, but once a Coal Tit has discovered the advantage of such a place it will certainly call on a regular basis.

Small holes in the ground or in walls are the favourite nest sites of the Coal Tit, and as they will readily accept a nest box foresters erect various types, some at ground level in an attempt to increase the forest population. On examining a nest box occupied by Coal Tits, one finds a very similar type of nest to that of the Blue Tit: a mossy base with hair, wool and feather lining, and on average one or two more eggs per clutch, ten or eleven not being unusual.

The incubation of the eggs is undertaken

COAL TIT
Comparative size Slightly smaller than Blue Tit. **Status** Resident. **Habitat** Mainly coniferous woodland. **Nest** In hole in ground/tree, nest box, moss, hair. **Eggs** White, pale brown markings, clutch 6-12. **Food** Insects, other tiny invertebrates, nuts, seeds.

---

mainly by the hen while she is fed by her mate, and as the chicks are in the nest for almost three weeks the parents work unceasingly in their constant quest for food, in the shape of insects and caterpillars.

When food such as beech mast is in abundance, Coal Tits will often hide part of the surplus along the hedgerow bottom for future use. On one such occasion I watched a little Coal Tit busy itself collecting and hiding kernels among the vegetation of a steep bank by the roadside, closely followed by a Great Tit who seemed to delight in unearthing them almost as soon as they were secreted away, appearing not in the least to upset the Coal Tit.

Willow Tit

Parus montanus

Marsh Tit

Parus palustris

The **Willow Tit** and **Marsh Tit** are so alike that less than one hundred years ago they were thought to be one and the same bird. However, the Willow Tit is a well-established resident in south-west and central Scotland, whereas the Marsh Tit has only managed to cross the border into the south-east corner.

Both birds are greyish-brown on the upperparts with pale, brownish-pink underparts. Their caps are black, the faces whitish and a small black bib is worn by males and females alike. To add to the confusion, Willow Tits do not prefer willows and Marsh Tits are not too fond of marshes, so how do we tell the two birds apart? Usually this is difficult, even for experienced birdwatchers – although, for instance, the cap of the Willow Tit lacks the glossy sheen of that of the Marsh Tit, this is not a lot of help when the birds are seen individually.

The songs, however, are more helpful, with the Marsh Tit calling 'pitchu-pitchu' while the Willow Tit calls 'tsi-tsi-tsi'. The most helpful identification feature of all, though, and the surest way of telling the two species apart, is when the birds are nesting, for this is where the main difference lies.

The Marsh Tit nests in a natural hole in a tree, wall or bank, lining the nest with moss, wool, hair and down, and the eggs, which are laid in

April or May, are incubated by the female alone while the male brings her food. Later when the chicks hatch, both parents pick insects and caterpillars to feed the family.

Although both birds show a preference for deciduous woods, the breeding haunts of the Willow Tit are somewhat damper than those of the Marsh, for it is there that the soft, rotting stumps can be found into which the Willow Tit excavates, like a diminutive woodpecker to form a nest chamber. When the nesting cavity is complete, some fine grasses are mixed with woodchips to form a base for the nest, which is then lined with rabbit fur mixed with tinier woodchips. The eggs are laid in May and again incubation is by the female alone, followed by a similar course of events to those of the Marsh Tit as it completes the breeding cycle.

WILLOW TIT

Comparative size Similar to Blue Tit.
Status Resident.
Habitat Damp woodlands.
Nest Hole excavated in rotten stump, wood chips, fine grasses, fur.
Eggs White, spotted reddish-brown, clutch 6-8.
Food Insects, caterpillars, spiders, seeds, berries.

Willow Tits are curious little birds that excavate their nesting chamber in the soft wood of a rotting tree stump.

Crested Tit

Parus Cristatus

On the Continent the **Crested Tit** can be seen in parks and gardens, but in the British Isles its range is limited mainly to the old Caledonian Pine Forests of Abernethy, Rothiemurchus and the Findhorn Valley.

Apart from its head, the Crested Tit is a drab little bird, only ll.5cm in length and with a greyish-brown mantle, tail and wings, the latter without any wing bar, and light buff underparts. The cheeks are white, bordered with a black collar. There is a black line in the shape of a pointed ear running from behind the eye, and the spiky, black-and-white crest, from which the bird gets its name, distinguishes it from any other small bird.

In its movements and flight, the Crested Tit is similar to other members of the Tit family, but as it chooses to feed among the topmost branches of mature pines, it can appear scarcer than it really is. Being familiar with their distinctive, trilling call therefore, helps in locating the birds as they flit among the branches.

In April or early May the little female selects a hole in a decayed pine in which to build her nest, frequently having to remove a quantity of rotten wood before the chamber is big enough. She gets little help from her mate during this time, although he is quick to warn her of any impending danger.

The nest chamber is lined with moss, hair and wool, and the eggs are then incubated by the female alone. After this both parents feed the chicks on caterpillars and insects, picked from among the long pine needles with their fine-pointed beaks.

As most of the nest sites are in stumps on fairly open ground, the parents encourage the young to forsake the nest as soon as they are fledged and seek safety in the tall pines, in order to escape the ever-present threat of predation by red squirrels or pine martens, which are always on the look out for an easy meal.

CRESTED TIT
Comparative size Similar to Blue Tit.
Status Resident.
Habitat Pine forests.
Nest Hole in decayed pine.
Eggs White, band of reddish speckles, clutch 5-6.
Food Insects, caterpillars, pine seeds.

Scottish Woodlands

At one time Scotland was covered with thick forests of both deciduous and conifer trees. Fortunately, by modern standards, Scotland still contains woodlands both sizeable and diverse, from the ancient oak woods and mixed broad leaves of the south to the magnificent old Caledonian Pines of the north, where many interesting species of birds can be found.

The following list is a mere sample of such woodlands

Notable Scottish Woodlands

Name, Region	Species	Map Reference
The Hirsel, Border	Green Woodpecker, Garden Warbler, Blackcap etc.	NT825405
Glentrool, Dumfries & Galloway	Peregrine, Buzzard, Hen Harrier etc.	NX400790
Wood of Cree, Dumfries & Galloway	Sparrow Hawk, Buzzard, Woodcock, Wood Warbler, Tree Pipit, Redstart etc.	NX382708
Falls of Clyde Strathclyde	Green Woodpecker, Willow Tit, Great Spotted Woodpecker etc.	NX882415
Argyll Forest Park, Strathclyde	Great Spotted Woodpecker Crossbill, Redstart, Goldcrest etc.	NS143946
Black Wood of Rannoch, Tayside	Capercaillie, Crested Tit Crossbill, Tree Pipit etc.	NN600570
Loch Garten Woods, Highland	Capercaillie, Goldeneye, Crossbill, Crested Tit etc.	NH978184
Arundle Oakwoods, Highland	Wood Warbler, Tree Pipit, Redstart etc.	NM830635
Nairn Bar and Culbin Forest, Highland/ Grampian	Crossbill, Capercaillie, Long-eared Owl, Crested Tit, Sparrow Hawk, Buzzard etc.	NH901573

Long-tailed Tit

Aegithalos caudatus

Although related to the Tit family, the **Long-tailed Tit** is a distant cousin with differences in its anatomy, the most obvious being the 8cm long tail which is more than half the length of the bird itself.

At a distance the plumage appears entirely black and white, but on closer inspection you can see that the underparts and head are white, the latter having a broad black band above the eye; the mantle and wings are black; the shoulders and rump pinkish, and the long, black tail has white outer feathers.

Long-tailed Tits are seen at their best when they roam the countryside in autumn and winter in the company of other small birds, when hedgerows and tree-lined riverbanks find the parties flitting along a few metres at a time, systematically feeding, calling and constantly on the move. On finding yourself in the path of an oncoming party in such a place, simply stand still, and the birds will approach and pass by almost within touching distance. If the party consists of about 30 Long-tails plus a mixture of other Tits, Tree Creepers and Goldcrests, then you are in for a special treat as the birds pause, pick and flutter, totally unconcerned at being watched from such close proximity.

A more noticeable difference from other members of the Tit family is the Long-tailed Tit's nest, for unlike its relatives it shuns holes, preferring to build its nest in a more open situation.

The nest of the Long-tailed Tit is a marvellous structure, often built in protective sites such as gorse or blackthorn, but flowering currant bushes and young conifers are also favoured where the domed, egg-shaped construction is seldom more than two metres from the ground.

Moss, hair and even spiders' webs are skilfully woven into the oval-shaped, mossy ball, which is attached to the branches with an entrance hole on the side, near the top. The whole construction is covered with tiny pieces of lichen, making it extremely well camouflaged. The task of lining the nest with feathers then begins and, with as many as 2,000 being recorded from a single nest,

The Longtailed Tit is the only member of the tit family that does not nest in a hole, but chooses to build one of the most intricate nests found in the countryside.

one marvels at the little females' ability to lay up to a dozen eggs following such a mammoth building effort.

Because of the materials used and how they are put together, the nest is both cosy and stretchable, cosiness being required to keep the eggs or newly-hatched naked chicks warm, and elasticity to allow the nest to expand as the chicks grow.

Having photographed Long-tailed Tits at their nests on a number of occasions, I was intrigued on occasions to see both parents' tails decidedly bent at the tip. This was caused by the birds sleeping arrangments in the nest on cold April nights: the female would enter to brood the young closely followed by her mate who, on entering the nest, drew in his tail, folding it upwards, thereby 'closing the door', and one can only imagine the situation throughout the night as a dozen or so occupants shuffled around inside.

When the young leave the nest, this 'closeness' continues, for the family are often discovered roosting in some sheltered nook, huddled together for warmth.

The Tree Creepers' long toes and stiff tail features enable it to cling to tree bark as it probes for spiders and their eggs among the cracks.

LONG-TAILED TIT

Comparative size Longer than Blue Tit.
Status Resident.
Habitat Open woodlands, gorse scrub.
Nest Oval in shape, moss, lichens, feathers, entrance hole near top.
Eggs White, slightly speckled reddish, clutch 8-12.
Food Insects, spiders.

Tree Creeper
Certhia familiaris

Mixed woodland, preferably dotted with dead and dying trees, is the haunt of the **Tree Creeper**, for it is there that it finds food, shelter and nest sites, and even a mid-winter walk through such a place should provide sightings of these unique little birds.

The Tree Creeper is an inconspicuous little bird in its brown mantle, streaked with lighter and darker shades, and snowy-white underparts. It has a white eyestripe, buffish barring on the wings, and a brown tail which, along with the beak and feet, have peculiarities necessary for the lifestyle of the Tree Creeper. The feathers of the graduated tail are stiff and pointed, and when the bird is probing into deep cracks for food or chiselling into soft rotten wood to form a sleeping place, the tail acts as a support. The beak is long, slender and downcurved, ideal for probing and pecking into cracks while searching for insects and their larvae. The legs are short but the toes

---

TREE CREEPER

Comparative size Larger than Blue Tit.
Status Resident.
Habitat Deciduous and coniferous woodland.
Nest In crevice or behind loose bark, twigs, stalks, lined-feathers.
Eggs White, reddish specks, clutch 5-6.
Food Insects, larvae, spiders, eggs.

are long, an ideal combination for a bird that spends so much of its life clinging to the bark of trees.

The Tree Creeper looks more like a mouse than a bird as it creeps up the tree trunks and along the branches, ascending in a spiralling manner playing a 'now-you-see-me, now-you-don't' game with the watcher. However, by remaining quite still at this point you could be pleasantly surprised by the Tree Creeper landing at the base of a tree only a few metres away and ascending once more in typical fashion, as this little fellow is extremely confiding towards man. Because of their unobtrusive habits Tree Creepers often go unnoticed, but if you discover a pair in the course of constructing their nest or feeding chicks, the continual flights back and forth are a joy to watch.

The nest is usually built behind a loose piece of bark or in a crevice in an old tree, the latter being the more secure as on occasion a nest behind bark comes to grief simply through the birds' over-enthusiasm while building. Twig after twig and stalk after stalk are added to the base of the nest, the continual adjustment of the material pushing the bark further from the trunk until finally the mass of twigs, stalks, moss and feathers bursts forth, spilling out into the open.

If such a tragedy occurs before egg-laying the pair will immediately set about building at another site, and even if a clutch of eggs is lost the birds could quite well nest again as they do, on occasion, raise two broods in a season. In the more secure nests, the chicks are fed by both parents for about a fortnight before they leave to spend their lives among the woodland trees.

In winter Tree Creepers can be seen in the company of other small birds, moving about in small flocks in their continual search for food. In order to conserve body heat through the long winter nights, Tree Creepers roost in crevices or in small hollows which they excavate themselves, either in the soft bark of wellingtonia trees or in the spongey wood of some decaying trunk.

Wren

Troglodytes troglodytes

Severe winters take a terrible toll of the **Wren** population, but this tiny bird only – 9.5cm from the point of its beak to the tip of its tail – is so resilient that within only two to three years numbers recover to their previous level.

Over the past 25 years, the Wrens' instinct for survival during the winter has taken a new twist in the shape of the 'communal roost', where literally dozens of these tiny birds converge on some cavity and huddle together for warmth. 'Cock' nests (see below) are an obvious choice, with nest boxes even more so – 60 Wrens have been recorded entering one box, but almost 100 in a single roost appears to be the record.

Everyone knows this tiny, brown bird, with its round body and stumpy, cocked tail, predominantly coloured in rusty brown, with darker barring on the wings and tail and buffish underparts. Many are surprised, however, to discover on a quiet woodland stroll, that this tiny ball of feathers is capable of such volume in its song, as even from some distance away the song of the Wren always appears to come from a much more sizeable bird.

When Wrens are in their breeding territory the male is indeed an industrious little chap, for not only does he frequently sing from some songpost to warn other cocks not to venture too close, but he also sets about nest building.

Using such materials as moss, twigs and bracken, the domed nest is built on the underside of a fallen tree root, in a thick hedge, in a bushy tree growth or any other place which will accommodate the structure with its neat little side entrance. The male not only builds one such nest, he builds several, escorting his mate from one to another until she finally accepts one, promptly lining it with feathers. She then lays her eggs and incubates them for 14 days, and for a further two weeks she and her mate bring caterpillars and insects to the nest to feed the chicks. Later she will select another of the 'cock' nests, line it with feathers, and rear another brood.

Standing by the riverbank late in the afternoon

WREN

Comparative size Smaller than Blue Tit.
Status Resident.
Habitat Woodlands, thickets, gardens, open ground with shrubs.
Nest In upturned tree root, crevice, thick growth, bracken, leaves, moss, feathers.
Eggs White, reddish-brown spots, clutch 4-8.
Food Mainly insects, caterpillars.

Wrens, like many other small birds coincide the rearing of their young with the time of year when caterpillars are abundant.

of an autumn day, the last few turns of a fishing reel with the ratchet engaged never fails to attract Wrens which approach very close, flitting from reed stalk to willow twig as they try to locate this mechanical sound which imitates their alarm call so realistically.

The Dipper

Cinclus cinclus

The **Dipper** is a plump, brownish-black and white bird, Wren-shaped, but of course much larger – in fact it is 18cm in length. It has dark-brown plumage above and on its sides and belly, with a reddish-brown band separating the contrasting dark underparts from the pure white chest and throat. The tail is short and the bill and powerful legs and feet are dark brown. The sexes are similar in colouring.

Dippers are resident throughout Scotland and

are found on all our fast-flowing hill burns and major rivers. They can swim on or under the surface of the water, and it is here that the powerful legs and feet come into use as this unique little bird walks upstream in the fast-flowing current, its body held at such an angle as to deflect the rushing water as it searches for the caddis larvae or other aquatic life that form its diet. Minnows and other small fish are also taken, and when in pursuit of this prey Dippers use their wings to assist in propelling them under the surface.

Perched on a stone in mid-stream, it bobs and dips in unison with the ripples – hence its name – and from such a vantage point it can either dive or walk into the stream. Another method of entering the water is for the bird to fly up or downstream and simply dive in, in a sort of bellyflop. Once submerged another asset can be brought into use, namely the nictitating membrane. This third eyelid, which is transparent, springs from the inner border of the eye and is capable of being drawn across the eyeball. All birds possess this peculiarity – extremely useful for protecting the eyes in flight against the pressure of air and, as an extra, in

the case of the Dipper it can be used to wipe the eyes clear after being submerged.

To the unaccustomed observer the Dipper is sometimes difficult to spot as it stands on a stone by the riverbank singing its warbling song, which always appears to be in tune with the tumbling water, and many an angler pauses between casts as he ponders whether or not that wee white disc under that overhang is a Dipper, or just some piece of jetsam left high and dry from a previous spate?

Shortly after the New Year Dippers become extremely territory conscious, and many squabbles can be witnessed by the waterside as pairs seek nest sites. When the site has been chosen, usually by the beginning of March, nest building begins and the first pure white egg is usually laid by the middle of the month.

Some nests, such as those built on a rocky ledge or in some crevice under a bridge, are traditional, as these sites are permanent and are used annually, with the material varying in quantity according to where the nest is situated. If, for instance, a stone slightly larger than a man's clenched fist falls from the underside of a bridge, forming a small cave, then this 'cave'

The constant companions of the angler on Scottish burns and rivers. Dippers have many antics which they delight in performing, both by and in the water.

could be occupied by a pair of Dippers using only a few dead leaves for the lining and a little moss for the entrance. On the other h and, another type of nest, commonly found under bridges built on cross-supports, resembles a small haystack, fashioned mainly from moss and again lined with dead leaves, and this type can be approximately 22cm high and 30cm wide.

The more natural Dipper nests are those which are built among the tangle of roots by the riverbank, and the most difficlt to locate are those which are built on a rocky ledge behind a

---

DIPPER

Comparative size Smaller than Starling.
Status Resident.
Habitat Swift flowing streams.
Nest Domed, built with mosses and grass.
Eggs White, clutch 3-6.
Food Crustaceans, aquatic insects, minnows.

tumbling waterfall, the birds at times having to pass back and forth through the cascading water to reach their nest and young.

When the clutch is complete it usually contains four or five eggs, with the hen incubating most of the time for a period of about 16 days. Then both parents feed the young for almost three weeks, and it is not unusual for the pair to rear two broods in a season.

After the nesting season, as the males progress through the moult they become almost silent and are apt to hide away in nooks and sheltered places, but by mid-autumn they appear in their new glory and from a boulder amid the rushing water, sing both loud and clear, only stopping short when suddenly disturbed, perhaps by a salmon leaping only a few feet away.

The bulky nest of the Mistle Thrush is often placed in a prominent position.

Song Thrush
Turdus philomelos

Mistle Thrush
Turdus viscivorus

The **Song Thrush** is one of our best known songsters, a familiar and common bird, 23cm in length. The upper parts are olive-brown and the creamy-white underparts are tinged with pale orange on the underwing, while the breast is covered in dark brown spots. The throat is also slightly tinged with orange and the sexes are similar in colouring.

As its name suggests, the Song Thrush is one of our finest songsters as is most helpful to the novice student of birdsong, as it repeats each series of notes three or four times until it has

completed its repertoire, then starts again from the beginning.

The habitat of the Song Thrush is any wooded area, and it has a decided liking for wild hedgerows, thickets and copses. Urban as well as suburban gardens also attract the Song Thrush and the nest is placed in a bush, tree, wall ivy or occasionally on the ground, though this is quite rare.

One of the most unusual Song Thrush nests I have recorded was one which I located in a gorse bush on rough ground by a river. Unlike the nest of the Blackbird; which is lined with fine grasses, the Song Thrush nest lining is a smooth coating of mud, horse dung and tiny pieces of wood, in all a very substantial construction, lasting many months after the young have flown. For some reason or other this Song Thrush pair decided to take over the existing nest of a pair of Blackbirds which at the time contained three eggs – perhaps one or other of the Blackbird pair had fallen victim to a Sparrow Hawk. In any case, the Song Thrushes lined the nest while the Blackbird eggs were still contained in it and the end product was most peculiar: one Blackbird egg only just visible in the mud lining and one showing about 50 per cent, while the third had somehow managed to remain loose and was included in the clutch of four Song Thrush eggs. Unfortunately, I had no occasion to return to the nest, so the final outcome is a mystery.

Watch a Song Thrush on the ground, especially on a lawn or playing field, and you will note that it takes short runs or hops, pausing now and then as if to listen for the slightest movement of worm or insect. Berries are also taken, and the bird's fondness for snails is obvious when one comes across a Thrush's 'anvil', for the mass of broken shells indicates how many of these pests are cleared from an area by a solitary Song Thrush.

The Song Thrush is found throughout Scotland where it is sometimes referred to as the 'Mavis', and though there are numbers of migrant Song Thrushes which visit us from northern and eastern Europe in the autumn, winter finds it a scarce bird indeed. It would appear that our resident Thrushes join their Scandinavian cousins as they head further south for the winter with only the odd individual remaining.

The **Mistle Thrush** at 27cm is the largest member of the Thrush family. It is a greyer bird than the Song Thrush and the spots on its breasts are larger, darker and more prominent. The outer tail feathers have white tips and the underwing is also white, conspicuous when the bird is in flight.

Its local name of 'Stormcock' comes from the fact that unlike most species, which take shelter during the spring storms, the Mistle Thrush seems to delight in challenging the howl of the wind. The fiercer the storm the louder the Mistle Thrush sings, and always from a high vantage point such as the topmost bough of a tree as it sways back and forth in the gale. The bird's fondness for mistletoe berries is said to be the reason for its name and hawthorn and yew berries are also favoured. Worms and snails also form part of the diet.

During the breeding season the Mistle Thrush is widespread throughout the country and it is equally at home in deciduous or fir woods, city parks and suburban gardens. The nest is quite conspicuous to the experienced eye, being a bulky affair usually placed in the fork of a tree and constructed with moss, roots and grasses, lined with wool and feathers.

The eggs are usually laid in March, and when the young are in the nest another characteristic of the Mistle Thrush becomes obvious to anyone who strays too near, namely the aggressiveness of the parents, for they are pugnacious birds,

---

SONG THRUSH

Comparative size Slightly smaller than Blackbird.
Status Resident, most move south in winter.
Habitat Gardens, parks, woods, hedgerows.
Nest Cup-shaped, twigs, grasses, lined mud.
Eggs Blue with few black spots, clutch 4-5.
Food Snails, worms, invertebrates, insects, fruit.

MISTLE THRUSH

Comparative size Larger than Blackbird.
Status Resident.
Habitat Gardens, parks, woods.
Nest Cup-shaped, twigs, roots, mosses, usually in bush or tree.
Eggs Blue-green to creamy-brown, speckled with brownish and greenish blotches.
Food Fruit, berries, earthworms and other invertebrates.

driving off any intruder be it avian or human – they have been known to dive-bomb and even strike human intruders.

Although the Mistle Thrush is the largest of our resident Thrushes, it is not the most common, the Song Thrush and Blackbird being more numerous, and in winter they are outnumbered by visiting Fieldfares and Redwings.

In autumn and winter the Mistle Thrush is found roaming over moorlands and open hill country where it spends much of its time on the ground, ever on the alert for worms. In the Southern Uplands, solitary rowan trees planted near the doorways of derelict shepherd's cottages (to ward off evil spirits) in days long gone provide another food source, as well as nest sites. Though common in the south of Scotland the Mistle Thrush becomes scarcer north of the Clyde Valley.

Fieldfare
Turdus pilaris

Redwing
Turdus iliacus

In late September and October thousands of Fieldfares and Redwings arrive in Scotland from Scandinavia and Iceland, to take advantage of our more temperate climate and abundant food supply. As they share the same breeding range both birds generally arrive together, and can be seen for the next seven months in fields and hedgerows throughout the country, ever on the move in their endless quest for food.

FIELDFARE

Comparative size Slightly larger than Blackbird.
Status Mainly winter visitor: a few pairs breed in Scotland.
Habitat Woodlands, open fields, hedgerows, gardens.
Nest Woven cup of grasses and moss, strengthened with mud usually in tree-fork.
Eggs Bluish-green, marked with brownish-violet: clutch, 4-6.
Food Earthworms, snails, insects and their larvae, berries.

The **Fieldfare**, at 25.5cm, is the larger of the two, and being slightly smaller than a Mistle Thrush but much more colourful with its bluish-grey head and golden-brown mantle. The chestnut breast is spotted with black and the pale buff underparts are similarly spotted along each flank; the pale underwing contrasts with the dark tail, and the bluish-grey rump is conspicuous when the bird is in flight.

The **Redwing**, being only 21cm in length, is smaller than a Song Thrush which it closely resembles, having brown upperparts and a spotted breast, but a distinct white eye-stripe and deeper red underwing and flanks identify the Redwing without doubt.

During their stay here both birds frequent farmland, woodland and open pastures where berries, earthworms, slugs, insects and their larvae are their choice of food, plus windfall apples when available.

When flocks are seen in flight, the characteristic 'chuck-chuck' call of the Fieldfare is usually interspersed with a high-pitched 'tseep-tseep', call indicating the presence of the Redwing, and simply from seeing their silhouettes the two birds can be distinguished one from the other by their size. On the ground, the larger Fieldfare adopts a more upright stance than the smaller Redwing as it searches among the grass stalks for worms and insects.

Redwings have bred in the northern half of Scotland for over 60 years with their numbers at a peak during the 1960s, but since then it is doubtful if more than 100 pairs have nested in any one year. The Fieldfare breeds in much smaller numbers, with possibly only a dozen or so pairs nesting annually.

When Scottish winters find the temperature dropping below freezing for more than a few consecutive days, those Fieldfares and Redwings

---

REDWING

Comparative size Smaller than Blackbird.
Status Mainly winter visitor: a few pairs breed in Scotland.
Habitat Birch and Alder Woods in summer: farmland and hedgerow in winter.
Nest Cup of grasses and moss: low in tree or on ground.
Eggs Bluish-green, finely marked with reddish-brown: clutch, 5-6.
Food Earthworms, snails, insects berries.

The prominent pale-coloured, eye-stripe and reddish-coloured flanks distinguish the Redwing from the Song Thrush.

from further north that choose to remain in Scotland find conditions increasingly difficult as the ground freezes over, denying the birds their main food source. It is then that hawthorn and other types of berries are devoured in great quantities and, once they have gone, if the ground is still frozen the more robust Fieldfares peck at such unusual fare as turnip fodder for sustenance, while the smaller Redwings, not equipped to deal with such items, succumb to the cold and many perish as a result.

In April, large numbers of Fieldfares pass through Scotland from the south as they head northwards to their breeding territories. The Redwings have a similar movement, with the Scandinavian birds following the east coast while the Icelandic population favour the west.

Blackbird
Turdus merula

The familiar **Blackbird** is our most numerous garden songbird, the constant companion of the gardener at all times of year, and in spring the first sign of gardening activity finds a Blackbird landing close by with characteristic tail-cocking stance, peering intently for the slightest sign of invertebrate movement among the overturned soil.

At other times we are aware of the Blackbird's presence, even if it cannot be seen, from the sound of dead leaves being overturned under trees or bushes as the Blackbird busily searches for worms, insects and small snails. So confident towards man has the Blackbird become over the years that it has overtaken the Robin in its choice of nest sites in man-made structures, with garages, sheds and outhouses frequently occupied by a resident pair.

The Blackbird requires little by way of description. 25cm from the tip of his bill to the tip of his tail, the cock's all-black plumage is only broken by an orange-yellow bill and a yellow rim round its eyes. Sometimes the hen does cause a little confusion, having a browner appearance with a slightly spotted, pale coloured breast. She is much darker than the Song Thrush, the bird with which she is most likely to be confused, but when both birds are seen together on the lawn or playing fields there is no problem in distinguishing between the two.

Conifers, rhododendrons and all types of hedges are used as nest sites. Some nests can be found to contain eggs early in the year, but in usual conditions March is the month when most pairs can be found in their territory, and throughout the spring and early summer the cock delights us with his song, while his mate incubates eggs or broods young.

In birds with totally black plumage, such as Blackbirds and Jackdaws, the black colouring is maintained by a natural pigment in the feathers, the slightest deficiency resulting in some of the feathers turning white. Less of this pigment is required to maintain the colouring of lighter-coloured birds such as Thrushes, and the chance of seeing a partially white Song Thrush is therefore much less than that of finding a pied Blackbird. In fact, though contradiction in terms it may be, 'white Blackbirds' do occur.

Some years ago I was asked if I would like to photograph a pied cock Blackbird, which was feeding young in a nest built in a garden hedge. The situation was ideal, both cock and hen alighting on the back of a garden seat before entering the hedge to feed the nestlings – or so I was informed. I set up the camera and waited, only to find that a perfectly normal coloured cock Blackbird appeared and fed the young, closely followed by his mate. I was just about to tell my informant in no uncertain terms what I thought of him, when a movement on the bungalow roof caught my eye, and seconds later I had taken a marvellous shot of a pied Blackbird with a beakful of worms on the back of the garden seat.

It was a strange way to discover that two cocks and one hen were feeding young in the same nest, but nature is a wonderful thing and obviously one or other of the cocks had recently lost his brood – and perhaps even his mate – to some predator, such as a marauding cat but, still having the urge to feed young, on hearing the nestlings beg for food he decided to help his neighbour.

Ring Ouzel

Turdus torquatus

Unlike the Blackbird, the **Ring Ouzel,** or 'Mountain Blackbird', does not like to share its habitat with man and chooses to inhabit the wildest rocky hills and heather-covered slopes where they can be found from mid-March to September, following their trans-continental journey from Africa.

The sooty black plumage of the male Ring Ouzel has a 'scaly' effect on the mantle and underparts, and the white crescent on his breast is more noticeable than that of the female, which tends to be off-white. Females are also much browner in appearance than their mates, and the feathers on their mantles and underparts have paler edges, making the 'scaly' effect on their plumage more pronounced. Both birds, however, have distinctive greyish wings, which are a good field characteristic.

The Ring Ouzel resembles the Blackbird in much of its behaviour and habits, 'cocking' its tail on landing and poking about in the vegetation for insects and worms which, when

---

BLACKBIRD

Comparative size Larger than Starling.
Status Resident.
Habitat Gardens, parks, woodlands.
Nest Cup-shaped, grasses, leaves, fibres.
Eggs Blue-green, red-brown speckles, clutch 3-6.
Food Earthworms, insects, kitchen scraps, berries.

RING OUZEL

Comparative size Slightly smaller than Blackbird.
Status Summer resident.
Habitat Remote mountain and moorland.
Nest Among heather or rocky ledge, grasses, roots.
Eggs Blue-green, dark brown markings, clutch 4.
Food Insects, worms.

Occasionally Ring Ouzels will nest where a measure of concealment is exchanged for a measure of inaccessability.

found, are carried back to the nest in a direct flight, less undulating than that of the Blackbird.

Nests are usually well concealed among clumps of mountain heather or in rocky linns, where a measure of concealment is exchanged for a measure of inaccessibility, as some nests are located on rocky ledges in quite open situations.

As two broods are normally reared in a season, nests with eggs or young can be found from mid-April to July, and in August once again the family parties start moving south.

Wheatear

Oenanthe oenanthe

When the Ravens are in full display and the Peregrines are in their territories, the first of our summer residents arrive to share the rocky and heathery terrain with these impressive residents.

Almost 'wing to wing' in company with Ring Ouzels, the **Wheatears** move steadily up the valleys of the Southern Uplands to their breeding territories, being leap-frogged by others heading further north to populate every region in Scotland for the duration of the summer.

The first indication that Wheatears have arrived in the area is the spotting of a conspicuous white rump on a bird slightly larger than a Robin, that drops behind a drystone dyke, flies a short distance and perches on the ground with an upright stance, allowing you to note the grey upperparts and black patches on the face, and the black wings. The underparts shade from buff to off-white, and the most noticeable differences between the sexes is that the female lacks the black face patches and is more brownish in appearance.

WHEATEAR	
Comparative size Larger than Robin.	
Status Summer resident.	
Habitat Open hilly country.	
Nest In hole, grasses, moss, lined hair, wool.	
Eggs Pale blue, clutch 5-7.	
Food Insects, spiders, small snails, berries.	

Wheatears are sprightly, restless birds, constantly on the move with a flitting flight from stone to stone or tussock to tussock, keeping near the ground and settling only for a moment before moving on.

The usual nesting sites are located in high uncultivated land, where the nest is built in a hole at the base of a dyke, under a boulder or even in an old rabbit hole. The nest, usually situated about 30cm from the entrance, is built by both birds using grasses and moss, and then lined with wool and hair. The eggs are incubated by the female for about 14 days and, when hatched, the young are fed by both parents for the next two weeks, both before they leave the nest and for a short time afterwards, but they are soon able to take care of themselves.

In mid-August the Wheatears begin their longish journey south, spending the winter months with other species of Wheatears south of the Sahara Desert.

Redstart
Phoenicurus phoenicurus

Mixed woodland, preferably including some older, decaying trees, is the favoured summer quarters of the **Redstart**, one of our most attractive summer residents, and in April it arrives to add its presence and song to the ever-growing number of species that choose to inhabit the diverse Scottish countryside throughout the summer months.

The male Redstart is a brilliant little bird with his blue-grey head and mantle, black throat and cheeks and white forehead. His underparts, from his breast to the tip of his tail, are bright orange-red, and as his name is said to come from 'red-

One of the most colourful summer residents, the Redstart prefers old deciduous woodland with open areas of short vegetation.

tail', we are left in no doubt as to the reason why. The female, on the other hand, is a drab, brown little bird, but she also sports a red tail which she uses to advantage during the spring courtship display, when both she and her mate chase each other from branch to branch, constantly displaying and flirting their colourful tails.

The Redstart's similarity to the Robin is noticeable in flight, and when perched on some vantage point it has the same dipping action of the body.

Nest sites of the Redstart are holes of various kinds in walls, old buildings and trees, with nest boxes also readily accepted. When the site has been chosen nest building is undertaken by the female, the only contribution from her mate being that he stops singing, possibly to avoid drawing attention to his industrious little mate as she constantly flits back and forth with nest material. Moss, grass, fibres and hair are the materials she uses, and a day or so after it is completed she lays her eggs, incubating them alone for 14 days. For the first few days after hatching she broods the naked young while the male brings food, then both parents feed the chicks which remain in the nest until they are about 15 days old.

Redstarts prefer woodland where the upper branches of the trees are open and the undergrowth is interspersed with patches of open ground – hence they are often found frequenting large gardens.

During the 1960s and early 1970s the Redstart population was drastically reduced due to the prolonged drought in their wintering quarters in the Sahel Zone of Central Africa, but by 1975 numbers were once again on the increase and by the mid-1980s Redstart numbers were back to their pre-drought level.

REDSTART

Comparative size Similar to Robin.
Status Summer resident.
Habitat Open woodland, parks, gardens.
Nest In hole, moss, fibres, hair.
Eggs Pale blue, clutch 5-7.
Food Insects.

Whinchat
Saxicola rubetra

Although much of the habitat previously populated by **Whinchats** has now been planted with conifers, unlike most other moorland nesting birds that have no alternative the little Whinchat, not being so dependent on open country, can be found in a variety of other places.

Roadside verges by mixed farmland and railway cuttings are situations that afford nesting cover and food for these charming little summer residents, that please the birdwatcher by always being easily seen when perched on telegraph wires or other prominent places, when you are in their territory.

The male is streaked with shades of brown on his upperparts with white patches on the wings, and is pale buff on the underparts with white

A summer resident, the Whinchat is more plentiful than its close cousin the Stonechat, a bird that braves our cold winters – often with fatal results.

sides on the base of the tail. His black cheeks are bordered by a prominent white eyestripe above and a white mark below. The female is paler and shows less white in her plumage.

It is usually late April or early May before Whinchats arrive, occasionally being seen in small migratory parties before pairing and selecting their territories. Once the territory has been chosen, the nest, which is built mainly by the female from grasses and moss lined with finer grasses and hair, is located on the ground in a grassy tussock or at the base of a clump of bracken stalks. The eggs are incubated by the female alone for about 13 days, after which both parents feed the chicks for a similar period.

As two broods may be reared in a season, recently-fledged young can be seen being tended by their parents as late as August, and when you come in close proximity to a nest containing chicks the parents appear as if from nowhere, flitting from one vantage point to another uttering their scolding 'tuc-tuc' alarm notes in an attempt to lead you away from the nest.

Whinchats are fairly widespread throughout Scotland, though their actual breeding haunts are rather patchy, some areas finding them plentiful while in others they are scarce.

WHINCHAT

Comparative size Smaller than Robin.
Status Summer resident.
Habitat Scrub and grassland.
Nest Cup-shaped, on ground, grasses, moss, lined hair.
Eggs Blue-green, faintly marked, clutch 4-6.
Food Insects.

Stonechat

Saxicola torquata

Unlike the Whinchat, the **Stonechat** is resident with us throughout the year, consequently, as these birds feed on insects, harsh winters drastically reduce their numbers. Another major factor governing the Stonechat population is loss of habitat, many inland areas that previously supported breeding pairs now being deserted due to afforestation and modern farming methods. Most of the Scottish population is therefore found in coastal regions, where scrubby gorse provides the ideal habitat.

Another handsome little bird, the male Stonechat has a black head and dark wings and tail, a brown-and-black mottled mantle and chestnut underparts. White patches on the sides of his neck and wings complete his summer dress, but in winter he closely resembles the female, having a brown head and less in the way of white patches.

The Stonechat has a liking for gorse bushes, and when you are close to a nest containing an incubating female the male will perch on one of the topmost twigs, constantly bobbing up and down while flicking his tail and uttering the curious 'chac-chac' alarm call from which he gets his name, the sound resembling two stones being struck together.

The nest is built in a well concealed nook, on or near the ground at the foot of a gorse or other bush, fashioned from moss and grasses and lined with hair and feathers.

Stonechats rear at least two broods in a season, and sometimes three – nature's way of helping the population to recover following a severe winter. The first clutch is laid in April and incubated by the female alone for about 14 days, the young leaving the nest two or three days before they can fly.

They are tended mainly by the male at this time while the female sets about building a new nest, then after mating, the second clutch is laid and again incubated by the female with both parents feeding the young after hatching.

STONECHAT

Comparative size Slightly smaller than Robin.
Status Resident.
Habitat Scrub with open ground.
Nest Cup-shaped, on ground, grasses, moss.
Eggs Greenish-blue, speckled reddish-brown, clutch 5-6.
Food Insects, other invertebrates.

Robin

Erithacus rubecula

Thanks to Christmas cards and Advent calendars, the **Robin** is as well known to children as Santa Claus and will remain one of the most familiar and best-loved birds throughout their lives.

The little olive-brown bird with the red breast

Although closely associated with gardens in winter time, Robins move out into open woodlands and scrubby areas for the breeding season.

and face was also the Robin with which I was familiar as a boy, not thinking for a moment that a Robin could be any other colour, until one day while walking along a railway embankment birdnesting, I spied a peculiar little bird perched among the branches of a whin bush.

I approached the bush very carefully, studying the Robin-shaped bird with the brown-mottled breast and spotted mantle, mentally flicking over the pages of my well-studied book on British Birds, yet failing to put a name to this stanger. Even though I stood stock still the bird became agitated and fluttered into a thicker bush a few metres further on so, allowing a short time for it to settle, I followed. Pacing the railway sleepers until I was level with the bush, I sat down on the line and looked upwards into it, only to see an adult Robin feeding its spotted youngster.

It is July or August before the youngsters moult this juvenile plumage, adopting the familiar colouring of their parents and taking up their own territories. As well known as the Robin is, its nest sites are equally well known around human habitation, and over the years the more regular nests in old kettles and various other receptacles in sheds and garages have been supplemented by more macabre sites, such as in a human skull and on a dead cat!

For many years the Robin has, as far as nest sites go, been the bird most closely associated with man. Recently, however, and possibly due to prowling cats, the situation has changed with the Blackbird taking over sheds and outhouses while the Robin, following the example of his cousins on the Continent, chooses to move into the cover of woodland during the nesting season. Here a suitable hole in a tree or bank is the favourite site, where the bulky nest of leaves, grass, moss and hair is built.

ROBIN

Comparative size Sparrow size.
Status Resident.
Habitat Gardens, parks, woodlands.
Nest Built in hollow, leaves, moss, hair.
Eggs White, spotted with reddish, clutch 4-5.
Food Insects, worms, caterpillars, seeds.

The eggs are laid in March and incubated by both parents for about a fortnight. Then both parents rear the chicks, which later become the responsibility of the male while the female lays her second clutch, often producing a third, the rearing of which can take her well into June.

During July and August, 'Cock Robin' becomes silent, but in September when he returns to his garden territory, he announces his presence with a song – somewhat more melancholy than his more cheerful spring version – and will continue singing this quieter rendering until mating instincts are aroused in January. During this time both cocks and hens claim their own winter territories, and will even fight furiously for possession, while in the garden birds of other species also come under attack from these pugnacious little birds.

As conspicuous as he is in the open, the Robin is sometimes difficult to observe in the failing light. When he perches in a tree or bush singing his wistful little song – quite slowly, as if listening for another bird to reply – he is usually left to 'put out the light' as the other songsters have already gone to roost.

The extreme north is the only region in Scotland where the Robin is not a common bird.

Sedge Warbler
Acrocephalus Schoenobaenus

Eight species of Warbler regularly breed in Scotland, each with its own characteristics, song and habits which help the birdwatcher distinguish any one from the others.

Two have stripes in their plumage and the other six are plain coloured, three of which are 'brownish' and three 'greenish', so let's introduce them in that order.

The first of our striped friends is the **Sedge**

SEDGE WARBLER

Comparative size Slightly smaller than Great Tit.
Status Summer resident.
Habitat Dense vegetation in damp areas.
Nest Cup shaped, grasses, lined down.
Eggs Stone-coloured with dense, brown spots, clutch 5-6.
Food Insects, small invertebrates.

Warbler, known to most flyfishers as the little bird which frequents the tall reeds and willows by the river's edge, singing his 'chittery' song while constantly moving among the vegetation, occasionally pausing on a topmost point at the edge of his territory as if to allow positive identification.

The Sedge Warbler is dressed in warm brown, with darker streaks on its crown and mantle, cream-coloured underparts, an orange-brown rump and a prominent, buff eyestripe, which is a good field characteristic.

Ponds with a reedy fringe, damp, densely vegetated areas, and patches of rosebay willowherb also provide nesting habitat for the Sedge Warblers, which appear in late April, select territories and build their nests among the stalks, usually about half a metre from the ground, using moss, grass and reeds, and lining it cosily with hair and feathers. Although the male accompanies the female during nest building, appearing to take much interest, he contributes nothing in the way of physical effort, leaving the entire construction to his mate.

The eggs are laid in May and the hatching which takes about 14 days, is undertaken mainly by the female, although her mate 'lends a beak' to help feed the chicks inbetween bursts of song, which can sometimes be heard well after dark.

Grasshopper Warbler
Locustella naevia

The second of our little striped warblers, which at 13cm is exactly the same size as the Sedge Warbler and which also appears in late April, is the **Grasshopper Warbler,** one of the birds that is more often identified by sound than by sight.

When seen, the Grasshopper Warbler is a drab-looking little bird in its brown, streaked upperparts and pale brown underparts, and the fact that it has a graduated tail is of little or no consequence in identification, as this Warbler is the most secretive of the entire family, moving mouse-like through the dense vegetation, seldom in view for more than a second. However, what it lacks in assisting the birdwatcher to identify it by sight the Grasshopper Warbler more than makes up for in its song, a curious 'reeling' sound, easily heard and long-lasting, allowing for positive identification. The sound is almost mechanical, like the slow, continuous winding of a fishing reel, rising and falling in pitch as the bird turns its head from side to side. From late April to July the song can be heard, often for prolonged periods with short pauses, most frequently at dawn or dusk, but often into the night.

The nest is concealed amongst low, dense vegetation and is built with leaves, grasses, moss and hair. It is cup-shaped and is constructed by both male and female, the eggs being laid in late May or June.

Rough ground is the typical habitat that attracts Grasshopper Warblers, and it was in just such an area, which had been ploughed and planted by forestry workers, that my one and only close encounter with the bird occurred some years ago.

On a June evening, a friend and myself decided to attempt to find the nest of a pair of Grasshopper Warblers which had their territory among the young trees and, as the male was in full song as we approached, I imagined that it would be a straightforward task. The area was conveniently divided into sections by drainage ditches, so we set about searching systematically, tapping the undergrowth with a light stick as the male 'reeled' continuously, first ten metres to the left, then seven metres to the right and so on, for fully an hour.

At the end of this time, stumbling constantly among and torn by dense brambles, tormented by midges, almost driven daft by the male's phantom-like behaviour and soaked with mud and perspiration, I sat down on the edge of a drain – only to be joined by a little, brown-streaked bird that clung to a bramble stalk less than two metres away as it swayed from side to side with open beak, 'trilling' non-stop and leaning forward to display its wedge-shaped tail.

Needless to say, we failed to locate a nest but for fully 60 seconds I was priviliged to observe the antics of a Grasshopper Warbler that was quite unaware of my presence.

Whitethroat

Sylvia communis

The first of our Warblers that does not have streaked plumage is the **Whitethroat,** and sadly it is now somewhat scarce when only 20 years ago it was one of the most plentiful of Warblers, with practically every roadside patch of brambles providing a nest site for a pair.

Like the Redstart and Yellow Wagtail, the Whitethroat winters south of the Sahara, in the Sahel Zone. All three species were reduced in numbers by almost 75 per centfollowing the severe drought of the late 1960s and, whereas the Redstart and Yellow Wagtail numbers are almost back to their previous levels, the Whitethroat has only made around a 50 per cent recovery.

The upperparts of the male Whitethroat are greyish-brown, the grey being more pronounced on the crown and tail coverts. The wings are rufous, the outer tail feathers are white, and the underparts are light-buff, tinged with pink on the breast and flanks. The female is browner and has no pink tinge on the breast but, like her mate, she has a distinct white throat, a field characteristic that distinguishes them from all our other warblers.

Whitethroats move restlessly through the hedgerow bottoms and dense undergrowth, a habit that has earned them the name 'Nettlecreeper', only appearing for a moment as they dart after a passing insect, which on one occasion I saw to be a white butterfly, allowing me to follow the bird's progress through the undergrowth which, without the white 'signal-flag', would have been much more difficult.

The nest of the Whitethroat is built by both male and female amongst a tangle of brambles,

---

GRASSHOPPER WARBLER

Comparative size Smaller than Great Tit
Status Summer resident.
Habitat Rough moorland, young plantations
Nest Cup shaped, lined with grass and leaves in grass tussock.
Eggs White with pinkish spots, clutch 4-7.
Food Insects.

WHITETHROAT

Comparative size Similar to Great Tit.
Status Summer resident.
Habitat Scrub, hedgerows.
Nest Cup of grasses, lined with hair.
Eggs Pale olive, spotted with grey, clutch 4-6.
Food Mainly insects.

The Whitethroat is one of our summer residing Warblers which chooses to nest in dense undergrowth.

in a thick hedge bottom or other dense vegetation. It is a deep, cup-shaped structure of grass and roots and lined with hair and the eggs are laid from late May onwards, with both parents sharing the incubation and rearing of the chicks, feeding them mainly on insects.

Garden Warbler

Sylvia borin

The most plain-coloured warbler on the Scottish list is the **Garden Warbler,** with a dark brown mantle, wings and tail, paler underparts and a very faint stripe above the eye. The sexes are similar in colouring, but anything that this little warbler lacks in appearance is more than made up for in its voice, which shares the top of the popularity list with the Blackbird.

Unlike the Blackbird, the Garden Warbler does not sing from a prominent perch but chooses to spend its time among the foliage of trees and undergrowth, singing from the higher boughs and nesting among the thicker vegetation only a metre or so from the ground. Indeed, if it were not for the Garden Warblers' song, many would spend the summer here, raise their families and leave without being noticed.

Garden Warblers do not, as their name suggests, show a preference for gardens, but prefer much wilder places where the undergrowth is dense and protective, and when the females arrive the males have already claimed their territories, having appeared one or two days earlier.

The females then set about nest building low

down in the tangle of vegetation, the nest being built with grasses and bents into a cup-shaped structure, and then lined with fibres and hair.

The eggs are laid in late May or June. For the 13 days most of the incubation is undertaken by the female, then both parents feed the chicks on insects and caterpillars for a similar period, the young leaving the nest before they can fly and skulking in the undergrowth, always under the watchful eyes of their parents. Usually only one brood is reared in a season, the autumn migration beginning early in August when the birds start drifting south.

Apart from an area around the Moray Firth, Garden Warblers – and Blackcaps – are absent in most northern regions of Scotland.

GARDEN WARBLER

Comparative size Slightly larger than Great Tit.
Status Summer resident.
Habitat Woodland with dense undergrowth.
Nest Cup-shaped, grasses, low down.
Eggs Pale ground colour, covered in brown and grey markings, clutch 4-6.
Food Mainly insects.

The Garden Warbler is one of our summer residents that would go unnoticed but for its beautiful song.

Blackcap
Sylvia atricapilla

There is much similarity between the **Blackcap** and the Garden Warbler in habitat, song, nest and eggs, but there is a noticeable difference in the plumage of the two birds, and though most of our Blackcaps are summer residents like the Garden Warblers, some spend the winter here.

Unlike most Warblers, the sexes are easily distinguished, the male having a noticeable black crown whereas the female's crown is a pale, reddish-brown, the remainder of the plumage of both birds being greyish-brown on the upper parts with paler underparts.

Every year the number of Blackcaps that choose to spend the winter here seems to rise, perhaps an instinctive step towards self-preservation as thousands are trapped annually for pickling in parts of the Mediterranean while on migration. It would be fine if it were so, but a subtle change in our climate seems a more rational explanation and, unlike our other Warblers, Blackcaps find fruit, berries and bird-table mixtures enough to sustain them through the winter months.

Blackcaps frequent the same type of habitat as the Garden Warbler, broadleaved woodland with a dense undergrowth of bramble and bushes, and

their song is every bit as melodious, some even preferring it to that of the Garden Warbler, though in all honesty it takes an exceptional ear to tell them apart.

The nest, built mainly by the female, is a copy of that of the Garden Warbler, a shallow cup of grass and fibres lined with hair. The eggs, too, are almost identical to those of the Garden Warbler, both male and female sharing the 12 day incubation period. Both parents feed the chicks, which will leave the nest days before they can fly, seeking shelter among the tangle of undergrowth if they are disturbed.

The autumn migration of the Blackcap is somewhat complex, with most of our summer residents wintering in one part of Africa or another, where they are joined by other European breeders.

BLACKCAP

Comparative size Similar to Great Tit.
Status Summer resident, some birds winter here.
Habitat Woodland and scrub.
Nest Cup-shaped, grass, lined hair.
Eggs Pale ground colour, covered in brown and grey markings, clutch 4-5.
Food Insects, berries.

Willow Warbler
Phylloscopus trochilus

Chiffchaff
Phylloscopus collybita

The Willow Warbler, Chiffchaff and Wood Warbler are the three 'greenish' or 'Leaf' Warblers that occur in Scotland, the Willow Warbler and Chiffchaff being almost identical in appearance and the Wood Warbler larger and brighter.

By late March, the distinctive 'chip-chap', 'chip-chip-chap' call of the **Chiffchaff** announces his arrival as he flits among the topmost twigs of leafless trees, allowing us to note his plumage – olive-green on the upperparts with a pale eye stripe and paler below.

About a fortnight later the warming April days become alive with the song of the **Willow Warbler,** a series of notes which trickle down the scale, distinguishing these two identically plumaged birds beyond doubt.

Smaller than Blue Tits, these tiny Warblers, only 11cm long and weighing a mere 8gm, have flown over 5,000 miles from their wintering grounds in Africa to charm us with their presence through the summer, a journey which, with stopovers for feeding, has taken them almost two months.

Another similarity the three 'Leaf' Warblers have in common is their 'domed' nests for, unlike all our other Warblers which build open, cup-shaped nests, the Leaf Warblers choose to construct their nests in the shape of a ball, with a side entrance.

The breeding habitat of the Willow Warbler is wide and varied – open woodland, young plantations, large gardens, scrubby heathland and embankments – where the nest is usually built on the ground, or very close to it in a low bush, the latter being more unusual. Normally, the nest is built in a grassy tussock, moss intertwined with grasses and leaves being the main materials, with feathers used for the cosy lining.

The eggs are laid in April or May and incubated by the female alone for 13 days, both parents feeding the chicks for a further 14 days until they fledge and leave the nest. The Willow Warbler, being our most numerous and widespread summer resident, far outnumbers the Chiffchaff, whose range is almost limited to the southern half of Scotland, less even than the range of the Wood Warbler, which also extends along the western half of the country.

The Chiffchaff's choice of nest site is above ground level among bramble or other dense vegetation, where the domed structure is well hidden, being built of leaves, grasses and twigs, and lined with feathers and hair.

The eggs are laid early in May and incubated

WILLOW WARBLER

Comparative size Smaller than Blue Tit.
Status Summer resident.
Habitat Woodland, scrub, large gardens.
Nest Domed, moss, grass, leaves, lined feathers.
Eggs White, finely spotted red or brown, clutch 6-7.
Food Mainly insects, caterpillars.

Our most familiar warbler, the little Willow Warbler, looks cosy in her feather-lined nest.

by the female alone for about 14 days while the chicks remain in the nest she also undertakes most of the feeding duties, her mate flitting amongst the foliage high above uttering his 'chip-chip-chap' call, which can be heard from a considerable distance away.

CHIFFCHAFF

Comparative size Smaller than Blue Tit.
Status Summer resident.
Habitat Woodland and copses with tangled undergrowth.
Nest Domed structure of grasses, leaves, moss lined with feathers: near ground.
Eggs White with purplish brown spots: clutch 5-7.
Food Mainly insects.

Wood Warbler
Phylloscopus sibilatrix

At 13cm in length, the **Wood Warbler** is the largest of our Leaf Warblers, and is also the most colourful and tuneful.

The upperparts are yellowish-green with a yellow eyestripe; the wings are brownish with yellow tips to the feathers, and the bright yellow throat and breast contrast with the whiter underparts.

In Scotland, the habitat of the Wood Warbler is well defined – mature oak or beech woods with scant undergrowth, preferably on an incline – and from mid-April the characteristic song can be heard, a series of 'sip-sip', notes which end in a rattling warble as the male perches on a branch, throws back his head, and announces to all that this is his territory.

When you are in Wood Warbler territory it is a relatively easy matter to obtain good views of the bird as he flitts constantly from perch to perch, singing from each one, and sometimes approaching quite close in an inquisitive manner.

Like the other Leaf Warblers, most of the Wood Warbler's feeding is done high among the branches while nesting is carried out at ground level, and when located, the nest of the Wood Warbler is easily distinguished from that of the Willow Warbler and the Chiffchaff, for although it is similarly domed it is totally lacking in feather lining, the Wood Warbler choosing fine bents and hair with which to line the interior of the ball-shaped structure. An outer covering of bracken and dead leaves help to conceal the nest among the scant vegetation of the woodland floor, and when the female is sitting tight she is most reluctant to break cover, making finding the nest very difficult. She builds most of the nest on her own and incubates the eggs for about 13 days, although after hatching she is joined by her mate in rearing the chicks, which fledge soon afterwards at about 12 days old, immediately rising to the upper canopies where cover and food are more plentiful.

Only three months after the song is first heard, and when insect life is at its peak, the Wood Warblers start migrating, wending their way in leisurely fashion through woodlands and along tree-lined river courses where small family parties can at sometimes be spotted making their way south.

WOOD WARBLER

Comparative size Slightly larger than Willow Warbler.
Status Summer resident.
Habitat Broad-leaved woodland, scant undergrowth.
Nest Domed, grass, leaves, bents, lined hair.
Eggs White, spotted, violet-brown, clutch 5-7.
Food Insects, spiders.

Goldcrest

Regulus regulus

Conifer forests of spruce or pine are the haunts of our smallest bird, the **Goldcrest**, where the high pitched 'see-see-see' contact calls of these tiny birds can be heard as roving parties flit among the topmost branches, picking at pine needles and cones as they search for spiders and their eggs.

Weighing a mere 5gm, about the weight of a 1p piece, and measuring only 9cm in length, the Goldcrest – a close relative of the Warblers – is with us throughout the year, and how this tiny bird survives even an average Scottish winter is one of nature's wonders.

The male Goldcrest has dull green upperparts, with two faint white wing bars, his underparts are creamy-buff, and his bright orange crest has a distinct black edging. The female is similarly coloured but her crest, as well as being less distinctive, has a yellow centre.

Although Goldcrests are difficult to observe on top of the tall firs they are quite heedless of man, and in winter, when they roam the countryside in the company of other small birds, they can be approached extremely close as they pick among the branches of leafless trees and shrubs with their long, thin beaks.

Goldcrests prefer to nest along the open forest edges rather than among the denser trees, and although the forests support the larger populations, much smaller fir woods and even yews in churchyards and country gardens are often chosen as nest sites.

The Goldcrest is sometimes known as the 'Golden Crested Wren', and in the south of Scotland it is called the 'Basket Hanger' because of the way it builds its compact little nest. This is an intricate construction, built from green moss woven together with spiders' webs and feathers. It is always suspended on the underside of the branch, stitched to the fir needles by some of the mossy material, and the rim of the cup-shaped structure tilts inwards, making it both cosy and secure.

Both male and female share in the building of the nest in late April or May, and as the female can lay as many as ten eggs, amounting to twice her own body weight, the devoted little parents are kept very busy for two weeks after hatching until the chicks fledge.

GOLDCREST

Comparative size Smaller than Wren.
Status Resident.
Habitat Coniferous and broad-leaved woodland.
Nest Deep hammock, shaped cup on underside of conifer bough, moss, feathers.
Eggs Pinkish-white, darker spots, clutch 7-10.
Food Mainly insects, their eggs and larvae.

Suspended on the underside of a branch the nest of Scotland's smallest bird, the Goldcrest is constructed of moss, lichens and spiders' webs.

The chicks are fed entirely on insects, many of which are injurious to the forest so like the Coal Tit, the Goldcrest is looked upon as the forester's friend.

In the autumn, large numbers of Goldcrest cross the North Sea from Scandinavia to spend the winter in the company of our little 'Basket-Hangers'.

Pied Flycatcher

Ficedula hypoleuca

The introduction of nest boxes in woodland frequented by hole-nesting species not only provides extra sites for the birds, but also provides the birdwatcher with the opportunity to observe the nesting habits of the species, from nest building to the young reaching the free-flying stage.

One of the most noticeable opportunists regarding nest boxes in mixed woodland is the **Pied Flycatcher,** the male being easily recognised in his pied plumage, black above and white below. His forehead is white, and a broad white wing bar contrasts strongly with his black mantle. The female's plumage is brown, she lacks the white forehead, and her white wing bars are less pronounced.

The birds arrive in late April and are soon in their territories, the males defining theirs by singing from prominent song posts.

While feeding, although they take insects on the wing with a few erratic twists and turns, in similar fashion to the Spotted Flycatcher, unlike this latter species they do not return to their point of departure but land on a different branch altogether on another tree or even on the ground.

Natural holes in trees and holes in walls also provide nest sites for Pied Flycatchers, the males arriving in the area first and selecting the site. After the female has accepted this choice, she builds the nest using moss, leaves and grasses, and by mid-May her clutch is usually complete. Following a 13 day incubation period, again undertaken by the female alone, the chicks are fed on flying insects for about a fortnight by both parents. When they leave the nest, like many other families reared in the woodland, they disappear completely amid the dense foliage of the oak trees, where the young soon learn to chase and catch flying insects in a similar fashion to their parents.

Although Pied Flycatchers show a preference for woods on the slopes of hilly country, they also inhabit woodlands in the lower valleys, and in one such mixed wood of 13 acres consisting of oak, beech, ash, birch and a few firs, the introduction of nest boxes proved most successful. In January 1986 I installed a number of nest boxes among the mature trees in the wood and in May a pair of Pied Flycatchers successfully nested in one of them, rearing six young. Young birds reared in such sites will return to similar sites the following season, and the follow-up has been most encouraging with two pairs in 1987, two in 1988, three in 1989 – and in 1990 six pairs reared 42 young.

The success of occupied nest boxes can only be measured by the number of young which reach the free-flying stage, so it is much better to avoid interference that could cause a nesting pair to forsake their eggs or young, especially as the parents spend so much of their time visiting the box when the chicks are in the nest, thus allowing the watcher perfect, unrestricted views.

PIED FLYCATCHER

Comparative size Smaller than House Sparrow.
Status Summer resident.
Habitat Open woodland, often near streams.
Nest Nest box, hole in tree, birch bark, grass, hair.
Eggs Glossy pale blue, clutch 5-7.
Food Insects.

The population of summer residing Pied Flycatchers in open woodlands can be greatly increased by providing and maintaining nest boxes.

Spotted Flycatcher

Muscicapa striata

One of our shortest staying summer residents, seldom arriving before the end of April and leaving again sometimes as early as mid-July, is the **Spotted Flycatcher,** an inconspicuous little bird that does not even merit the name 'Spotted'.

At l4cm in length the, Spotted Flycatcher is slightly larger than the Pied Flycatcher, more streamlined, and much duller in its plumage, being greyish-brown on the upperparts and whitish on the underparts, with some dark streaks on the head and breast.

All Flycatchers are adept at catching flying insects, but in this manoeuvre the Spotted Flycatcher outstrips the others, and it is this ability that is the best identification feature for the birdwatcher. From an observation point on a post, wire or branch, the Spotted Flycatcher sits and waits. Suddenly springing to life, it darts forward and, with a series of erratic twists and turns, snatches a flying insect from mid-air and returns to the exact same spot from where it started.

Open woodland, gardens and parks are all frequented by Spotted Flycatchers as breeding habitats, where the choice of nest sites is extremely varied, some favourite sites such as

SPOTTED FLYCATCHER
Comparative size Slightly smaller than House Sparrow.
Status Summer resident.
Habitat Woodland, parks, gardens.
Nest Built in hole in wall, tree, box, twigs, roots, leaves, hair.
Eggs Greyish with reddish-brown flecks, clutch 4-5.
Food Flying insects.

Spotted Flycatchers nest in a variety of sites including holes in walls and convenient ventilation pipes.

open fronted nest boxes being used year after year.

Other sites around human habitation such as a hole in a wall or among the foliage of a climbing wall plant, are also favoured, and in fact the Spotted Flycatcher is one of the most obliging birds for the birdphotographer – I have successfully photographed Spotted Flycatchers at their nests in a ventilation pipe, a hole in a wall, a crack in a tree and in an old Song Thrush nest.

The nest is constructed of moss, wool and hair and both male and female share in the building of it. Both sexes also share in incubating the eggs and raising the chicks, feeding them entirely on flying insects, their only form of food. Because of this specialised method of feeding, inclement weather is sometimes responsible for nest failure, as the parents fail to catch enough insects to support the chicks.

Spotted Flycatchers are more widespread throughout Scotland than their cousins, the Pied Flycatchers.

Starling

Sturnus vulgaris

Because of its ability to exploit such a variety of food sources, the **Starling** is a very successful species and if, when it turned up in the garden, at the bird table or on the lawn, it did so either singly or in pairs, it would certainly be loved rather than loathed – for the Starling is an interesting bird, often ignored simply because it is so numerous.

At 21.5cm in length, Starlings are smaller than Blackbirds, due mainly to their much shorter tail, and in winter pale tips to many of the feathers give the birds a spotted plumage, which in spring is much less pronounced, with the glossy, greenish-black plumage of the males totally lacking in any spots whatsoever on the breast.

Always appearing to be in a hurry, a party will swoop down on kitchen scraps, which disappear in seconds as the birds dash hither and thither in a frenzy of feeding, only to be found minutes later a few hundred metres away on some grassy patch probing with partly open beaks for leatherjackets, the larvae of the cranefly and other insects.

Starlings are superb mimics, many characteristic bird calls being included in their repertoir, along with human whistles and telephone bells. One particular character which perched on a TV aerial on the house opposite my front door appeared to take a delight in watching me glance skywards, as he copied to perfection the call of Curlew as soon as I stepped onto the pavement.

In April the pairs start nest building, both birds carrying masses of twigs, straw and grass into the chosen hole, which is just as likely to be under the eaves of a house in an urban situation as a tree hole in a rural area.

In woodland which provides natural holes in trees and old Woodpecker holes the birds move in en masse, and in May, when each nest contains four or five ravenous chicks, the characteristic speedy life of the Starling is highlighted once more. They dash back and forth from nearby fields carrying beakfuls of grubs and insects, only pausing if an observer is too close to the nest site, the birds then settling on a nearby branch with a harsh, scolding alarm call, darting to the hole as soon as the intruder has left the area.

The watcher gets an almost uncanny feeling on visiting such an area of woodland after the young have left the nests and the Starlings have gone leaving the wood once more to the residents, who are quite content to lead quieter lives with less bustle.

It is at this time that large numbers descend on towns and cities once again, where among the spotted adults the plain, brown-plumaged young are noticeable as they chase their parents, constantly begging for food. It is difficult to believe that at the beginning of the last century the Starling was a rare bird in Scotland, when one witnesses the hordes that descend on city buildings to roost in such numbers that they represent a public nuisance.

Roosts also occur in rural areas, providing birdwatchers with an exciting spectacle as the birds gather to settle for the night. My first visit to such a 'roost', many years ago, was quite an

STARLING
Comparative size Smaller than Blackbird.
Status Resident.
Habitat Widespread, rural to city centres.
Nest In hole in tree or building, straw, grasses.
Eggs Pale blue, clutch 4-6.
Food Insects, grubs, worms, fruit, kitchen scraps.

Glistening in its autumn coat a Starling feasts on wild cherries.

'eye-opener', especially as when I was asked if I would like to join a party in assessing the number of birds at the roost, I had imagined a few hundred Starlings settling in a couple of beech trees.

On a December afternoon, some time before dusk, we took up our positions overloking a birch-bordered loch, and it was not long before the first Starlings arrived – a few hundred birds.

Prior to our arrival, other members of the party had placed four white poles in such a manner as to mark a square metre in the centre of a field bordering the roost, the significance of this strategy soon becoming obvious. Hundreds, and then thousands of birds were arriving by the minute from every direction, wheeling, turning, climbing and diving, thousands upon thousands, creating a spectacular sight as they peeled off and settled in two fields, the one with the marker poles and one adjoining it. At a pre-arranged time, the birds within the area of the marker poles were counted from two different vantage points, and as the total area of the two fields was known, an estimate could be made especially as one entire field was 'black' with Starlings, as was 75 per cent of the adjoining field, in which a solitary cow moved steadily through the mass, a 'green' patch appearing as it walked on, turning black again as it moved forward.

It took almost ten minutes for the ribbon of birds to fly past from the fields to the birch trees, where the chattering calls of thousands of Starlings sounded like a cascading waterfall, and at the end of a most exciting afternoon the final estimate was in the region of 250,000 Starlings using the roost – slightly more than I had envisaged!

Waxwing
Bombycilla garrulus

A most attractive and characteristic winter visitor to Scotland is the **Waxwing**, a slightly smaller bird than the Starling and quite exotic-looking in its plumage of buffish-brown, pink and grey, with black chin and throat. It has a rich, chestnut erectile crest, a conspicuous yellow tip to the dark tail, and the dark wings with white and yellow markings also have waxy, red tips to some of the feathers, which give the bird its name.

Waxwings arrive in this country from Northern Scandinavia and the USSR, most

winters occurring in small numbers, but occasionally 'irruptions' take place with hundreds appearing on the east coast, forerunning a more general spread inland.

On arrival, Waxwings show little or no fear of man, allowing one to approach quite close as the birds gorge themselves on cotoneaster, hawthorn and other berries, and although as the days pass they become a little more wary, they always present a pleasant and exciting scene when they are discovered.

WAXWING

Comparative size Smaller than Starling
Status Winter visitor.
Habitat Woodland, parks, gardens.
Nest Cup-shaped of grasses and lichen.
Eggs Pale blue with blackish spots and lines: clutch 3-6.
Food Insects and berries.

Meadow Pipit
Anthus pratensis

The most numerous species of bird seen on a walk across a Scottish moorland in spring or summer is the Meadow Pipit, easily identified by its 'tsip-tsip' call as it rises from the ground, showing noticeable white outer tail feathers. The rest of the plumage of these sparrow-sized birds is olive-brown on the upperparts, with dark streaks and paler underparts, which are also streaked with a darker colour on the breast and flanks.

Having spent the winter travelling around the lower countryside in small flocks, Meadow Pipits return to our hill moors in April, and by the end of the month many little grassy, cup-shaped nests will have been built among tussocks, cleverly concealed from prying eyes.

The little 'Moss Cheeper', as the bird is known

MEADOW PIPIT

Comparative size Sparrow sized.
Status Resident.
Habitat Open ground.
Nest On ground, grasses, bents.
Eggs Greyish-brown, clutch 4-5.
Food Mainly small invertebrates.

In Scotland the Meadow Pipit is most often chosen by the Cuckoo to foster its young. Two pipit eggs can be seen lying outside the nest.

in the south of Scotland, is a favourite of the shepherd, who finds many of these nests as he makes his rounds during 'lambing time', and if Cuckoos move into the territory they, too, will locate some of the nests, into which one of their own eggs will be deposited – for the Meadow Pipit fosters more young Cuckoos than any other species.

On heather moors Meadow Pipits, because of their plentiful numbers, serve another purpose as the main prey species of the Merlin, but there is little chance of this affecting their numbers.

After the breeding season, the high moorland areas are deserted once more as the Pipits move to lower ground, frequenting sewage farms, marshy areas and coastal flats where they share winter quarters with their larger cousins the Rock Pipits.

Rock Pipit
Anthus spinoletta

Rock Pipits are essentially coastal birds, spending the winter on mudflats and sandy shores and in spring moving to islands and rockier stretches of coast, where they nest among rougher ground, usually under a rock or in a rocky crevice.

Slightly larger than the Meadow Pipit, the

ROCK PIPIT
Comparative size Larger than House Sparrow.
Status Resident.
Habitat Rocky coastline.
Nest In crevice, built with grasses.
Eggs Greyish with brown and grey mottling. Clutch, 4-6.
Food Small molluscs, crustaceans and insects.

171

Rock Pipit is more robust, with an olive-brown mantle tinged with grey, a brown rump and pale underparts with darker streaks.

The nest is built of grasses, bents and hair, the first clutch of eggs being laid in April, followed by a second clutch in June, and the female undertakes the incubation on her own, sharing the rearing of the chicks with her mate and feeding them on insects, small molluscs and crustaceans.

Tree Pipit
Anthus trivialis

As its name suggests, the **Tree Pipit** is more of a woodland species than the Meadow Pipit and, unlike the latter, the Tree Pipit is a summer resident, arriving in April and leaving again in September or October.

Tree Pipits are somewhat similar in appearance to Meadow Pipits, having brownish upperparts with darker streaks, and pale underparts which are also streaked in a darker shade. The beak, however, is stouter and the hind claw is shorter and curved, more fitting for a bird that perches on trees.

Open woodland and the edges of denser woods are the favoured breeding haunts of the Tree Pipit, where the male arrives first and immediately claims his territory by performing spectacular song flights. He rises almost perpendicularly into the air from a vantage point, bursting into song seconds before he reaches the peak and then parachuting down, wings and tail spread, swaying from side to side as he lands on the branch from which he left, or on the ground.

The song of the Tree Pipit is the best and most finely delivered of Pipit songs, with extraordinary carrying power, and to find oneself in a bluebell – carpeted area of woodland when two males are in full display, is a double blessing.

TREE PIPIT
Comparative size Sparrow sized.
Status Summer resident.
Habitat Open woodland with rough clearings.
Nest On ground, grasses and moss, bents.
Eggs Variable, from reddish to grey, finely marked, clutch 4-6.
Food Insects, spiders.

On the ground, Tree Pipits walk and run like other members of the family, but their flight is erratic and flitting when they are in their breeding haunts, where the nest is built in a depression on the ground, well concealed under overhanging grass. The nest is built with grasses and bents and lined with finer grasses, and the female incubates the eggs alone for 14 days, the male sharing the rearing of the chicks for a similar period until they are fledged.

Photographing small birds in dense undergrowth can be a bit of a problem, especially when the parents are in the habit of arriving secretively at the nest without any obvious sound. However, the nestlings are most co-operative in alerting the photographer by springing to life, clamouring for food as soon as the parents arrive in the vicinity.

Pied Wagtail
Motacilla alba

Living in a small town in the south of Scotland has many advantages for the birdwatcher, the most obvious being that only a few hundred metres from the town centre in any direction finds one in open country, where within a five-mile radius over 100 different species of bird breed annually.

One of the species closely associated with the town centre is the **Pied Wagtail,** for every autumn about half an hour before dusk Pied Wagtails gather on rooftops on both sides of the high street, some years only 100 or so and other years almost 300, and as darkness falls they fly down from the roofs to roost for the night, fluttering among the branches of the two rows of hybrid lime trees and finally settling, quite unconcerned by those who pass underneath. This 'roost' is used faithfully until the trees lose most of their leaves, the birds then moving to another roost in reed beds a few miles further south.

Pied Wagtails are common residents, unmistakable in their pied plumage and long 'wagging' tails, with white faces and underparts contrasting strongly with black crowns, throats and breasts.

Females are slightly greyer on the back, but not so lightly coloured as the European race known as the 'White Wagtail', a few pairs of which breed in the Shetlands.

The undulating flight of the Pied is typical of

the Wagtails, and on the ground it is an entertaining bird to watch as it darts hither and thither with its long tail constantly moving up and down, reminding one of its name.

Although it is fond of watery place and is, often seen by the banks of rivers and streams, it also favours grasslands where cattle graze, and constantly visits playing fields and lawns.

Nest sites are varied, with a hole in a dry stone wall or under the overhanging vegetation of a riverbank being the most common, but shelves in outhouses and other sites around human habitation are also used. The nest is built by the female alone, an extremely well-made structure of moss, leaves, twigs and roots lined with hair,

feathers and wool, and the eggs are laid by the end of April.

The female also undertakes most of the 14 day incubation period alone, but her mate joins her in rearing the chicks and between them two, and sometimes three, broods are reared in a season.

PIED WAGTAIL
Comparative size Slim, longer than Sparrow. **Status** Resident. **Habitat** Variable, mainly open ground near water. **Nest** In hollow, grasses, roots, moss, twigs, hair, feather. **Eggs** White, flecked greyish, clutch 4-6. **Food** Insects, small invertebrates.

Grey Wagtail
Motacilla cinerea

Often wrongly identified as a Yellow Wagtail, the **Grey Wagtail** is our other common resident Wagtail, found throughout Scotland on every burn and fast-flowing river. A wagtail that shows bright yellow in its plumage is often assumed to be a Yellow Wagtail; however, this is not the case, for the elegant, long-tailed yellow-breasted bird with the bluish-grey head and mantle is the Grey Wagtail, the male having a noticeable black 'bib' during the breeding season.

The Grey is our most water-loving Wagtail,

The striking yellow-coloured underparts of the Grey Wagtail often lead to it being wrongly identified as the Yellow Wagtail.

spending most of its life among the rocks and boulders of clear running streams, where its lively action is a joy to watch as it flits from boulder to boulder or perches on overhanging branches, constantly raising and dipping its tail, the motion that gives rise to its name.

Unlike the Pieds, Grey Wagtails are never seen in flocks, only singly or in pairs, and in early spring during courtship they present a pretty sight as the male approaches the female, displaying his black bib while offering her some morsel of food, which she accepts with quivering wings and gestures of acceptance.

The nest is cleverly concealed in some rocky crevice, or on a ledge of the riverbank under overhanging vegetation, and it is built by both birds using moss, leaves, roots and fibres. The male and female also share the incubation period and rearing of the two broods.

GREY WAGTAIL

Comparative size Size of Pied Wagtail.
Status Resident.
Habitat Hill burns, rivers.
Nest In hollow, moss, leaves, roots, fibres.
Eggs Buffish, greyish-brown speckles, clutch 4-6.
Food Mainly insects.

Yellow Wagtail
Motacilla flava

At 16.5cm in length the **Yellow Wagtail** is slightly shorter than our other Wagtails, and it also differs by being a summer resident which shows a preference for open pasture and grassland, rather than the banks of fast-flowing rivers and hill burns.

The male is a striking bird, the top of his head,

YELLOW WAGTAIL

Comparative size Smaller than Pied Wagtail.
Status Summer resident.
Habitat Water meadows, lowland pastures.
Nest On ground, bents, grasses, hair.
Eggs Greyish-white, lightly spotted brown, clutch 5-6.
Food Mainly insects.

---

ear coverts and mantle being greenish-yellow, with his throat, sides of the neck, eyestripe and underparts bright yellow. The female is much duller in colouring, and the tails of both her and her mate are noticeably shorter than those of our other Wagtails.

The undulating flight and ground behaviour of the Yellow Wagtail are similar to other Wagtails, but the bird itself is not familiar in Scotland, only residing in about 10 per cent of the country, mainly in the south west.

Yellow Wagtails nest in lowland pastures and water meadows, usually in a grassy tussock. The nest is built with bents and grasses, and lined with hair. The eggs are incubated by both male and female, who also share in rearing the chicks which, when fledged, join other family parties roosting and feeding together in preparation for the southerly flight to their wintering grounds in West Africa.

Dunnock
Prunella modularis

Dunnocks, or Hedge Sparrows as they are sometimes called, are indeed sparrow-sized, but are not related to them in any way. In profile they resemble the Robin and like this species, Dunnocks spend the winter months in parks and gardens close to human habitation. In spring they become more secretive, the majority moving into open country for the breeding season.

The Dunnock is a familiar little bird to the countryman with its streaked brown back, wings and tail, and its slate grey head, neck and breast which are streaked with brown and pale grey underparts. It has a thin, insectivorous bill quite unlike the shorter, thicker bill of the Sparrow family.

Attracting little notice as it moves about roadside hedgerows, copses and gardens, the Dunnock forages among dead leaves or pecks amongst the grass in its search for insects, many of which are pests to the gardener and farmer, making the bird welcome wherever it appears.

Being able to secrete itself in the minimum of covering vegetation, often the only indication of a Dunnock's presence is the loudish, single 'tseep' call note which is extremely characteristic, although when defining his territory the male will perch prominently on a bare twig in a hedgrow, constantly repeating his short, warbling song, which is best heard from January until July.

In the case of the Dunnock the word territory is used rather loosely for what this little bird lacks in colourful appearance it more than makes up for in its colourful, almost bizarre sex life. A single male may have one, two or even three females, while a female could quite well have as many males in attendance. In spite of such a busy social life, the female somehow finds time to build a nest, usually only a metre or so from the ground in a hedge, bush, young conifer or amongst ivy, using twigs, moss and leaves and lined with wool, hair and feathers.

To a certain extent the Dunnock resembles the robin, choosing to spend the winter months near human habitation then moving to wilder places to breed.

The eggs are laid in April and incubated by the female, during which time the male feeds her on the nest and when the chicks hatch one of the 'unattached' males or females often help the parents to rear their young.

DUNNOCK

Comparative size House Sparrow sized.
Status Resident.
Habitat Gardens, woodside edges, hedgerows, farmland.
Nest In hedge etc, twigs, moss, leaves, hair, feathers.
Eggs Deep blue, clutch 4-5.
Food Insects, weed seeds.

Great Grey Shrike

Lanius excubitor

Whenever the word 'Great' appears in the name of a bird one thinks big, but in most cases it simply means that this is the largest member of the family, and the **Great Grey Shrike** is actually slightly smaller than a Blackbird.

This small size, however, does not detract from the fact that this winter visitor is a formidable killing machine which not only catches and kills small rodents, birds and large insects but has a unique way of storing them – by impaling surplus prey on spikes in a hawthorn bush, forming a 'larder'.

The Great Grey Shrike is recognised by its grey upperparts which contrast with its black-and-white wings and tail, and it also has black eye patches. The underparts are dullish-white, the tail is graduated with white outer feathers, and the beak is slightly hooked.

Appearing mainly on the east coast from October onwards, it is usually after the New Year before they are regularly seen inland, and in southern regions most winters produce birds which provide birdwatchers with the opportunity to observe their habits, as they 'take up residence' in the same location for days at a time.

The Great Grey Strike has the habit of perching on the topmost branches of a hawthorn or other small tree or on telegraph wires, from which it swoops down to secure a small rodent or beetle, then returning to its perch where the prey is either eaten at once or stored in the larder.

Having seen a Great Grey Shrike in the district as late as 29 April a few years ago, perhaps some day a pair will find Scotland to their liking and stay to rear a family.

Crossbill

Loxia curvirostra,

Loxia pytyopsittacs

The **Crossbill** (Loxia Pytyopsittacus) of the Caledonian Pine Forests is a more robust bird than that found in the afforested areas of southern Scotland, and its beak is slightly stouter, enabling it to prise open hard pine cones, whereas the southern birds concentrate mainly on the softer larch cones.

The bills of these birds are more specialised than those of any other member of the Finch clan, with the tips of the upper and lower mandibles distinctly crossed, the lower mandible twisting to the right or to the left of the upper mandible with no definite pattern, either way equally adapted for prising the scales from cones in order to extract the seeds with their sticky tongues.

Just as distinctive as the crossed bill, is the bird's colouring, males being dressed in orangey-red with brownish wings and tail while females are yellowish-green, with similar brownish wings and tail and pale brown mottling on the head and underparts.

Normally Crossbills are difficult to see when high in the trees, but their distinctive 'bell notes' attract one's attention, with falling cones, stripped to varying degrees, confirming their whereabouts and, when they are located, the feeding birds are most obliging by continuing to feed on the same tree.

Crossbills are fond of bathing in and drinking from shallow streams or puddles, with gardens on the outskirts of Crossbill territory frequently visited by parties where a source of water is available, the birds bathing, drinking and pecking at grit and then flying into nearby garden trees to dry and preen, quite unconcerned at being admired by the watcher only metres away.

Nesting coincides with the cone harvest even in mid-winter, nests with young being recorded in December and January, for unlike most other young Finches which are fed on insects for the first few days of their lives, young Crossbills are fed entirely on regurgitated fir-cone seeds.

Nests are usually placed high, on the outer branches of a fir or pine tree, and are built rather untidily with pine or spruce twigs, grass, moss and leaves, but with a neat cup, lined with fur, hair and wool.

The eggs are incubated by the female for about 14 days and when hatched the chicks are

---

CROSSBILL

Comparative size Larger than House Sparrow.
Status Resident.
Habitat Coniferous woods and forests.
Nest Twigs, grass, moss, leaves, lined fur-hair.
Eggs Greenish-white, spotted, streaked, chestnut, clutch 3-4.
Food Mainly coniferous seeds.

---

brooded by her while the male brings food, which she in turn feeds to the chicks. The fledging period is exceptionally long for small birds, and it is over three weeks before young Crossbills leave the nest.

Being entirely dependent on the cone harvest, Crossbill numbers fluctuate in accordance with a poor harvest, forcing this nomadic species to move elsewhere, a good harvest finding the birds in abundance.

Hawfinch

Coccothraustes coccothraustes

The **Hawfinch** at 18cm in length is our largest Finch, shy, secretive and a scarce breeding bird in Scotland.

In profile the large head, massive bill and short tail are distinctive, and if the watcher is fortunate enough to obtain a good view then the general colouring of orange-brown with black, brown and white wings with curiously curved flight feathers, may be seen.

Hawfinches tend to nest in the same part of a wood year after year, at times forming loose colonies,. Prior to nesting the male selects a breeding tree on which he is joined a few days later by a female. Selecting the actual site for the nest, the male lays down the first few twigs for a foundation, then the nest is completed by the female with twigs, roots, lichens and grasses. Incubation, which is undertaken by the female, is about 13 days, with both birds rearing the chicks for about the same period; two broods are usually reared in a season.

Kernels and seeds of many fruits and trees form the diet of the Hawfinch, its massive bill cracking cherry stones with ease – the birds also have a liking for peapods.

HAWFINCH

Comparative size Larger than House Sparrow.
Status Resident.
Habitat Broad-leaved woodland, parks and orchards.
Nest Twig base, lined with roots, grasses, lichens.
Eggs Buffish-blue, spotted and streaked with purplish-brown, clutch 4-5.
Food Fruit kernels, buds, insects.

Bullfinch

Pyrrhula pyrrhula

It is unfortunate that the **Bullfinch's** only claim to fame is that he devastates orchards, for he is a handsome little bird, quite scarce in some parts of the country.

The trouble arrives when the ash buds, the Bullfinch's favourite winter food, is scarce, for he then turns to fruit trees where he can remove buds at the rate of about 30 per minute, a party of six or so doing untold damage in a very short time.

The male Bullfinch is beautiful, a black cap, grey back, pinkish-red breast and white rump combining to make one of our most attractive small birds. The female is duller on the back, with a brownish breast, but her rump is also snow-white, making both birds immediately recognisable in flight, and when seen in profile the short, stubby beak is also characteristic.

Bullfinches are woodland birds but will nest in large gardens in a thick hedge, yew, or other tree that offers good cover. The nest is shaped in a shallow cup, with thin twigs interwoven and lined with roots and hair, and the eggs are usually laid in May. Hatching the eggs is left mainly to the female and takes about a fortnight, but both birds feed the hatched chicks on seeds and insects which are brought to the nest in two little pouches under the parents' tongues.

Second broods are not unusual, and if spotted in late June or July the male's plumage is noticeably faded, having started his autumn moult.

Very often, when feeding their chicks both birds arrive at the nest together and it appears more or less certain that these birds pair for life, for as winter approaches they are always seen together in pairs and do not associate much with other birds.

BULLFINCH

Comparative size Larger than House Sparrow.
Status Resident.
Habitat Woodland, thickets, large gardens, orchards.
Nest Shallow structure, twigs, roots, hair.
Eggs Greenish-white, brownish spots, clutch 4-6.
Food Kernels from seeds, buds, fruit, berries.

The Bullfinch brings food to its young in two small pouches situated under its tongue.

Unlike most other finches Goldfinch sexes are almost identical.

Goldfinch

Carduelis carduelis

Over the past few years the **Goldfinch** has increased in numbers in parts of Scotland, much to the delight of birdwatchers and gardeners alike for many gardens are enhanced by visits from these charming little Finches.

One of the most easily recognised of the Finch clan, both male and female are similar in colouring, with pale-brown mantles and whitish underparts on which pale brown patches appear in spring, on either side of the breast. The tail and wings are black, the latter having a broad, golden-yellow band, the face is red, the sides of the face white, and the rest of the head is black.

Goldfinches strongly favour feeding on thistle heads, their specially adapted, longish pointed beaks allowing them to extract the seeds as they cling to the stalks, swaying back and forth pendulum-fashion. In the nesting season they show a preference for orchards and chestnut trees – I know of one such tree which has provided a site annually for over 25 years. The chestnut tree in question is on the edge of a public footpath and the nests, although always situated on the outer branches, are built at varying heights, some years only four metres from the ground but usually a few metres higher. The nest is successful in producing young most years, and one wonders just how many generations of Goldfinches have nested in this tree.

The nest is beautifully constructed from roots, twigs, moss and feathers, and lined with vegetable down and feathers. The eggs are incubated by the female, the male bringing her food to the nest during the 13 days it takes for the eggs to hatch, then both parents feed the chicks by regurgitation.

Goldfinches also nest in thick hawthorns bordering railway lines, and one such nest only two metres from the ground proved ideal for photography, even though trains whizzed past at about 100 miles per hour, causing the outer branches to disappear in a flurry and giving me some anxious moments as I waited for reassurance that nest and contents were still intact.

As the bush took a severe buffeting every time a train sped south, the Goldfinch proved that she could, by using the flimsiest of materials, build a structure which would safeguard her young through the severest of storms – natural or otherwise.

Linnet

Carduelis cannabina

Rough, scrubby ground with gorse bushes bordering farmland is the favoured haunt of the **Linnet**, for here it finds nesting cover and, usually, the necessary winter food supply.

The male is a handsome bird with his grey head, chestnut-brown mantle, and fawn underparts which merge into white. The wings and tail are dark brown with white edges, and his crown, breast and forehead are crimson. The female is less colourful and lacks the crimson.

In their breeding territory males sing from such perches as overhead power cables and other prominent points while the females incubate eggs in nests deep in the protective covering of gorse bushes, although later in the spring, when they are covered in foliage, other shrubs are used as well as young conifers.

The first clutch of eggs is laid by mid-April and incubated mainly by the female for about 14 days, but both parents feed the hatched chicks on insects and regurgitated seeds and soon after fledging when the young can fend for themselves, the parents rear a second brood.

GOLDFINCH
Comparative size Smaller than House Sparrow.
Status Resident.
Habitat Wasteland, gardens, orchards, farmlands.
Nest Moss, lichens, feathers, wool.
Eggs Pale bluish, spotted brown, clutch 5-6.
Food Weed seeds (especially thistles), some insects.

LINNET
Comparative size Smaller than House Sparrow.
Status Resident.
Habitat Gorse covered scrub, young conifers, farmland.
Nest In bush, grasses, moss, lined hair, wool.
Eggs Bluish-white, purplish-red spots and streaks, clutch 4-6.
Food Mainly weed seeds, insects.

In winter Linnets can be found roaming the countryside in company with other Finches, feeding together in large numbers on weed seeds and the like amongst stubble.

Twite
Carduelis flavirostris

The **Twite**, or 'Mountain Linnet' as it is sometimes called, is common in the West Highlands and islands, and although there is a bordering area in which both Twite and Linnet can be found breeding, the Twite is the bird of the northern regions.

The Twite is a close relative of the Linnet, the females being difficult to tell apart, but the males are more helpful, lacking crimson on the crown

TWITE
Comparative size Smaller than House Sparrow.
Status Resident.
Habitat Open hilly country, lowlands in winter.
Nest In low cover or rock cleft, grass, stalks, hair, wool.
Eggs Pale blue, reddish brown markings, clutch 5-6.
Food Weed seeds, insects.

and breast, but with a crimson rump which is noticeable and a good identification feature in summer, whereas the yellow beak is equally helpful in winter.

Twite nest amongst heather in open country, building on the ground with grass and stalks, and lining the nest with hair, wool and feathers. The female incubates alone for about 13 days, both birds rearing the chicks for a slightly longer period, and two broods are normal.

In winter the high ground is deserted as the birds move to lowland, very often coastal, feeding areas, where they move about in small flocks and assist the birdwatcher by settling on stunted hawthorn, allowing the cautious observer to approach and, by using binoculars, identify these little Mountain Linnets.

Greenfinch
Carduelis chloris

Large gardens with rhododendrons, ivy-covered walls, yews and other ornamental firs are the favourite haunts of the **Greenfinch** for, being an early nester, evergreens are an obvious choice of nest site.

Greenfinches are early nesters often rearing two and sometimes three broods in a season.

Around such gardens in early spring the characteristic trilling songs can be heard as the birds fly overhead from nests to feeding areas, and as the birds remain sociable throughout the year, a large garden offering a choice of sites will be inhabited by more than one pair, sometimes as many as half a dozen nesting in close proximity to one another.

Female Greenfinch are distinctly browner than the males, which are bright olive-green with greyish wings, the outer feathers of which, like the base of the tail, are golden-yellow. This latter colour leads to their occasionally being wrongly identified as Yellow Hammers when they visit garden bird tables, where they can be quite aggressive towards other birds and destructive towards the 'Netlon' peanut feeders.

Away from gardens, Greenfinches frequent almost any part of the countryside which is well supplied with trees, hedges, bushes and evergreens, and on arable land it is a most useful bird, devouring many weed seeds as well as injurious insects.

Early in April the rather untidy nests can be found to contain three or four eggs, the female incubating them alone for 14 days while the male feeds her on the nest. Then both parents feed the chicks for a similar period, with as many as three broods being reared in a season.

GREENFINCH

Comparative size Size of House Sparrow.
Status Resident.
Habitat Woodland edge, gardens, parks, hedgerows.
Nest Twigs, moss, wool, fine vegetation.
Eggs Whitish with reddish-brown spots, clutch 4-6.
Food Seeds, grain, insects.

Redpoll
Carduelis flammea

Redpolls are perhaps best seen throughout the winter months when they accompany parties of Siskins feeding among the topmost branches of alder or birch trees. Here, their characteristic Tit-like manner of hanging upside down while feeding, coupled with their small size of ll.5cm, helps to identify them.

The mantles of these tiny birds are brown with darker streaks, while the underparts are whitish. Both male and female have crimson foreheads and black chins, but in his summer dress the male has a distinct crimson breast.

Redpolls have an erratic and bounding fight and tend to fly at greater heights than other Finches when moving around the countryside.

The nest of the Redpoll is very distinctive, and is built in a gorse or other bush, or young conifer. It is constructed of small twigs, moss and grass, and is always lined with white cotton grass 'down' and feathers.

The eggs are laid in May or June and incubated by the female alone for about 11 days, while the male brings her food to the nest. When the chicks hatch, the female broods them for a few days while the male continues to bring food for the family, and she joins him a few days later when the chicks are partly fledged.

REDPOLL

Comparative size Size of Blue Tit.
Status Resident.
Habitat Scrubland, young plantations, open woodland.
Nest Twigs, grass, vegetable down.
Eggs Bluish with brown markings, clutch 4-6.
Food Birch and alder seeds, insects.

Chaffinch
Fringilla coelebs

Brambling
Fringilla montifringilla

Autumn is a magical time in the countryside as the bountiful harvest of seeds and nuts is exploited by many species of birds, residents and visitors alike, who spend most of the daylight hours picking and foraging, as they build up their fat supply in preparation for the cold, dark winter months ahead.

In October, roadside beech trees provide an ample supply of beech-mast which is sought after by one of our most common birds, the **Chaffinch.** By the middle of the month, on disturbing a group feeding beneath the trees, a few of the birds may show a distinct white rump,

Our most common finch, the Chaffinch is a beautiful little bird in his breeding plumage.

as they fly to the safety of the branches, telling us that the Chaffinches have been joined by their northern cousins, the **Bramblings.**

For the remainder of the winter mixed flocks ranging from a few dozen to many hundreds of birds, will roam the countryside visiting stubble fields and others such as those containing turnips – the winter food supply for sheep – as these fields often contain patches of plants such as charlock, a persistent weed to the farmer but an ideal food source on which the birds will feed for many days. This provides the birdwatcher with the opportunity to study different species at the same time, as Buntings often join the variety of Finches fortunate enough to find such a bounty in their time of need.

As winter merges into spring the male Chaffinches acquire their breeding plumage, becoming one of ourmost attractive little songsters with their blue-grey heads, orangey-pink breasts and chestnut mantles. The white

wing patches becoming more prominent in their aggression and courtship displays. The white wing bars of the females are not quite so pronounced as the males', and their general colouring is much duller.

Chaffinches will nest almost anywhere, in woods, gardens, copses and hedgerows, the nest being built in a fork or close to the trunk of a tree where, because of the way the nest is constructed, it is very difficult to see. Built from moss, wool and hair, lined with hair and down,

---

CHAFFINCH

Comparative size Slightly larger than House Sparrow.
Status Resident.
Habitat Woodlands, gardens, parks.
Nest Cup-shaped, moss, lichen, wool, hair, feathers.
Eggs Greyish-stone, slightly spotted-streaked brownish, clutch 4-5.
Food Insects, caterpillars, seeds.

---

and covered with lichens, the structure merges into the mossy trunk, appearing as a natural growth when seen from below.

The eggs are laid in May and incubated for about 12 days, mainly by the female, but both parents feed the chicks, firstly on insects and later on seeds for the following 14 day fledging period. Unlike most of our other breeding Finches, which rear two or more broods in a season, the Chaffinch rears only one.

The Chaffinch's song is a familiar sound in gardens and woodland throughout the spring and summer, and to those with a trained ear who have the opportunity to compare the songs of southern and northern birds, it soon becomes obvious that there is a decided difference between the two.

Bramblings arrive on the east coast from Scandinavia and eastwards from the USSR in varying numbers in October, and are most often seen in the company of Chaffinches, although others move about the country in huge flocks, settling where food is available.

In winter, when Bramblings are seen in this country the males have orange-buff shoulder patches and breasts, and blackish-brown heads and mantles which turn glossy black when the birds are in breeding plumage. It can be late April before the Bramblings leave us for the return journey to their northern breeding haunts, so it is possible to see the males in splendid summer plumage before they leave. Females are rather duller, but like the males their white rumps are conspicuous, especially when in flight.

When snow covers the open country Bramblings often accompany the Chaffinches which visit gardens, adding their welcome presence to the multitude of small birds which rely on a little human support to tide them over the coldest spells.

Siskin

Carduelis spinus

A few years ago one had to visit alder or birch copses to find one of our smallest Finches, the **Siskin** which occurs in this country mainly as a winter visitor, the majority of the Continental birds arriving in October and leaving again in April and early May.

Nowadays, Siskins regularly visit bird tables and feeding places, attracted by the orange-coloured 'Netlon' peanut holders, where Tit-like antics coupled with their small size of 12cm immediately endear them to garden birdwatchers, who often comment on the confiding nature of these tiny birds, which allow the observer to approach them to within a few metres without any undue alarm.

The male is yellowish-green with darker streaks on the mantle and his underparts are paler, shading to white. His crown and chin are black, his rump is yellow and his brownish wings have a yellow wing bar. The female lacks the black on crown and chin, and her yellow colouring is much duller.

As well as being winter visitors, smaller numbers of Siskin regularly breed in Scotland, and though previously confined to the pine forests of the north, they now inhabit the spruce and larch forests of the south. Here they nest high in tall conifers, the nest itself being built by the female on the outer branches with moss, bents and wool, and lined with down and hair.

Egg laying coincides with the opening of the spruce cones in April, when the Siskins are able to extract the seeds on which they feed the chicks from the partly-open cones.

The female incubates the eggs on her own for about 14 days; then both parents feed the chicks by regurgitation for about the same period rearing at least two broods in a season, the

---

BRAMBLING

Comparative size House sparrow size.
Status Winter visitor.
Habitat Woodlands, especially beech, farmland with stubble.
Nest Cup-shaped of grasses, moss, lichens, lined with feathers.
Eggs Dark greenish with reddish-brown spots, clutch 4-6.
Food Insects, caterpillars, moths, winter cereal seeds and beechmast.

SISKIN

Comparative size Smaller than Greenfinch.
Status Resident.
Habitat Conifer forests, birch and alder woodland.
Nest Moss, lichens, down, hair.
Eggs Pale bluish, reddish-brown spots-streaks, clutch 3-5.
Food Seeds from cones, birch, alder.

second brood often fed on the seeds of the later opening pine cones and insects.

Corn Bunting

Miliara calandra

By late spring and early summer most of our small resident birds have reared families and are possibly in the midst of raising a second brood, but not so the **Corn Bunting** for it can be late May before some females lay their eggs, although a few records show earlier nesting.

Spending much of the winter in flocks the males, who have a tendency towards polygamy occupy their territories, singing their 'key-jangling' songs from overhead wires or posts, and although territorial rights can be claimed by February, it is usually well into April or even May before the flocks of females disperse among the males.

At 18cm in length the Corn Bunting is our largest bunting, and in appearance is the least impressive, two field characteristics that help the birdwatcher to identify it. Its plumage is sandy brown with darker brown streaks on the upperparts and the underparts, are buffish-white, streaked with brown on the throat, breast and flanks.

Corn Buntings hop when feeding on the ground, while in the air their flight is Sparrow-like, and if the observer is close enough the yellowish legs will be seen dangling, another good field characteristic as this is the only small bird to fly in this manner.

As its name suggests, cultivated land is the favoured haunt of the Corn Bunting, nests often being built on the ground amidst the growing corn but they can also be situated in long grass, dense weeds or brambles, where it is well concealed and difficult to locate.

The nest is an untidy affair, built by the female alone with moss, straw and grass, and lined with hair. The eggs are laid in late May or June and incubated entirely by the female. When hatched, the chicks are again mainly her responsibility, as the male visits each of his partners for a short period of time only.

In Scotland Corn Buntings favour the eastern side of the country, but their distribution is rather patchy.

Yellow Hammer

Emberiza citrinella

The **Yellow Hammer** is more widely distributed throughout Scotland than its larger cousin the Corn Bunting, and is a common bird wherever the habitat is suitable.

Farmland with thick hedgerows, areas of gorse, railway banks and young conifer plantations all appeal to the Yellow Hammer, and when the birds are in their territory the males are easily seen as they sing from overhead wires, the top of a bush or other obvious perch.

For many years textbooks have described the song of the Yellow Hammer as a 'little-bit-of-bread-and-no-cheese', and while this interpretation certainly leaves many birdwatchers wondering why, the Scottish interpretation of 'De'il-de'il-de'il-de'il, tak' ye' is only marginally better. If the intrepretation of his song is confusing, the actual song itself is not, for it is one of the most characteristic of all and easily associated with the bright yellow of the male bird as he sings from a vantage point in his territory.

Apart from his yellow breast, the male's head and underparts are also yellow, his mantle and wings are streaked with shades of brown and his rump is chestnut. The female is Sparrow-like in

---

CORN BUNTING

Comparative size Larger than House Sparrow.
Status Resident.
Habitat Open country, farmland.
Nest Moss, grass, hair, on ground, or close to it.
Eggs Greyish, marked with black spots-lines, clutch 3-5.
Food Weed seeds, grains, insects.

YELLOW HAMMER

Comparative size Larger than House Sparrow.
Status Resident.
Habitat Farmland, scrubland, young plantations.
Nest Grass, moss, hair, close to ground or on it.
Eggs Pale purplish, black spots and squiggles, clutch 3-5.
Food Insects, spiders, seeds.

Viewed from behind the cock Yellow Hammer proves to be a brown-streaked little bird with a yellow head. From the front it has an entirely different appearance.

plumage, being almost without any distinguishing yellow colouring, though she does have a chestnut rump similar to that of her mate.

The nest, which is built from grass, bents and moss and lined with hair, is situated on the ground or close to it, at the base of a bush or young conifer. The eggs are incubated by the female alone for about 14 days and the chicks are then fed by both parents for a similar period, with at least two broods being reared in a season.

Yellow Hammers congregate in small flocks in winter, usually in association with other Buntings, and when seen perching among the dark-coloured branches of a hawthorn or similar tree on a bright winter's day their brilliant colours can be appreciated to the full.

Reed Bunting
Emberiza schoeniclus

Even though many of our marshy places and damp, reedy areas have been drained during the last decade, the **Reed Bunting** has not declined accordingly, taking up residence in young conifer plantations and other drier situations such as field edges. From here the male's repetitive song is heard as he sings from a reed stem, post or bush during the spring and summer months.

In summer plumage the male is a handsome bird with brown-streaked upperparts, and a black head and throat with a clean, white collar, the underparts varying from white to pale buff. The female is duller, lacking the black head and throat, and in his winter coat the male resembles her, both birds having white outer tail feathers, a characteristic of most of the Buntings.

In typical Reed Bunting habitat the nest is usually built low among the reeds or tussocks constructed from reeds, bents and grass and lined with finer vegetation and hair. The first clutch of eggs is laid in May, and incubation is undertaken mainly by the female for about 14 days, after which time the male assists in raising the chicks, bringing beakfuls of insects and caterpillars to the nest. The young leave the nest before they can fly, but are tended by the male while the female lays her second clutch.

In winter many birds leave the marshy places and, in company with other Buntings and Finches, seek their food in fields containing turnips and other root crops, where weed seeds are usually available. At this time of year Reed Buntings roost in reedbeds in the company of other Buntings, thereby providing another dimension to the birdwatcher's hobby, but when visiting such a communal roost, great care must be taken not to disturb the sleeping birds, and to tread carefully, as icy winter nights can produce one or two quaint surprises for the 'nocturnal-bog-birdwatcher'.

In summer plumage the cock Reed Bunting is an attractive little bird with his black head and contrasting white collar.

REED BUNTING

Comparative size Slightly larger than House Sparrow.
Status Resident.
Habitat Open ground, usually near water.
Nest Reeds, grasses.
Eggs Olive-brown, blackish spots and squiggles, clutch 4-5.
Food Seeds, insects, caterpillars.

Snow Bunting

Plectrophenax nivalis

It is with much enthusiasm that I visit our Moffat Water hills from late February, ever hopeful of finding a small flock of passing **Snow Buntings**, for in such a habitat they are in their natural element and can be seen from the comfort of one's car as they move steadily northwards, pecking at grass seeds and hugging the contours only a metre or so above the ground with their bouncy, undulating flight.

The Snow Bunting is a hardy little bird with a robust body and the thick, fluffy plumage necessary for warmth at high altitudes; its colour also suits its mountain-top surroundings. The male is predominantly white, with a black mantle and black patches on the wings and tail. The female has a white breast and underparts, but her head and mantle are speckled with brown. All in all, the conspicuous white plumage of the species makes them very attractive in flight, earning them the name of 'Snowflakes'.

Although most follow the coastline during migration, Snow Buntings also occur inland in the south of Scotland. Here, among the snow-covered hills one finds flocks of various sizes feeding at sheep and cattle troughs, where hay and other fodder has been put down for the animals.

In their breeding territories the males arrive first, being joined by the females some time later and, following a detailed inspection of a number of possible sites the female selects one and commences nest building.

Nests are substantial, with an outer layer of moss, an inner layer of grasses, and finally a cosy lining of feathers, usually those of the Ptarmigan, and they are well concealed under a rock, boulder or other deep, sheltered place. The eggs

are incubated for about 12 days mainly by the female, who is fed on the nest by her mate. He also shares in the rearing of the chicks, and as it can be into June before the first eggs are laid, only one brood is reared in a season.

Many thousands of Snow Buntings pass through Scotland on migration in spring, but only a small percentage nest on our highest northern peaks.

The **Lapland Bunting** can be found on our eastern coast in small numbers in winter, and these Scandinavian Buntings must surely be overlooked more times than they are actually identified because of their strong resemblance to Reed Buntings in winter plumage.

The male Lapland Bunting in breeding plumage is, however, unmistakable, with his black face and throat separated from his black crown by a white mark above his eye, and his chestnut nape.

Tree Sparrow

Passer montanus

Of the two members of the Sparrow family that breed in Scotland, one is as unfamiliar to most people as the other is familiar.

The **Tree Sparrow** is a bird of open woodlands, slightly smaller and more dapper than his 'towny' cousin the House Sparrow and, unlike the latter, the sexes are similar in colouring. Tree Sparrows have brown mantles which are streaked with black, two narrow white wingbars and whitish underparts. The crown and nape are chocolate-brown, the cheeks are white with contrasting black central spots, and the throat is also black.

Though its movements bear a close resemblance to those of the House Sparrow, the Tree Sparrow is more agile both in flight and on the ground, and its song if anything is slightly more musical.

Where Tree Sparrows occur, woodland that provides suitable nesting holes will be colonised by these gregarious little birds and numbers can be increased by erecting nest boxes with holes 3cm in diameter.

Whether in a tree hole or nesting box the nest is built by both male and female with twigs, grasses and masses of feathers. The eggs, which are laid in May, are incubated by both birds for about 14 days, and the chicks are fed by both

---

SNOW BUNTING

Comparative size Larger than House Sparrow.
Status Resident, moves to lower ground in winter.
Habitat Summer mountainous, winter lowland-coastal.
Nest In cavity, moss, grass, hair, feathers.
Eggs Whitish with grey and blackish markings, clutch 4-7.
Food Mainly seeds.

parents for a further two weeks until they vacate the nest, allowing the female to lay again.

Outside the nesting season, Tree Sparrows move around in company with House Sparrows and Finches, feeding in stack yards and fields and perching among the branches of willows and other bushes by bathing places, where the mixed flocks can be seen bathing in and drinking from the burn, then preening and drying themselves in the watery sunlight filtering through the branches.

TREE SPARROW

Comparative size Slightly smaller than House Sparrow.
Status Resident.
Habitat Open woodland.
Nest In tree hole, nest box, grasses, moss, feathers.
Eggs Pale, densely spotted with dark brown, clutch 4-6.
Food Mainly seeds.

The Tree Sparrow is a more dapper little bird than his towny cousin the House Sparrow and unlike the latter both sexes are similar in colouring.

House Sparrow

Passer domesticus

Wee cock Sparrows are the subject of both song and rhyme, and are birds that could at one time pass for two different species simply as a result of where they were 'born and bred', for the neat, distinctly coloured 'country' sparrows differed in appearance from their grubbier city relatives.

Nowadays, thanks to the diminishing number of smoky chimneys and sooty railway yards, the wee cock Sparrows of the cities are losing their 'greyish' look, and their brown-streaked plumage with white wing bars, grey crown, chestnut nape and black throat, contrast with their greyish-white underparts.

Grubby or not, the **House Sparrows** of town and city parks are loved by thousands who, because of the Sparrows' confiding nature, feed them from the hand and any kitchen scraps placed on bird tables or on the ground are immediately raided by perky little Sparrows.

Because of their close association with man, who provides them with nest sites and food, House Sparrows have been known to breed in most months of the year, but generally May to July is the time to find them nesting.

House Sparrows nest in two very different situations, the one we are more familiar with today being in a hole under the eaves of a house or a hole in a wall. In fact any manmade object such as a lamp standard, statue or piece of machinery with a cavity large enough to accept some nesting material, could be used. The other site, originating from before man's provision of convenient holes, is in a thick hedge or hawthorn bush, where an untidy, domed affair is built with straw and lined with feathers.

The eggs are incubated mainly by the female and the chicks are brooded by her for about a week while the male brings food to the nest. At about ten days old the chicks are fed mainly by the female while the male 'chirrups' close by, encouraging the young to leave the nest.

Outside the breeding season many House Sparrows roam the countryside in company with other seed eaters, but some reside permanently around farms while others show a preference for urban habitats where, their friendly early morning 'chirruping' reminds us that it is time to 'feed the birds'.

HOUSE SPARROW

Comparative size Size of Robin.
Status Resident.
Habitat Urban, rural, in close association with man.
Nest An untidy domed structure of straw and feathers.
Eggs Greyish, black-brown markings, clutch 4-6.
Food Insects, seeds, scraps.

INDEX